South Dakota Stories
from World War II

Charles M. Rogers

To order copies in quantities of 500 or more, call 972.632.6364.

ISBN: 978-1-944913-62-5

Dedication

This book is dedicated to my parents,
Ted and Alice Rogers, who encouraged me to go
to college and pursue my interest in history.

Author's Notes

I was an adjunct professor at Killian Community College in Sioux Falls for twenty years. One course I taught several times was on South Dakota history. Over the years I kept articles from the *Argus Leader* related to WWII, obituaries of WWII veterans and articles from the *South Dakota Magazine*. Whenever I visited a historic site or museum I checked to see if there was any information that related to SD and WWII. Old and new books were added to the collection.

After the school closed, I began to wonder what to do with the information I had collected. So, one day I decided to organize it and began to write. In the process of writing I continued to collect articles and research various sources.

This book tells some of the stories from WWII. I am confident there are many more stories yet to be told. If you have a relative or friend with a story to tell I would encourage you to write or record it.

The capitalization of Soldiers

Army Chief of Staff Peter J. Schoomaker gave the order to capitalize the word Soldier as if it were a proper noun. The order applied to all military publications. He also requested that the Associated Press and Webster's dictionary adopt the proposal.

Introduction

South Dakota's Pheasant Canteen:
A Refreshing Stop on the Road to War

The only WW II Pheasant Canteen in South Dakota opened on August 19, 1943 and closed on March 22, 1946. Aberdeen "Hub City" got its nickname because four railroads passed through the city. The railroads were a reason for opening a canteen. Local citizens supported the idea. The Red Cross/USO Canteen was located in the depot of the Chicago-Milwaukee railroad. Its mission was providing free lunches and help to troops traveling through Aberdeen on special trains. The first menu consisted of ground ham sandwiches, cake, cookies, donuts, fresh fruit, pie, milk, and coffee.

A change in the menu took place in December of 1943. Local farmers started bringing pheasants to the canteen workers. The pheasant sandwich became the highlight of the meal. Aberdeen became known as the "Pheasant Canteen". People in the area organized pheasant hunts to make sure the canteen had enough pheasants on hand. Aberdeen was in the heart of pheasant country. The canteen was supported by volunteers from towns nearby.

WW II Pheasant Canteen.
(Visitors Bureau, Aberdeen)

The word about pheasant sandwiches spread among the troops, and when a train stopped, the first thing many Soldiers asked about was the pheasant sandwiches. General Dwight D. Eisenhower and Presidential candidate Harry S. Truman stopped for a meal. Four to six trains passed through the city each day carrying a daily average of 500 troops. Over a 30-month period the canteen served over 586,000 meals.

An exhibit about the Pheasant Canteen is located in the former Milwaukee depot. The Milwaukee depot is open from 8:00am to 5:00pm Monday through Friday.

Table of Contents

South Dakota Stories
from World War II

CHAPTER 1

The USS Holbrook, Pearl Harbor and the War's Impact on South Dakota

The USS Holbrook left Pearl Harbor a few days before the attack. Ray Swift, Bob Snyder, Earl Bonacker, and Rex W. Leubecher were among the 1,100 South Dakota National Guardsmen on board. They were a part of the 147th Field Artillery Regiment. The ship was painted white with an American flag on its side, making it a good target. As soon as the guardsmen heard about the attack, they set about painting the ship gray in an attempt to camouflage it.[1]

William P. Gese of Mina Lake, near Aberdeen, was member of the 147th Field Artillery Regiment. He was abroad the USS Holbrook when it docked at Pearl Harbor. Because the Holbrook had only a Protestant chaplain, William and other Catholics went to mass on the USS Oklahoma on November 30.[2]

Their original destination was the Philippines, but because of the attack on Pearl Harbor, they were sent to Darwin, Australia, where the unit was to provide defense for the port of Darwin. Later they were sent to New Guinea and divided into two groups. One group loaded trucks, and the other went into battle.[3]

Marvin E. Sletten was born in 1918 in Chancellor, South Dakota. He enlisted in the National Guard in November of 1940. Marvin became a member of 147th Field Artillery Regiment. His unit was sent to Ft. Ord, California, for basic training. Further training took place in Fort Lewis, Washington, where the unit participated in field exercises with the Army's Seventh Division. He shipped out with other members of the 147th on the USS Holbrook.

Marvin wrote a letter home about his voyage to Hawaii and his experience there. It was postmarked November 28, 1941, from Honolulu: "We're about 100 miles from Honolulu. We left San Francisco on September 22nd about 5 o'clock in the afternoon. The ocean was smooth for a while. On the 2nd and 3rd days out we hit a heck of a storm. The wind came up and we really saw how rough water could be. The waves came over the sides of the ship. Some of boys really got sick. I was very lucky and didn't get sick but did get a deuce of a cold. Some of our medics got sea sick and I mean it isn't funny. Sea sickness is the closest you come to dying without doing it. We don't know how long we're staying there yet. From Hawaii, we're going to sea in a big convoy. There will be about ten more ships. We're going to travel in blackout the rest of the way to the Philippines. It will take us about twenty-five days longer because we have to go slower on account of slower ships joining us.

We docked at Pearl Harbor at four in the morning. It's one of the biggest harbors the USA owns. There are warships, destroyers and every other kind of boat you can think of. On the other side of Pearl Harbor there's an airfield. Planes of all types were coming and going all the time. It's about six or seven miles to town. Honolulu isn't what I expected it to be. Not half as pretty. I guess I had it painted up too much. It has rather narrow streets and every other street is one way. The buildings aren't over two or three stories and sort of dirty looking. We don't know how long we'll stay here. On inspecting the ship, they found that a rudder was cracked, so that will have to be repaired. That's what the storm did. You can imagine how big the storm was because the rudder weighs about seven to eight tons." One of Marvin's daughters still has the letter.

Marvin was trained to be a medic. He did not talk about his war experiences until later in life. There were two experiences that stayed with him many years before he finally related them to his daughters. The first was having to amputate a soldier's arm on the battlefield. After the war the soldier got in touch with Marvin to thank him. He was the "advance man" for the Lawrence Welk Show. From then on Marvin got free tickets to all the Lawrence Welk shows.

The second experience occurred when Marvin was on New Guinea where the fighting was intense. The Japanese would not surrender and come out of their caves. Flame throwers were used to force them out into the open. In his dreams he could still visualize a Japanese soldier coming out of a cave with his clothing and skin on fire. The smell of burning flesh lingered in his memory. The soldier was still screaming as he was cut down by rifle and machine gun fire.

The Effects of Combat

Three of the battalions were equipped with 105mm howitzers whose shells would carry about seven miles. They could fire more than three rounds per minute. When several were fired one after another, the noise was deafening. Marvin, like many others, suffered loss of hearing. Malaria was a common tropical disease that affected multitudes of soldiers in the Pacific, including Marvin.[4]

Marvin was a staff sergeant at the time of his discharge in 1945. He had been awarded a Good Conduct Medal and a Bronze Service Arrowhead on his Asiatic-Pacific Theater Ribbon.

Members of the 147th Who Perished
in Service to Their Country

Donald M. Hoon was born on February 14, 1897, in Armour in Douglas County. He was married and had three sons. From 1929 to 1940 he worked in Minneapolis. He entered the service with the 147th Field Artillery Regiment. He was on the USS Holbrook when it left Pearl Harbor a few days before the attack. While the Regiment was in Darwin, Australia, he was promoted to the rank of major. Donald died of a heart attack on May 29, 1942.[5] Dennis E. Pingel of Lake Preston did not survive when he threw himself on a Japanese grenade but saved the lives of at least three comrades. He was awarded the Distinguished Service Cross posthumously.[6]

Gerald Porter was from Colman. In May of 1942, his wife, Arlyne, was informed that he had died defending his country. Gerald was buried in National Cemetery of the Pacific, Honolulu, Hawaii.[7]

Max Smith was born in Wilmot in Roberts County. He went overseas with the 147th. He was fighting on Luzon when he was wounded and died. He was buried in Manila American Cemetery.[8]

Clarence Thompson was from Renner. He enlisted in the 147th and became part of Battery B. He was always concerned about others. Clarence passed up furloughs to go home, allowing men with wives and children to go. He was in combat on Luzon where he died of his wounds. He was buried in Manila American Cemetery.[9]

The 147th fought on Luzon with the Sixth Army. Fighting was vicious, and the men of the 147th were recognized for their bravery. The recognition came in the form of a commendation from Major Leonard Wing of the U.S. Army.

Pearl Harbor and South Dakota

James G. Peacock Sr. was born in Armour on March 28, 1920. He joined the Navy in 1940 and was on the USS Maryland on December 7, 1941. James survived the attack and was transferred to the USS Missouri. James watched history in the making when he observed the signing of the peace treaty that ended the war on September 2, 1945. James passed away on March 31, 2008.[10]

Marvin Melius was born on November 4, 1919, in Faulk County. He joined the Navy on May 16, 1939. His rank was chief petty officer. He was a torpedo man on the USS Ralph Talbot when the attack on Pearl Harbor occurred. He manned a machine gun during the attack. The ship participated in the battles at Guadalcanal, Midway, and Leyte Gulf.[11]

US Navy Task Group 22.3 was commanded by Captain Daniel V. Gallery. The group was made up of his escort aircraft carrier, Guadalcanal, and five destroyer escorts—Pillsbury, Pope, Flaherty, Chatelain, and Jenks—were under the overall command of Frederick S. Hall. Marvin was on the Jenks. A German submarine, U-505, was detected by the Chatelain on June 4,1944. It had been damaged by a depth charge from a destroyer and abandoned. When sailors from the Pillsbury boarded the submarine, they captured papers and books while closing valves to keep the submarine from sinking. Submarine commanders were under orders to open the valves and let their submarine sink rather than have it fall into enemy hands. Somehow in the heat of battle some of the valves had not been opened. The codebooks, Enigma machine, and other materials from the submarine helped the Allied codebreakers.

The capture took place off the coast of Africa. Later the boat was taken to Chicago because the Captain of the Jenks was from there. The U-boat was on display outside for many years, and the elements were taking their toll. The boat was moved, and a building was constructed around it. The boat is on display at the Chicago Museum of Science and Industry.[12] Marvin Melius passed away on March 26, 2008.

Sailors from South Dakota Who Perished in the Attack on Pearl Harbor

On December 7, 1941, the USS Oklahoma lost 429 members of its crew. Navy Fireman 1st Class Walter B. Rogers from Bison died in the attack. The remains of those who perished were buried in two local cemeteries. After the war the remains were disinterred and transferred to the Central Identification Laboratory at Scofield Barracks. Only thirty-five were identified at that time. The remaining unidentified sailors were buried in 46 plots at National Memorial Cemetery of the Pacific, known as the Punchbowl, in Honolulu. They were classified as non-recoverable. In 2015 the unidentified remains were again disinterred in an attempt to identify them. Scientists from DPAA and the Armed Forces Examiner System used mitochondrial DNA analysis which matched Walter's family. A dental analysis also matched his records. Walter was positively identified in 2017 and buried in Arlington National Cemetery. His name is on the Tablets of the Missing in the Honolulu memorial, and the people in charge plan to place a rosette next to Rogers' name indicating that he has been accounted for.[13]

Leaman R. Dill of Huron was an Electrician's Mate on the USS Oklahoma on December 7, 1941. He went down with the ship, and his body was never recovered. His name, along with others from Beadle county who died in WW II, is listed on an obelisk near the public library in Huron.[14]

Arthur M. Grand Pre was from Doland in Spink County. Because of the Dust Bowl he joined the Civilian Conservation Corp (CCC) and worked in the Black Hills. Arthur and his brother Jack enlisted in the Navy. They were on the USS Oklahoma, and while Jack survived the attack, Arthur did not. He was buried in St. Joseph Cemetery in Conde, South Dakota.[15]

Porter L. Rich graduated from Lake Preston High School in 1931. He joined the Navy and served until he was discharged. The U.S. was in the middle of a depression, and there were very few jobs. Porter re-enlisted in 1939 and was assigned to the USS Oklahoma. He was buried in the Punch Bowl in Honolulu.[16] In 2017 scientists using DNA analysis identified Porter's remains which were returned to his family. Porter was buried in Lake Preston on March 31, 2018, with full military honors. His name is on the Tablets of the Missing in the Honolulu memorial, and the people in charge plan to place a rosette next to his name indicating that he has been accounted for.[17]

Myron K. Lehman was born in Buffalo County. There were five boys and three girls in the family. An uncle encouraged four of the five boys to join the Navy. Myron and his brother Laurence were on the USS Oklahoma. Laurence survived the attack; Myron did not. His name is listed on the Tablets of the Missing at the Honolulu memorial.[18]

Laverne A. Nigg was born in Peever in Roberts County. He had eleven brothers and sisters. Laverne was serving on the USS Oklahoma. His body was not recovered. His name is listed on the Tablets of the Missing at the Honolulu memorial.[19]

Edward L. Nigg was from Sisseton. He had four brothers and three sisters. Edward joined the CCC at age 16 and worked in the Black Hills. His brother Robert was in the Navy, and he convinced Edward, Herbert, and a cousin, Laverne Nigg, to join. Edward, Herbert, and Robert survived the attack. Edward was home on leave in July of 1943, when he went swimming in Lake Traverse east of Sisseton. His brother-in-law, Alvin Nelson, and a shipmate, James Nance, were with him. Edward suffered a cramp and drowned. His body was recovered about an hour later Edward was buried in St. Peter's Cemetery in Sisseton.[20]

George W. Jarding was born and raised in Emery. He joined the Navy in 1941 and was trained to be a machinist. He was assigned to the USS Oklahoma. George was 19 when he was buried in Punch Bowl Cemetery in Honolulu. His remains were identified several years later and returned to South Dakota. George was buried in St. Ann's Cemetery in Humboldt.[21]

Jimmie L. Henrichsen had been adopted by John and Alma Henrichsen. He was the youngest member of the family. Jimmie graduated from Platte High School in 1940. After basic training he was assigned to the USS Oklahoma. He was only 20 when he died. His body was not recovered. His name is listed on the Tablets of the Missing at the Honolulu memorial.[22]

There are two monuments to the sailors who died on the USS Oklahoma. One is located on Ford's Island in Pearl Harbor. Another monument is located in Oklahoma City, Oklahoma.

Emery L. Houde graduated from Brandt High School in Deuel County. He worked in a CCC camp before entering the Navy. His rank on the USS Utah was baker second class. Emery's body was not recovered. He is listed on the Tablets of the Missing at the Honolulu memorial.[23]

Arnold L. Anderson graduated from Waverly High School in 1940. He and his two best friends from high school enlisted in the Navy. They went to boot camp in Great Lakes, Illinois. Anderson was assigned to the USS Nevada. He died on December 7, 1941, when a Japanese bomb hit the ship. Arnold was awarded the Purple Heart posthumously.[24]

Herman Goetsch was born on the family farm in Davison County. There were eighteen children in the family, and he was number fifteen. Herman joined the Navy and was assigned to the

USS Nevada. It was close to the Arizona at Pearl Harbor. He died on December 7, 1941, when the ship took a direct hit from a bomb. Herman was buried at the Punchbowl Cemetery in Honolulu.[25]

Harold Roesch was from Wentworth. Because of the Depression he enlisted in the Navy. His first and only experience in the war was at Pearl Harbor where he was killed.[26]

An Act of Bravery During the Attack

Brigadier General La Verne Saunders was born in Stratford. The Japanese attack on Pearl Harbor succeeded in destroying most of the bomber fleet on the ground. La Verne was one of the first to get a bomber air-borne. After encountering a Japanese Zero, he did land the plane. Later in the war he organized and trained the first Bomb Wing of B-29's. He was awarded the Navy Cross, Distinguished Flying Cross, and Purple Heart. He passed away in 1988. La Verne was inducted into the South Dakota Hall of Fame in 2002.[27]

Our Entry into WW II Created a Need for Technically Trained Personnel

To meet the demand for technically trained personnel new bases were built throughout the U.S. The Sioux Falls Chamber of Commerce campaigned for a base. Sioux Falls gained approval for a base and radio training school. It was one of two schools whose purpose was to teach soldiers how to build and operate radios. The Army Air Force Technical Training Command and Radio Training School was located between Covell Lake and the airbase (Foss Field). It covered 1,600 acres.[28]

The training was completed in a three to nine-month period. Their next assignment was gunnery school. The Soldiers became crew men on medium and long-range bombers. In the period from 1942 to 1945, 25,000 Soldiers graduated from the school.[29] The records of the South Dakota National Guard indicate that half of the radio operators who served in Europe were trained in Sioux Falls.[30] The large number of soldiers coming and going had a profound effect on the growth of the city during the 1940's and 1950's.

Soldiers came to the training base from throughout the U.S. By July 21, 1944, at least 355 trainees, representing all but six states, had married local women. The following states with the most soldiers who married local women were Illinois 39, California 39, New York 32, Pennsylvania 30, Minnesota 20, Texas 20, Ohio 19, Wisconsin 19.[31]

Ivan John Ostrander came to the training base from New York. Louise Schweitzer was an Army nurse when they met. Ivan shipped out to the Pacific and served in the 13th Air Force. He manned a machine gun on a B-24 bomber. His plane bombed Tokyo. Louise was sent to England and nursed wounded soldiers. She also served in France. In 1947 they came back to Sioux Falls and were married. Ivan started a business, Screen Process Arts, but left to become an art teacher at Whittier Junior High School and taught many years at Axtell Park Junior High School. Ivan passed away in 2009.[32]

Harold F. Wingler enlisted in the Army Air Force in Indiana. He was sent to the radio school in Sioux Falls. Lois Ann Johnson was from Shindler, just east of Sioux Falls. They were married in 1947. He established Wingler & Sons Auction in 1958. Harold was involved with the business until he passed away in 2002.[33]

Charles A. "Chuck" Connor was born in Charlestown, Massachusetts. After being drafted into the Army, he was sent to the training base. The Arkota Ballroom was a popular social setting for soldiers from the base and local girls. Chuck met Jeanne Swenson there on a blind date. Their marriage took place in Sioux Falls in 1943. Chuck was sent to Normandy, France, and spent two years there. After the war he went into business with his father-in-law and brothers-in-law. The business was known as Swenson Hardware for many years. The name was changed to "Handy Man" and is still operated by family members.[34]

Sidney Epstein was born to Sam and Tillie Epstein on January 16, 1914. His birthplace was New York City. The family moved to West Orange, New Jersey, when Sid was a month old. The family included his brother Irving and sister Rose. Sid graduated from West Orange High School. Sam owned and operated a hardware store where Sid worked before entering the military. Sid's older brother, Irving, served on the front lines in Africa and Germany. Sid was drafted in 1942 and did his basic training at Fort Dix in New Jersey. The next assignment was in Miami, Florida. He was part of a group that was assigned to guard the coast against an Axis invasion. How they were supposed to do that he wasn't quite sure as they did not have any rifles.

The next move brought him to the air base in Sioux Falls in 1942. As supply clerk he was responsible for providing the soldiers with clothing, bedding, and even foot powder. At any given time there was 25,000 to 30,000 soldiers at the base. Sid was in charge of eight to ten men who helped him supply the troops. It seemed as though they were always short of pillows and blankets.

After their training sessions the men could participate in a variety of leisure and recreational activities. On-base activities included singing. Each Soldier was issued a songbook. Movies were shown, and a large PX offered the Soldiers a variety of personal items. The men could participate in athletic competition including basketball, football, boxing, and bowling. There was competition between the various military bases.

An important social outing was going to the USO Club where dancing was the main activity. Nurses from the base hospital, Sioux Valley Hospital, and McKennan Hospital attended the dances. Soldiers were curious about who would be there and become their dance partners. The Convention Center is the present-day location of the base hospital. Other off-base entertainment included movies and dancing at different clubs. The Arkota Ballroom was a popular spot.

Judee Koplow was a teacher at Mark Twain Elementary School. Officials at the air base told her that they would increase her salary if she would teach at the base, she accepted the offer and took courses in radio and Morris code, which qualified her to teach at the base. Later on, she also worked at the message center. She lived with her parents on Phillips Avenue and took a bus to the base. Judee's mother worked at the USO Club. She kept telling Judee about a staff sergeant who came to the club and was a good dancer Judee's mother invited Sid Epstein to their home for dinner. Six months later in January of 1944 Judee and Sid were married in West Orange, New Jersey They were married sixty years. Three children—Henry, Robi, and Barbara—were born to this union. In the early years of their marriage they lived with Judee's parents.

Sid served as supply sergeant for two and a half years. Whenever a group of Soldiers had completed their training, it was his job to make sure they had the proper clothing and personal items for their next assignment. They were assigned as radio operators on all types of military aircraft in the European and Pacific theaters of the war. Sid had to deal with sadness as he knew that some of the Soldiers he checked out would not return.

American commanders and troops were surprised by a German offensive in December of 1944. It became known as the Battle of the Bulge. Sid was sent to Texas for training in preparation for entering the battle. He was on a boat to Europe, but the battle ended, and he did not have to go. His next assignment was to Ford Ord in California. Military planners were getting ready for the invasion of the home islands of Japan. They were estimating that the Allies would suffer at least 100,000 casualties. Sid was being trained to be part of the landing force. Then President Truman made the decision to drop two atomic bombs, and the war ended.

Judee was pregnant when Sid left for training in Texas. Because of his training in Texas, being put on a boat to Europe, and then being sent to California by train, the news of his first-born child, Henry, did not catch up with him until Henry was a month old.

After the war Sid returned to Sioux Falls. Sid and Judee talked about moving to New Jersey so that he could work in the family hardware business, but Judee wanted to stay in Sioux Falls. Judee's family owned a wholesale liquor business, and Sid started to work there. He decided that he wanted to have a liquor store of his own, so he bought a store in 1947. Sid's Crown Liquor was located on Second Avenue and was in operation for several decades.[35] Sid passed away in 2009 at age 95.[36]

Bernard E. "Jim" Hale graduated from Caribou High School in Maine in 1941. He enlisted in the Army Air Corp and was sent to Sioux Falls for military training. Jim graduated from the Radio Operators School with a very satisfactory rating. His military duty took him to India where he served in the China-India-Burma Theater. He flew a total of one hundred seventy-three missions with the 10th Air Force. The total flight time for the missions was 378 hours. Fifty-eight missions were flown in a B-24 Liberator bomber. He was a waist gunner manning a 50-caliber machine gun to ward off enemy fighter planes. He flew one hundred and fifteen missions in a C-46 cargo plane serving as the radio operator. C-46 cargo planes flew over the "Hump" from India to China. They took aviation fuel and other supplies to the Chinese. On the return trip they brought back Japanese prisoners of war. Jim was awarded an Air Medal and the Distinguished Flying Cross. He was promoted to the rank of sergeant in February of 1945.[37]

While attending radio school in Sioux Falls, Jim met Lu Halverson of Toronto at a local bowling alley. Jim and Lu were married in California in 1944 while Jim was still in the service. They lived most of their married life in Sioux Falls. Jim was an insurance agent. Lu taught third grade at Garfield Elementary School. Four daughters made the household complete. They were my in-laws. Jim passed away at age 67 and Lu at 92.

Robert Lewis was from California and trained at the air base. Lorraine K. Putzte was a farm girl from Humboldt when they met. Robert was assigned to Europe and flew missions over Germany. Lorraine joined the Women's Marine Corp. They were married after the war and stayed in Sioux Falls until they both passed away. Robert passed away four months before Lorraine, and she died on his birthday.[38]

As an elementary school teacher Mary Tinkham was earning $75 a month. She decided to become a truck driver at the training base for $150 a month. Paul Graves was from Illinois and was an instructor at the base. They met at the base and were married in 1944. Mary proceeded to take other jobs that paid even more. She became a welder, an assistant to the painter on the flight line, and an office worker in the base laundry. When the war was over and Soldiers returned, she interviewed them and recorded their military experiences.[39] She returned to teaching and taught elementary students many years. Paul took a job at Washington High School teaching English.

Ivan W. Kieser was born on a farm near Wessington Springs. He graduated from Wessington High School in 1939. After enlisting in the Army Air Force in 1943, he was sent to the airbase in Sioux Falls where he was trained to be a radio operator. Further training was completed in Yuma, Arizona, Boise, Idaho, and Miami, Florida. He was deployed to Aviono Air Base in Italy. Ivan was a top turret gunner on a B-24 Liberator bomber. He flew twenty-five missions over Germany, Poland, and Yugoslavia. His plane was shot down over Yugoslavia on October 4, 1944. None of the crew survived. The plane was never found.[40]

John Ronk Jr. was born in Wentworth and graduated from Colman High School. He left Iowa State College to enlist. John was sent to the air base in Sioux Falls for radio operator training. He was on a mission in a B-24 Liberator bomber over Formosa when the plane was shot down. Nobody survived. The crew was buried together at Fort Snelling.[41]

Clarence Mogck was born in Hutchinson County. After earning a teaching degree from Southern State Teachers College in Springfield, he taught school in Yankton County for two years. The new base in Sioux Falls needed teachers. Clarence was employed as a civilian instructor until the end of the war. He passed away in 2010.[42]

A Movie Incentive that Led to a National Show

Movie theater owners in Sioux Falls used a variety of promotions to encourage moviegoers to attend their theater. The promotions included prize drawings and bingo games on the screen. Joe Floyd ran the Hollywood Theater. It was located north of the current Chamber of Commerce building on Phillips Ave. Joe and Cliff Gill came up with an idea that would end up in a date for a local girl and a Soldier from the training base. It was named "G.I. Blind Date." Joe and Cliff wanted the idea to go beyond those attending a movie. Verl Thomson of KELO radio was contacted, and the first show hit the air waves in January of 1943. A petition on stage separated the women from the men. A participant would call a Soldier who would try to convince her that he should be her date. The winners went on a date paid for by the promoters. The show was a success, and Floyd sold the idea to NBC. On NBC it became "Blind Date", hosted by Arlene Francis. The show made it to television in the early 1950's with Francis as the host. The name was changed to "The Dating Game" and continued to be on television from 1965 to 1999.[43]

An Unsolved Tragedy with Connections to the Training Base

Naomi Cheney was a native of Jasper, Alabama. She graduated from high school in Pensacola, Florida. After graduating from college, she was a high school teacher for a short period of time but decided to join the Women's Army Corp (WAC). She first trained at Fort Des Moines in Iowa. Her next assignment was to the air base in Sioux Falls. Naomi rented a room at 525 S. Euclid Ave. On October 5 she ate at the officer's club on base. She had visited her roommate who was in the base hospital. About 9:00 p.m. she left the base and was walking home. She was last seen alive by a cab driver at the corner of Northwest and Sixth Street. The body of Second Lieutenant Naomi Cheney was found in the afternoon of October 6, 1943, near the 12th St. bridge and Grange Ave. She was only three blocks from home. A suspect was arrested on the sixth just as he was ready to leave town. His name was never released. His wife and children lived in Iowa. He had worked in Minnesota before moving to Sioux Falls. The police found some evidence of a crime in his room at Smith's Auto Court; today it is Nites Inn. They found blood on his shoes and blood-matted hair near and inside the cabin. He could not explain where the blood had come from. The blood and hair samples were sent to the FBI in Washington but were not good enough at that time to prove anything. The suspect had been drafted and was ready to go to basic training. He was released on October 27th. An extensive search took investigators to several states, but no information was found to explain why Naomi had been killed.[44]

The 1945 Closing of the Base

Some of the buildings were moved after the war. Two barrack buildings were on the campus of Sioux Falls College on Menlo Avenue. They were the home of Kilian Community College for many years A large building was moved to the campus at Augustana College to be used as temporary class rooms for the art department.[45] The temporary building was replaced in 2006. A theatre building and two barracks found a new home in Freeman at the Junior College. One of the base chapels became the first site of Our Savior's Lutheran Church. Another chapel was moved to the south-eastern part of Sioux Falls for a new Catholic congregation. A mess hall was dismantled by members of the First Reformed Church for a new building at 19th St. and Grange Avenue.[46] A few were moved and became residences.

As time passed, some of the land was converted to other uses. It became the building site for the Sioux Falls Arena, airport, Veteran's Park south of Russell St., Dow Rummel Retirement Village, athletic fields, and Elmwood Golf Course.[47]

Facilities Established to Aid the War Effort

An airfield was built east of Rapid City in January of 1942. Its mission was to train crewmen to fly the B-17 Flying Fortress, a heavy-duty bomber. The mission has changed over the years to adapt to new aircraft. The base was named Ellsworth Air Force Base in 1953. The base contributed to the growth of Rapid City's population and continues to be important in their economy.

The Black Hills Ordinance Depot was located in Provo. It covered 21,095 acres and was in existence from 1942 to 1967. The ordinance depot was named Igloo for the mound-shaped huts used to store munitions. Men and women worked on a machine in Igloo that put 50 caliber ammunition on belts.[48] The ammunition was used in fighter planes and in heavy bombers. A man-proof structure was completed in 1958 to store leaking mustard-gas containers. Since the 1990's unexploded weapons have been discovered in the area.[49] The government has spent a large amount of money on clean-up. Land on the Pine Ridge Indian Reservation was used as a practice bombing range.[50]

Training bases were also located in Pierre and Mitchell. A Personnel Distribution Command was located in Watertown and a contract flying school was headquartered in Aberdeen.

Historic Markers Marking the Locations of Military Airplane Crashes in South Dakota

Two AT-18 bombers from the Sioux Falls Training Base collided in midair on December 8, 1944. The radio operators on board were practicing the skills they had learned at the base. One plane crashed into a barracks building on base. All seven on the plane died in addition to three in the barracks. The pilot of the other plane flew it north of the city, and six crewmen bailed out. The pilot also made it out before the plane crashed east of Renner. A historic marker is located on Industrial Boulevard in Sioux Falls marking the area where the planes collided.[51]

On June 13, 1943, two B-17 bombers attached to the 393rd Bomb Group, the "Flying Sioux", left their home base in Sioux City,

Iowa. They were on a training mission to practice flying in formation. In the process of switching places they collided in midair. The crew from one of the bombers survived. All eleven crew members in the other plane perished. Brett Selland and Pat Maroney spearheaded a project to place markers at the crash sites. Business owners in Howard contributed to the cost of the markers. One marker is located west of Howard near Fedora along Highway 34. Another marker was placed north of Epiphany along Highway 25.[52]

A historic marker twenty-six miles south of Lemmon commemorates the crash of a B-24 Liberator bomber in October of 1944. Engine failure contributed to the crash. Four members of the ten-man crew died in the wreck. The Meadow Historical Society and Sons of the American Legion paid for the marker.[53]

Bill Clary and Joe Liberi were the only survivors when a B-29 Superfortress bomber crashed near Philip on September 28, 1944. Eight crew members died. The plane was on a training flight from Kearney, Nebraska. Twelve planes were flying in a diamond formation when a plane clipped the engine of the plane Clary and Liberi were in. One monument was placed in the field where the crash occurred. Another monument is on the grounds of the Haakon County Courthouse.[54]

A B-17 Flying Fortress from the air base east of Rapid City crashed near the city on September 6, 1943. None of the crew members survived. The crash was investigated, and no apparent cause for the crash was discovered.[55]

A B-24 Liberator was returning to its training base in Sioux Falls when it slammed into a mountain near Elgin, Oregon. The date was August 25, 1945. Eleven veterans from the European Theatre died in the crash. Their names and the names of the ten who died when a AT-18 bomber crashed into a barracks are listed on a historic marker titled *Forgotten Heroes*. It is located at Algonquin St. and "E" Avenue in Sioux Falls.[56]

The Tale of a Survivor

Dale Coates of Ramona was in a B-29 bomber that collided with another B-29 over South Dakota. He bailed out over White River. All crew members survived. He had the misfortune of being on a B-29 that went down in the Pacific Ocean on December 3, 1944. Dale and his crew mates were in the water for eleven days before they were picked up by the USS Roe. His body weight went from 185 pounds to 92 pounds.[57]

CHAPTER 2

The Political and Economic Climate in
The United States and Japan during the 1930's

The 1930's saw the United States and Japan going down different paths. Japan was preparing for war. The military had gained political power and built a navy, an air force, and organized a land army. The U. S. government was not preparing the nation for war. There was vocal opposition to getting involved in another European war. The U.S.'s main problem was figuring out how to deal with the Depression and drought. A threat of war was not the major thing on most people's minds as they were just trying to survive economically.

The collapse of the stock market had a domino effect. Banks closed, and people lost their savings. Businesses closed, and millions lost their jobs. In addition to the national depression, people in South Dakota faced even more challenges. When WW I ended, the demand for wheat and corn in Europe declined, causing a decline in farm prices. Low prices continued during the 1920's and on into the 1930's. Farmers had borrowed money on their land when prices and land values were high. By 1935 many farmers owed more money to the bank than the land was worth. The banks foreclosed on many farmers and became owners of land.

In 1930 the rain stopped, and the wind began to blow, creating dust storms. South Dakota became part of the Dust Bowl stretching from North Dakota to Texas. The dust covered everything and entered homes around doors and windows. People developed dust pneumonia, and livestock died. Just when it looked as if nothing else could go wrong, a green cloud descended and covered the land. Grasshoppers started by eating all things green and growing. Because of the drought it didn't take the grass-hoppers long to eat the vegetation. They moved on to anything they could chew. One target was clothes that had been hung on the line to dry. The wooden handle on a garden hoe became part of their menu. If they got into a house, the curtains were eaten.

South Dakota and the Civilian Conservation Corps

Unemployment was high in the 1930's, and the farm economy was bleak. The Civilian Conservation Corp (CCC) offered single men ages 18 to 25 a job, room and board, and pay of $30.00 a month. The age limits were changed a few times. Every man in the CCC got to keep $5.00, but $25.00 had to be sent home to his family. The $25 bought much-needed food, clothing, and tires for the car.[58]

The men from the various camps completed a variety of projects. They quarried and crushed rock, built roads and bridges, thinned trees, and constructed buildings. One of the larger projects was the construction of Lake of the Pines Dam, which created Lake Sheridan.[59] Historic markers throughout the Black Hills tell the stories of the various camps and what the young men did. Harold Eastwick, John Elrod, Floyd Forester, Edward Mark, Gordon Rich, Ernest Thietje, Leonard Warner, and Robert Westover served in the CCC and in WW II. They returned to live full and complete lives.

The following individuals were among those who served in the CCC, joined the military, and died in service to their country.

Their biographies can be found in *Fallen Sons and Daughters of South Dakota in WW II*, volumes one through six, at a public library.

Donald Adams, Glen Andersen, Dale Anderson, Glen Anderson, Vern Anderson, Eldin Arms, Benedict Axtman, Kenneth Bakkie, LaVerne Bauer, William Bauer, Norman Bergen, Gerhard Biberdorf, Glen DeBoise, Curtis Eggema, Jacob Erlenbudsch, Fay Floerchinger, Harrison Geyer, Jr., Emil Goeden, Alfred Hanson Jr., Lester Holt, Al Holtquist, Joseph Jandel, Alfred Johnson, Robert Jordan, Leon Killer, Alvin King, Gilbert Knodel, Robert Kotalik, Clyde Lee, Floyd Lewis, Nelson Linton, Harry Lofgren, Robert Lowry, Eugene Martell, Calvin Miller, Milton Muller, William Neilan, Leonard Neugebauer, Walter Nies, Edward Nigg, Ralph Olson, Lyle Paulson, Norman Portwood, Joe Prickett, Ralph Randall, Enoch Raymond III, John Redman, Joseph Rigney, Austin Rouag, Elmer Rusch, Emmens Sand, Robert Schlotter, Norman Severson, John Simmons, Lowell Stoner, Donald Theis, John Vosika, Cecil Waldron, Sigurd Westin, Winfred Wudel, Harry Ziegler, Selmer Langager, Donald Mangan, Kenneth Vander Hamm, Selmer Waxdahl, and Howard Kopke.

CHAPTER 3

Stories of Prison Conditions, Hell Ships, Heroism, Endurance, Survival, Sacrifice, and Misfortune

As 1942 dawned, the US and its allies were in dire military straits. The Nazis through appeasement and military force controlled most of Europe. Japan had overrun a large portion of the Pacific including the island groups: Solomons, Gilberts, Marshalls, Marianas, Carolines, and the Philippines. Major General Edward King Jr. was in command of the American and Filipino troops on the Bataan Peninsula. On April 9, 1942, Major King Jr. was forced to surrender 75,000 troops to the Japanese. A small number had escaped to the island of Corregidor. The troops there held out until they surrendered on May 6, 1942.

When the Bataan Death March began, 78,000 troops were alive. The march covered a distance of sixty-five miles. During the march about 10,000 troops perished. They died from starvation, thirst, wounds they had when the march started, and at the hands of Japanese guards. Troops were bayoneted, shot, and thrown in front of oncoming tanks. Their destination was Camp O'Donnell.[60]

A Startlingly Discovery When They Reached a Camp

Conditions at O'Donnell, Cabantuan, Bilibid, and others were appalling. It is hard to believe that POWs did survive the conditions they had to endure. They were tormented by a variety of bugs including mosquitos, bed bugs (which smelled bad when they were crushed), lice, fleas, and centipedes.[61] Lice were especially exasperating in that they could not be kept out of a Soldier's socks and his feet were constantly itching.[62]

Prisoners were fed a limited amount of extremely poor-quality food. The rice contained rat droppings which they tried to sort out before eating it, but if they were really hungry, they didn't bother. When meat arrived at a camp, it was usually rotten and swarming with blowfly maggots. The maggots were washed away, and the meat was cooked before being eaten.[63]When soup was served, it was mainly water with a little rice and sometimes other things that were hard to describe, but they were hungry and ate all of it.

The lack of food and quality of what they did get led to malnutrition and made them more susceptible to many diseases. They were subjected to cholera, malaria, tropical ulcers, dengue fever (which caused the joints to swell), varying degrees of dysentery, scabies (which made them want to itch), and beriberi. Beri-beri is caused by a B-1 deficiency. Prisoners did not get good meat, fish, nuts, whole grains, or vegetables which would have prevented the disease.[64]

Unsanitary conditions in the camps contributed to the spread of various diseases and increased the death tolls. Prisoners also had to deal with the brutality of Japanese guards. They were beaten with a variety of instruments resulting in broken bones and other injuries. "Statistics collected after the war revealed that the death rate of U.S.

POWs in German and Italian camps was about four percent. In Japanese camps the death rate was closer to thirty percent".[65]

South Dakotans Who Died in Japanese POW Camps

James E. Wagner was born in 1920 in Tyndall. He was an outstanding athlete in high school. After working for Shell Oil Company in California, he returned and joined the military in Sioux Falls in 1941. Jim, along with many other soldiers, was forced to surrender on Bataan. He survived the Bataan Death March and was a POW for three years. The U.S. was closing in on the Philippines in 1945. The Japanese started to move their POWs to other locations. James was sent to Formosa. He died there on April 3, 1945, of beri beri.[66]

Orlando C. Nelson, like many kids at that time, was born on the family farm in 1917. He graduated from Oldham High School in 1935. Orlando was a farmer until he enlisted in the Army Air Corps in 1939. His training took place in California, Illinois, and again in California before he was sent overseas in 1941. Orlando was a staff sergeant with the 21st Pursuit Squadron, 35th Pursuit Group. He was a radio operator and a mechanic. He survived the Bataan Death March. Military records indicate that he died on July 1, 1943. According to newspaper records, the cause of death was beriberi. Orlando was buried in Oldham Lutheran Cemetery in 1943.[67]

Julius A. Anderson was born in 1919 in Viborg. He was a trucker and worked at a creamery before joining the Army in 1941. After his training was completed, he was sent overseas. He was captured by the Japanese in Java in 1942. Julius was a POW in Moulmein, Burma. He died of beriberi in 1943. His family was not notified of his death until September of 1945. He is buried in National Cemetery of the Pacific in Honolulu.[68]

John Bennett was born in Pierre in 1909. He joined the Army Air Corps in 1939. John was trained as a field mechanic and sent to Clark Field in the Philippines. He became a prisoner after the fall of Corregidor. John survived the Bataan Death March and was held at Camp O'Donnell on Luzon. He died in the camp of dysentery in May of 1942. His final resting place is in Manila American Cemetery.[69]

Daniel G. Eakins was born in 1912 in Gary. He was one of twelve children. Daniel graduated from Gary High School. He was in the Army and was a member of the 803rd Engineering Battalion. Daniel became a POW when Corregidor surrendered. He was a POW from May to June of 1942. Daniel died of malnutrition in a prison camp on June 1, 1942. He is listed on the Tablets of the Missing at Manila American Cemetery.[70]

Lloyd W. Lewis was born in November of 1917 in Mitchell. He graduated from Mitchell High School in 1936. Lloyd enlisted in the Navy in 1937. He became a prisoner of the Japanese. The records show that he died of beriberi. He is buried in Manila American Cemetery.[71]

Darrell M. Wightman was born in Larchwood, Iowa, in 1921. His parents moved to Sioux Falls. He worked at a CCC camp in Rapid City in 1938 before enlisting in the Army the same year. He was assigned to the 31st Infantry Division and sent to the Pacific. For a number of reasons the American and Filipino troops on Bataan were forced to surrender. The date was April 9, 1942. Darrell's mother did not receive official notice of his death until November of 1945. The information from the War Department stated that he died on July 31, 1942, on Bataan as a result of malaria and dysentery. He was awarded the Bronze Star for his service. The O'Donnell Memorial Monument was built to honor all those who died. Darrell's name is on the monument. He is also listed on the Tablets of the Missing at Manila American Cemetery.[72]

Douglas F. Kiewel was a 1937 graduate of Washington High School in Sioux Falls. He enlisted in the Army Air Corps in 1940. His training took place in California, and he was assigned to the 34th Pursuit Squadron, 24th Pursuit Group. He was sent to Nicholas Field near Manila. Private Kiewel became a POW when the Philippines surrendered to the Japanese. In 1945 Kiewel's mother, Alma, received a telegram informing her that Douglas had died in 1942 He had been in Camp Cabanatuan and died from dysentery and malaria. In 1949, the family received an official letter that Douglas had been buried in Manila American Cemetery. The WW II Memorial in Pierre was dedicated in 2001. His cross and name card were returned to the family at that time.[73]

Richard C. Smith graduated from Brooking High School in 1938. Smith took his aviation exam at South Dakota State College in 1939 and in 1939 enlisted in the Army Air Corps. His training took him to Illinois, Louisiana, and Georgia. He became a crew chief and was sent to Manila. In January of 1943 his family was informed that he was a POW in Camp Cabanatuan in the Philippines. He died from amoebic dysentery. Richard was buried in the Philippines with two others. He was re-interred at Fort McPherson National Cemetery in Maxwell, Nebraska, in March of 1950. His remains could not be identified from the other two soldiers who had been buried with him in the Philippines. The remains of all three were buried together in a single grave with a single marker.[74]

Lars C. Jensen was born in Viborg in 1909. He attended South State College in Brookings and Iowa State College in Ames. Lars was a supervisor in a CCC camp prior to joining the military. In January of 1941 he was sent overseas as part of the 145th Infantry. He was a second lieutenant. He became a POW in May of 1942 and was held at Camp Cabanatuan. In July of 1943 his family was notified that he had died in October of 1942.

The telegram did not give a specific cause of death. Lars was survived by his wife, Myrtle, and a daughter, Marjorie Louise, who was born in 1939. His remains were returned to the US and reburied at Fort Snelling in Minneapolis.[75]

Clayton Gibbons was born at Wounded Knee in Shannon County. He was sent overseas in 1941 with the Army Air Corps. His father, William, received a letter stating that Clayton had become a POW and died from malaria. The date of his death was July 1, 1943.[76]

Jacob Heinrich was from Herreid. He graduated from the University of South Dakota and earned an M.A. degree from the University of Ohio. He was called to active duty in 1941 before Pearl Harbor. He was on Corregidor and part of the group who surrendered to the Japanese. His wife received a report informing her that Jacob had died in a Japanese prison camp.[77]

Roger Pederson graduated from Macintosh High School in Corson County. He enlisted in 1941 and was trained at Angel Island, San Francisco. Roger was sent to the Philippines for more training as a radio technician in the Army Air Corps. He was on Clark Field when he was captured by the Japanese after the fall of Bataan and Corregidor. He died in a Japanese prison camp. After the war his parents had his remains returned to South Dakota.[78]

Charles Robinson graduated from Hudson High School in 1937.He registered for the selective service, and his number was drawn from the Selective Service Lottery. After basic training he transferred to the Army Air Corps and became an aircraft mechanic. He was sent to the Philippines and arrived the day of the attack on Pearl Harbor. He became a POW and survived the Bataan Death March. Charles was held at Camp O'Donnell prison camp and died there from malaria. After the war his remains were returned and buried in Eden Cemetery at Hudson.[79]

Gerhardt Steinbach was from Yankton. He enlisted in Army in 1941. After basic training he was sent to Clark Field in the Philippines. After Pearl Harbor he became a POW. Gerhardt died at Camp O'Donnell. He was buried in Manila American Cemetery.[80]

Robert Wendroff graduated from Watertown High School in 1936 and later from the University of Wisconsin. He was a member of the 194th Tank Battalion. Robert was on Bataan and became a POW. He died in 1942. Robert was buried in Manila American Cemetery.[81]

George Zimmerman served with the Army at Ft. Meade near Sturgis before he was sent to the Philippines in May of 1941. Corregidor fell in 1942, and George became a POW. It was reported that he died on January 29, 1945. George is listed on the Tablets of the Missing at Manila American Cemetery.[82]

Frederick Miller was from Buffalo Gap in Custer County. He was a veteran of WW 1. Frederick re-enlisted in the military in January of 1941. His unit trained in Texas and was sent to the Philippines in September of 1941. The Japanese invaded the Philippines in December of 1941. The Americans retreated to Bataan where the Death March took place. Frederick died as a POW. He was buried in Manila American Cemetery.[83]

Kenneth Quande was born in Sisseton in 1912. He enlisted in the Navy in 1930 and served four years. Kenneth re-enlisted in 1940 and was sent to the Philippines. After the fall of Corregidor he became a POW and died in a prison camp of malaria. The official date of his death was listed as November 17, 1942. His brother Harold also served in the military.[84]

Clarence Rice was from Newell in Butte County. He enlisted in the Army in January of 1941. Clarence was sent to the Pacific in

October of 1941.He was with a chemical company. Clarence became a POW and died in a Japanese prison camp on January 1, 1943. His final resting place is in Mt. Moriah Cemetery in Deadwood.[85]

Raymond Shaffer was born in Colman. He joined the military in 1938 and served two years. He re-enlisted in May of 1940 and was sent to the Philippines in February of 1942. Raymond wrote a letter from Bataan describing how difficult the conditions were. He was reported as missing in action in May of 1942. The official letter stated that he died on May 23, 1942, on the Philippine Islands. He had been a Japanese POW. Raymond is buried in Manila American Cemetery.[86]

Glen White was from Montrose in McCook County. He was serving in the Army and was stationed in the Philippines. Glen was part of the group that surrendered to the Japanese on Bataan Peninsula. The "Death March" followed. Although Glen was reported as missing in action, his body was recovered and buried in Manila American Cemetery.[87]

Frank Williams Jr. was from Fruitvale in Butte County. He joined the Army Air Corps and was stationed in the Philippines. Frank became a POW and died in a prison camp on Corregidor. His remains were returned and buried in Pine Slope Cemetery in Belle Fourche.[88]

South Dakotans Who Died as German POWS

John Murphy graduated from Vermillion High School and law school at the University of South Dakota. John and Ruth Anderson were married in 1942. They had two children. John was serving in the Army and was part of a Reconnaissance Squadron. He was sent overseas in August of 1944. John became a German POW and died of heart failure. He was buried near the prison camp in Obermassfeld, Germany.[89]

Lowell Rempel graduated from Wentworth High School in 1935. He worked for a local farmer in the Wentworth area until he was drafted in July of 1941. Lowell was sent overseas as part of an infantry unit. He was in combat in Luxembourg when he was reported as missing in action. He sent a postcard saying that he was a German POW. An official notice from the government stated that he had died from pneumonia while being held in a German prison camp. The date was May 16, 1945.[90]

Herman Vollmer was born in Pierre. He joined seven brothers and sisters. Herman joined the Army in 1942 and trained in Kentucky, Kansas, Louisiana, and Texas. He was sent overseas in 1944 as part of the 52nd Armored Infantry Division. His unit was in combat in Northern Luxembourg at the beginning of the Battle of the Bulge. They were outnumbered and had to surrender. Herman had been wounded in the cheek. The prisoners were marched from one camp to another with little to eat. Herman became so ill that he was taken to a hospital where he died. His remains were returned to the U.S. in 1949. Herman was buried beside his parents in the cemetery near St. Peter's Lutheran Church south of Midland.[91]

The Massacre at Palawan

Erving A. Evans attended grade school in Huron. After enlisting in the Army in 1931, he served three years at Fort Meade. He re-enlisted in 1940 and was sent to cook and baker school in California. In April of 1941 he was assigned to Fort Mills on Corregidor. After the fall of Corregidor, he became a POW. He was held at Puerto Princesa on Palawan. The prisoners did not have any bedding or medical supplies, and there was a complete lack of any sanitation facilities. They endured regular beatings. There were several attempts made to escape. The war was drawing to a close, and the Japanese guards were ordered to kill POWs. One hundred and fifty prisoners were forced into air raid shelters lined with wood. Gas was poured in and ignited with flaming grenades. The shelters exploded into an inferno. Those who got out were machine gunned or killed with clubs and bayonets. Evans was among those who perished. Ten did escape.[92]

A Bataan Survivor

Jake Padilla opened the El Matador restaurant at 423 S. Phillips Ave in March of 1968. He was the only person in Sioux Falls who had survived the Bataan Death March. Jake passed away in 1972.[93]

Hell Ships

After the Americans landed in the Philippines, the Japanese began to move POWs to new locations. The ships used to transport prisoners were described as Hell Ships for several reasons. There was not enough space, air, food, and water. The largest hold on the Arisan Maru looked as if it had room for 200 men. The Japanese forced 1,805 men into the hold. Because of heat, lack of air, short rations, and little water, five men were dead after two days. On October 24, 1944, the ship was torpedoed by an American submarine. The Japanese did not mark any of the Hell Ships with the Red Cross symbol, and American pilots and submarines did not know that the ships were carrying Americans. A Japanese ship came to the aid of the Arisan Maru, but the commander refused to rescue Americans from the water. Only nine survived.[94]

On the Oryoku Maru prisoners were so tightly packed that there was not enough air and they felt as though they were suffocating. Those few near the open hatches had enough air to breathe, and those below did not. Fighting broke out between those who had air and those who didn't. The crowded conditions and temperature of 100 degrees caused them to sweat and feel as though they were drowning. Lack of water caused their tongues to swell, adding to the torment of the situation. The holds of the ships were very unsanitary. Liquid flows downhill, and there were several levels in the hold of a ship. More than 126,000 prisoners were transported on Hell Ships, and more than 21,000 died in transit.[95]

Robert A. Mathias was born in Rapid City in 1922. After high school graduation in 1940, he enlisted in the Marines. He was assigned to M Co., 3rd Battalion of the 4th Marines and sent to the Philippines. Robert was stationed at Bataan and Corregidor before he became a prisoner. When the fighting was over, the 4th Marine Regiment was so decimated that it ceased to exist as a unit. Robert was one of only 43 Marines who survived the Bataan Death March to Camp O'Donnell. Little is known about his years as a POW. He was abroad the Arisan Maru when it left Manila on October 10, 1944. It was sunk by an American submarine on October 24, 1944. Robert is listed on the Tablets of the Missing at Manila American Cemetery. He was awarded the Purple Heart.[96]

Harry J. Fleeger was born in 1908 in Parker. He was appointed to West Point and graduated in 1931. After training at two bases in the U.S., he was sent to the Philippines. Harry's wife, Louise, and two children went with him to Manila. By June of 1941 all Army families had been sent back to the U.S.Harry survived the Bataan Death March and being a prisoner until October of 1944. He was abroad the Arisan Maru when it was sunk on October 24, 1944.

Harry is listed on the Tablets of the Missing at Manila American Cemetery.[97]

Thomas C. Arnold was born in 1911. He grew up on a cattle and horse ranch near Hermosa. Tom loved horses and joined the Cavalry at Fort Meade in 1941. He was sent to the Philippines and was held as prisoner from 1941 until 1944. Tom was on the Arisan Maru when it was sunk. He was awarded a Purple Heart and is listed on the Tablets of the Missing at Manila American Cemetery.[98]

Edward G. Kindle was born in Lake Andes in 1914. His nickname was "Babe". He attended school in Hamill, Colome, and an Indian school in Kansas. Both of his parents died when he was young. Babe and his siblings worked for local farmers. He took a job with the CCC in Pierre before enlisting in the Army in 1939. His training took place at Fort Bliss in Texas and Fort Monroe in Virginia. He was sent to the Philippines in July of 1941. On Corregidor he was in charge of truck drivers and mechanics. He became a POW on May 6, 1942, when Corregidor surrendered. Edward was a POW until 1944. He was on the Arisan Maru. Edward was awarded the Purple Heart, and his name is listed on the Tablets of the Missing at Manila American Cemetery.[99]

Richard Hilliard grew up near Veblen and attended school there with his sisters. Because of the depression he worked at a CCC camp in the Black Hills until 1937. He entered military service in February of 1941. Richard was sent to Manila and was a driver hauling equipment. He became a POW in May of 1942. Richard survived the Bataan Death March and helped others to survive. He was a POW until 1944. Richard was on the Arisan Maru when it was sunk by a submarine, the USS Snook. He was awarded a Purple Heart, and his name is listed on the Tablets of the Missing at Manila American Cemetery.[100]

Ernest L. Christensen was born in 1918 and grew up in White, South Dakota. He enlisted in the Navy. Ernest was a POW at Bilibid prison camp from January of 1942 until October of 1944. He was on a Hell Ship that was torpedoed by an American submarine on October 24, 1944. There were several hundred prisoners aboard. He was awarded the Purple Heart, and his name is listed on the Tablets of the Missing at Manila American Cemetery.[101]

Robert F. Wallbaum was born in Yankton. He graduated from Yankton High School and law school at the University of South Dakota. Robert joined the Army in 1939. Training took place at Camp Rapid and the Presedio in San Francisco. He was assigned to the Judge Advocate's department and transferred to Manila. Robert served as a JAG officer until he became a prisoner. He survived two years in a prison camp. Robert was on a Hell Ship that was sunk in the South China Sea. The date was October 24, 1944.[102]

Vinal F. Sayre was born in Volga in 1917. He entered military service in 1940. Basic training took place at Fort Banning in Georgia and Fort Snelling in Minnesota. He was sent to the Philippines in the later part of 1940. Vinal fought on Bataan and Corregidor. He was held in a prison camp on Luzon island. Vinal was on a Hell Ship that was sunk on October 24, 1944. He was awarded the Purple Heart.[103]

Clarence E. Sayer was born in Britton in 1915 and graduated from Britton High School in 1932. Because of the depression he joined the CCC in 1933 and worked at Camp Lodge in Rapid City a year and a half. Clarence attended Black Hills State College two years and earned high honors. His next educational stop was at Stanford University for one year. He entered military duty as a draftee in 1940. He was a medical student at Northwestern University in Chicago and then was sent to Medical College in

Eugene, Oregon, for further training. His first assignment in Manila was at Sternberg Hospital. After joining the 31st Infantry, he was placed in charge of the medical department. Clarence became a POW on Luzon and survived the march to Camp Cabanatuan. There is no information about his years as a POW. He was on a Japanese ship that was sunk by an American submarine on October 24, 1944.[104]

John C. Bingham Jr. was born in Harding County in 1903. He graduated from Spearfish High School and became a Marine in 1925. John played the cornet in the Marine band. He enjoyed his time in the Marines and served three four-year enlistments. John was sent to China in 1938 and served there until 1941 when he went to the Philippines. He fought on Corregidor until the surrender. John was a POW from May of 1942 until October 24, 1944. He was aboard the Arisan Maru when it was sunk by an American submarine. John was awarded the Purple Heart. His name is listed on the Tablets of the Missing at Manila American Cemetery.[105]

Otis C. Bryant was born in 1909 in Indiana. His parents divorced. His mother and the three children moved to Nebraska and lived with relatives. Later they moved to Peever, South Dakota, and his mother remarried. Otis stayed with an aunt and uncle. He started school in Peever. Mary and her new husband homesteaded near Lemmon. Otis lived in Perkins County until he left the family farm in the late 1920's. He entered the military in 1930. Otis had been promoted to the rank of captain when he was sent to the Philippines. He was captured and survived the Bataan Death March. There are no records about his years as a POW. Otis was on an unmarked Japanese ship when it was sunk on October 24, 1944. He was awarded the Purple Heart. His name is listed on the Tablets of the Missing at Manila American Cemetery.[106]

Richard B. Williams was from Gettysburg in Potter County. He was born in 1914 and graduated from the Naval Academy in

1937. Richard was commissioned a second lieutenant on November of 1940 and was assigned to the USS Oahu. His duties included that of executive officer and chief engineer. The ship was sunk in May of 1942, and Williams became a prisoner. All of the prisoners were marched to POW Camp: #1 Cabanatuan. He survived the brutal conditions of the camp two years. In late 1944 he was transferred to Bilibid camp in Manila. Richard's last letter to his wife was dated December 13, 1944. On that day Williams was one of the 1,619 POWS who were marched from the camp to be boarded on the Oryoku Maru bound for Japan. The ship was sunk on December 15 by aircraft from the USS Hornet, an American aircraft carrier. His body was not recovered. Only 425 survived.[107]

Harry J. Harper was born in 1901. He attended school in Wolsey. Harry served in WW I at the age of sixteen. He graduated from West Point in 1925. Harry and Cecile Navin were married in 1925 and had four children. In 1941 he was sent to the Philippines with the 31st Field Artillery Regiment. Harry became a POW when Corregidor surrendered. He was a prisoner in Bilibid prison camp. On December 13, 1944, he and 1,619 other prisoners were put on the Oryoku Maru. The ship was sunk by U.S. Navy planes from the aircraft carrier USS Hornet. He survived the sinking of the ship but died a few days later of malaria. Harry is listed on the Tablets of the Missing at Manila American Cemetery.[108]

Belle Fourche was Robert K. Magee's hometown. He graduated from high school in 1936 and the University of South Dakota in 1940. Robert was commissioned a second lieutenant in 1940. After volunteering for overseas duty, he was sent to the Philippines in 1941. He was with the 31st Infantry Division and promoted to first lieutenant. After fighting broke out, he was taken prisoner and survived the Bataan Death March. He was held at Camp Davao from 1941 to 1944. He was at Camp Cabanatuan from

June until September and then moved back to Manila. He and other prisoners were boarded on the Enoura Maru which was sunk on January 9, 1945. He was awarded the Purple Heart, and his name is listed on the Tablets of the Missing at Manila American Cemetery.[109]

Willibald C. Bianchi graduated from South Dakota State College in 1940. He joined the Army when he was working in Brookings. Bill, as he was known in college, was in the 45th Infantry Division. His regiment was engaged in intense fighting on Bataan. He was wounded three times: once in the left hand, a second time in the chest, and a third time when he was firing a machine gun from the top of a tank and was blown off sustaining a severe wound, He was awarded the Congressional Medal of Honor. Even with his wounds he survived the Bataan Death March and being a prisoner until January 9, 1945. Based on the date he was probably on the Enoura Maru. Bill is listed on the Tablets of the Missing at Manila American Cemetery.[110]

Donald G. Whitman was born in 1917 and graduated from Aberdeen High in 1935. Don attended South Dakota State College two years and graduated from the University of South Dakota in 1939. He was in the ROTC program at USD and was commissioned a second lieutenant. His overseas duty was in the Philippines, where he was in command of Battery D, 24th Field Artillery, Philippine Scouts. Don survived three years at Camp Cabanatuan. He was on a Japanese ship bound for Japan when it was sunk on December 15, 1944. The Oryoku Maru was sunk on that date. He is listed on the Tablets of the Missing at Manila American Cemetery.[111]

James B. Campbell and his mother lived in White Lake. He enlisted in the Army in 1936 and was sent overseas in April of 1941. He became a POW when the Philippines fell. Campbell survived as a prisoner three and a half years. There were 1,600 prisoners on the Enoura Maru when it was sunk in Takao Harbor in Formosa by

American planes. The date was January 9, 1944. He was awarded the Purple Heart and is listed on the Tablets of the Missing at Manila American Cemetery.[112]

Wallace F. Churchill graduated from Wessington Springs High School in 1937. He enrolled at the University of Nebraska and after graduating joined the Army Air Corps. He trained at several airfields and learned to fly a variety of aircraft. Wallace was at Clark Field in the Philippines and was wounded. After recovering, he was assigned to an infantry unit. When Mindanao fell, he became a prisoner. He was held at Camp Davao until 1944. Wallace and 750 other Americans were on the Shinyo Maru when it was torpedoed by an American submarine off the coast of Mindanao. A total of 668 perished. The date was September 7, 1944. He was awarded the Purple Heart and is listed on the Tablets of the Missing at Manila American Cemetery.[113]

Lincoln F. Karl was born in 1918 in Aberdeen. He graduated from Aberdeen Central High School in 1937. He wanted to become a member of a flight crew which led him to enlist in the Army Air Corps in 1941. Lincoln was stationed at Nichols Field with Headquarters Squadron, 20th Air Group. When the Americans surrendered at Corregidor, he became a POW. Lincoln survived the Bataan Death March and was a POW for over two years. He was on the Shinyo Maru when it was torpedoed. He was awarded the Purple Heart and is listed on the Tablets of the Missing at Manila American Cemetery.[114]

American troops on Bataan surrendered to the Japanese. Joseph Stensland was on the Oryoku Maru on December 15, 1944, when it was bombed by Navy planes from the aircraft carrier USS Hornet. He is listed on the Tablets of the Missing at Manila American Cemetery.[115]

Two Hell Ships

Cecil C. Welch was born in March of 1904 in White, South Dakota. After graduating from Brookings High School, he attended South Dakota State College two years. Cecil graduated from the School of Medicine at the University of South Dakota in 1925. He went on to graduate from Northwestern University Medical School in Illinois in 1927. Cecil and Lara Minor were married in Chicago in 1927 and had two children. Dr. Welch enlisted in the Navy in 1927. He was assigned to positions in Boston, Rhode Island, California, and the USS Nevada. His last assignment was to the Canacao Naval Hospital in Manila. Dr. Welch became a prisoner on January 2, 1942. He was imprisoned at Bilibid camp from 1942 to December of 1944. Dr. Welch was on a Japanese ship that was sunk in Subic Bay by American planes on December 15, 1944. The Oryoku Maru was sunk on that date and at that location. He survived the sinking and made it to shore before becoming a prisoner again. The prisoners who had survived were boarded on the Enoura Maru. He did not survive when the Enoura was sunk. Dr. Welch was awarded the Purple Heart and several other medals.[116]

Robert N. Thwing's birthplace was Hartford, South Dakota. He was adopted by W. A. and Annie Thwing. He enlisted the Army and did his basic training in California. Robert was sent to serve in the Pacific Theater in September of 1941. He, along with hundreds of others, were forced to surrender on the Bataan Peninsula. Robert survived the Bataan Death March and was held at Cabanatuan. His first prison ship was the Oryoku Maru. He was one of the survivors when the ship was sunk. His second prison ship was the Enoura Maru. Robert perished when the ship was sunk by American aircraft.[117]

Edgar S. Gable was born in Wagner in 1905. Following graduation from Wagner High School he enrolled at the University of South Dakota. He also attended the University of Wisconsin in Madison. Edgar married Marian Miller in 1935. They moved to Manila in 1936. Edgar was employed by the Niessen Mining Company. Civilian wives were evacuated in 1941; Marian never saw Edgar again. Edgar joined the military on December 8, 1941. He was a lieutenant in the Quartermaster Corps. When Corregidor surrendered, he became a prisoner. Edgar was first held at Bilibid prison before being transferred to Cabanatuan. He was held there two and a half years. Edgar was on the Oryoku Maru when it was sunk on December 15, 1944, by American planes. He swam to shore, but was taken prisoner for a second time. His second prisoner ship was the Enoura Maru which was sunk on January 9, 1945, by American planes from the USS Hornet. He was awarded the Purple Heart and is listed on the Tablets of the Missing at Manila American Cemetery.[118]

A Third Hell Ship

Ted Spaulding joined the California National Guard in 1937. He became a member of the 40th Division Tank Company. In 1940 the company was designated C Company, 194th Tank Battalion. Ted was sent to OCS and became a second lieutenant and was promoted to first lieutenant in 1941. His tank battalion was ordered overseas in September of 1941. They reached Manila Bay on September 26th. Ted became a prisoner when the troops on Bataan surrendered. He survived the Bataan Death March and was first held at Camp O' Donnell which was overcrowded. He was transferred to Cabanatuan. On September 24, 1944 ,Ted was sent to Bilibid prison. From there he was put on the Oryoku Maru along with 1,619 other prisoners. When the ship sunk, he swam ashore and was taken prisoner again. His second prison ship was the Enoura Maru. The Enoura Maru was sunk, and Ted was boarded on the Brazil Maru. It arrived in Japan on the 29th of January. Ted was a prisoner in Korea when the war ended. He had been a prisoner most of the war.

Ted and Ardes moved to Huron after the war. He enlisted in the South Dakota National Guard and was promoted to major in 1953 and later became a colonel. His last promotion was to brigadier general in 1957. They bought some land east of Huron. Ted became a high school teacher and a cattle rancher. He passed away in 2002.[119] Ted was inducted into the South Dakota Hall of Fame in 2003.

South Dakota and the Doolittle Raid

In 1942 America needed a morale boost. To accomplish this boost and let the Japanese know they were not invincible, military leaders devised a plan to bomb cities in Japan. The plan was to fly bomber planes off an aircraft carrier which had never been done before. Colonel James "Jimmy" Doolittle was selected to plan and lead the raid. The 17th Bombardment Group in Pendleton, Oregon, was chosen for the raid as they had the 35 most experience flying over water. Sixteen B-25 "Mitchell Bombers" were modified to provide more space for bombs and fuel. They carried a total crew of 80. Training took place at Eglin Field in Florida. The crews had about a month to train. When a B-25 took off from the ground, it reached a speed of 100 miles per hour and had a runway that was a mile long. The deck of the aircraft carrier USS Hornet was less than 500 feet long, and they could reach a speed of only 50 miles per hour. The USS Enterprise carried fighter planes to protect the bombers.

The raid took place on April 18, 1942. It was a complete surprise. Some damage was done, but not significant. The bombers were low on fuel. They had two options: to find a place to crash-land or to use the last of their fuel and get high enough to bail out.

Three crew members were captured by the Japanese and executed with a bullet to the back of the head. Sixty-five crew members survived. They were welcomed by Chinese civilians. Chinese troops took them 1,000 miles to Chungking. From there they were flown to the United States.[120]

Don Smith of Belle Fourche was one of the sixteen pilots. His plane bombed Kobe. He crash-landed the plane in the ocean. Smith and four crewmates made it to shore and were greeted by Chinese civilians. Don was stationed in England when his plane crashed because of bad weather in late 1942. His body was returned to Belle Fourche for burial.[121] Don was inducted into the South Dakota Hall of Fame in 2004.

Henry Potter of Pierre was the navigator on Jimmy Doolittle's plane. Potter was sent to North Africa. He flew missions against the Germans and Italians in 1942 and 1943. When he retired, he had reached the rank of colonel.[122]

After the raid American morale soared. Americans felt that it was a little payback for Pearl Harbor. The Chinese who had helped the Americans paid a dear price. A Japanese force of 100,000 was sent to the area. After four months 250,000 Chinese were dead.[123]

South Dakota and the Battle of Midway

The Doolittle Raid gave Americans a morale boost, but the U.S. needed 36 a military victory. In May of 1942 Admiral Chester Nimitz was facing a formidable challenge. The U.S. Navy was still suffering from Pearl Harbor, a defeat in the Java Sea, and the loss of the aircraft carrier Lexington in the Battle of the Coral Sea.

Intelligence sources reported that the Japanese were gathering some two hundred ships for an operation. The U.S. Navy could not match them in numbers and did not know their plan of attack.

Commander Joe Rochefort was in charge of combat intelligence at Pearl Harbor. By early June of 1942 his staff had cracked the Japanese naval code. They knew the Japanese were planning three attacks, the main one being Midway Island. The challenge was to determine the date and time of the attack.

Rochefort came up with a plan to verify how the Japanese would identify Midway in their transmissions. He sent a message to the commander at Midway telling him to report to Pearl Harbor that the water plant on Midway had broken down. The Japanese code word for Midway was "AF". If the Japanese fell for the trick, "AF" would be confirmed. They took the bait. Further work on the code determined that the attack on Midway would begin on June 3. Nimitz went to work making plans on how to deploy his limited resources.[124]

Because of the weather the Japanese attack on Midway Island started in the early dawn of June 4. The first attack was a disaster for the American forces. John Waldron was from Ft. Pierre and had been appointed to the Naval Academy in 1920 and graduated in 1924. John meet his future wife Adelaide at a dance in her home town of Pensacola. He was stationed there for training. They had two daughters, Nancy and Anne. John was 42 in 1942. The men in his squadron respected him, and he was known as "The Skipper."

Waldron was stationed on the aircraft carrier USS Hornet. The night before the attack he wrote a letter to his wife and daughters. Waldron's Torpedo Squadron 8 was made up of fifteen Douglas Devastators when they made their attack on the Japanese carrier Akagi. They made their attack at a very low level, and the Japanese Zeros followed them. The Americans did not have any fighter protection, and some of the planes were shot down. The remaining planes continued the attack, but encountered heavy antiaircraft fire from several Japanese ships. Waldron's plane was lost to antiaircraft fire. The only pilot to survive was Ensign George Gay. The Akagi was not damaged in this battle.

Later in the day American dive-bombers spotted the Japanese carriers as Zeros were attempting to gain altitude. They made their attack without any opposition from the Zeros because of the sacrifice of Waldron's squadron and others. The decks of the carriers were covered with planes that were being refueled and loaded with ordinance. The Akagi was the first carrier refueled and loaded with ordinance and was the first carrier to be attacked. The planes on deck were set on fire. Bombs also penetrated several lower decks setting off explosions of bombs, torpedoes, and fuel storage tanks. The Akagi was destroyed as was the Kaga, Soryu, and Hiryu. All four carriers had been at Pearl Harbor.

In the movie "Midway" Waldron's plane is shown with his name on it. A Japanese officer praised the American pilots for their bravery and sacrifice. Waldron's wife was informed of his death. Several weeks later she received the letter he had written the night before the attack.[125]

Waldron received several honors for his sacrifice. He was awarded the Navy Cross and Purple Heart, posthumously. In 1943 an airfield in Corpus Christi, Texas, was named after him. A Navy destroyer carries his name. A plaque at the Air & Space Museum in Washington, D. C. describes the role Waldron and his squadron played in the battle of Midway. It details how their sacrifice made a difference in the outcome of the battle. The USS Yorktown is harbored at Patriots Point in Charleston, South Carolina. The Carrier Aviation Hall of Fame is located on one of the lower decks. It contains plaques dedicated to individuals who made significant contributions to the war effort in WW II. One plaque is dedicated to Waldron and describes his role as the skipper of Torpedo Squadron

8.[126] A street in Ft. Pierre was named after him. In 2002 the Missouri River bridge west of Pierre was named the Lt. Commander John C. Waldron Memorial Bridge.[127] Waldron is listed on the Tablets of the Missing at Honolulu Memorial. There is a marker of him at Black Hills National Cemetery near Sturgis. John was inducted into the South Dakota Hall of Fame in 1985.

Leo E. Perry was born in Wolsey in 1904. He farmed in the Wolsey area. Leo married Cecelia Maunders in Huron in 1931. They had two sons. Leo had enlisted in the Navy in 1927. He was trained to be a radioman and sent overseas. Leo was assigned to Torpedo Squadron Three on the aircraft carrier Yorktown. His squadron, along with others, attacked Japanese carriers during the Battle of Midway. The planes met heavy resistance from antiaircraft fire and Japanese fighters. Leo died in the fighting. He was awarded the Distinguished Flying Cross. Leo is listed on the Tablets of the Missing at Honolulu Memorial.[128]

Harry G. M. Selle was born in October of 1923. His parents were Herman and Klare Selle. They were born in Norway. Harry attended high school in Canton and Hudson. He enlisted in the Navy at the age of seventeen. His training took place at the Naval Training station at Great Lakes, Illinois, and at the Naval Air Station in Norfolk, Virginia. He became a member of Torpedo Squadron Five and was assigned to the aircraft carrier Yorktown. Harry lost his life during the Battle of Midway. His body was never recovered. He is listed on the Tablets of the Missing at Honolulu Memorial. He was posthumously awarded the Purple Heart.[129]

Guadalcanal, America's First Offensive in the Pacific

Guadalcanal is part of the Solomon Islands chain. Its location was strategic for both the Japanese and the Americans. Whoever controlled the island controlled the supply lanes from

America to Australia. The fighting for control of the island was intense on land, air, and sea. The key to the island was Henderson field that had been named after Lofton Henderson, a Marine pilot who had died defending Midway Island. The side that controlled the airfield controlled the island. When Joe Foss landed on the island, it was controlled by Americans. The Japanese made constant attacks by air and sea to win control of the island. A large part of their strategy was to land more and more ground troops on the island.

Joe Foss was born on April 15, 1915, on the family farm that was located northeast of Sioux Falls. At a young age he was fascinated by airplanes, and Charles Lindbergh was his idol. Joe graduated from Washington High School in 1934. After graduating from high school, Joe and his brother decided that Cliff would take over the farm and Joe would go to college. Their father had died in a tragic accident in 1933.[130]

Joe had a part-time job at a gas station and paid for his first flying lessons at Soo Skyways in 1936. There is a historical marker to Soo Skyways Airport on Kiwanis Avenue between 41st St. and 49th St. It was the first commercial airport in Sioux Falls. During his senior year at University of South Dakota he enlisted in the Marine Corps.

After graduation Joe reported for duty at Wold-Chamberlain Field in Minneapolis. His training continued at Pensacola Naval Air and Opa-Locka Naval Air Station in Miami. Upon receiving his wings, he wanted to go into combat, but was assigned to be a flight instructor at a flight school. In 1942 he was sent to Guadalcanal.[131] On Guadalcanal Joe was assigned to fighter group VMF-121. The group became known as The Flying Circus. They flew a plane made by Grumman, the F4F Wildcat. Cactus was the Allied code name for Guadalcanal. The entire force of planes became known as the Cactus Air Force.

Upon his arrival Joe soon learned that the Japanese controlled the hills around Henderson Field. As evening approached, the Japanese fired rockets and mortars on the field. When Joe heard the shells approaching, he and another soldier took cover in a bomb crater while three others did the same thing in another crater. After the shelling stopped, Joe went to check on the three soldiers in the other crater. It had taken a direct hit, and all three were dead.[132]

On some days Joe's fighter group was assigned to protect American bombers that were bombing Japanese positions on Bougainville northwest of Guadalcanal. Other days they were sent up to stop Japanese bombers that were headed for Henderson field from Bougainville. The Japanese also sent bomber groups from the island of Rabaul.[133]

During one of his early combat encounters, Joe's plane was shot up, and while he was attempting to crash land, he began to wonder why he had left the safety of the farm.[134] He was not injured in the crash landing. During his time on Guadalcanal Joe was credited with shooting down twenty-six Japanese planes. He was awarded the Congressional Medal of Honor. Joe was inducted into the South Dakota Hall of Fame in 1978.

The National WW II Museum in New Orleans opened on June 6, 2000. It is divided into several exhibits. One exhibit is "The Road to Tokyo." This exhibit details the fighting in the Pacific. In this exhibit there is a plaque to Joe Foss. It contains his picture and details his contribution to winning the battle of Guadalcanal.

Veteran's Memorial Park is located between Terrace Park and Russell Avenue in Sioux Falls. This area was once part of the Sioux Falls Training Base. The park was dedicated in 2006. On one of the walkways there are plaques dedicated to Medal of Honor recipients. Those honored from WW II are Joe Foss, Arlo Olson, and Woodrow Wilson Keeble.

Alvin S. Anderson was born in 1919 near Lake Norden in Hamlin County. The Army drafted him when he was twenty-three. His basic training took place in Texas with additional training in Des Moines, Iowa, and in the Hawaiian Islands. He was sent to Guadalcanal with the 25th Division of the Army. A hand grenade took Alvin's life when he was trying to rescue a fellow soldier from a foxhole. He was buried in the Estelline cemetery in 1943. Alvin was awarded the Purple Heart.[135]

The battle of Guadalcanal lasted from August of 1942 until February of 1943. The U.S. won the battle because of the superiority of our air power, the strength of the navy, and the tenacity of the ground troops. The victory was important for several reasons. It was the first defeat the Japanese had suffered in the Pacific. It kept the sea lanes from America to Australia open. The Japanese lost many troops. The U.S. had a base from which they could launch attacks on other island groups held by the Japanese. The idea that the Japanese were invincible was destroyed.[136]

The US South Dakota and Its Role in the War

The USS South Dakota, Battleship 57 (BB 57) was commissioned in March of 1942. She was sent to the Pacific and was assigned to protect the aircraft carrier Enterprise. During the Battle of Santa Cruz in October of 1942 near Guadalcanal, thirty-two Japanese planes were downed in the process of protecting the Enterprise. A direct hit from a 250-pound bomb put three sixteen-inch guns out of action. During the Battle of Guadalcanal on November 13-14 of 1942, the Japanese thought they had sunk the South Dakota. To keep her identity a secret from the Japanese, she became Battleship X.[137] She played a role in every major battle in the Pacific from 1942 to 1945 and became the most decorated battleship of WW II.[138] A memorial to the USS South Dakota is located on the corner of 12th Street and Kiwanis Avenue in Sioux Falls.

Lt. David J. G. Currer was a radarman on the South Dakota. He was a graduate of the US Naval Academy. He lost his life during the Battle of Savo Island near Guadalcanal. David and thirty-seven other sailors were buried at sea. He had kept a copy of the New Testament in his pocket. A chaplain, J. V. Claypool, had kept the copy before David was buried. He asked the family if he could keep the copy, and the family gave their permission. He kept it until he became aware of the memorial to the South Dakota. The chaplain donated Currer's New Testament to the memorial. In September of 2010 David Currer, who was sixty-three at the time and named after the uncle he never knew, came to visit the memorial. He was joined by two sisters and his aunt Elizabeth Currer-Wolf. The family took turns holding the bible and viewing other items. They are grateful to the memorial as it is a connection to David, especially since there is no grave to visit.[139]

The aircraft carrier USS Lexington is harbored in Corpus Christi, Texas. A plaque praises the role of the USS South Dakota and other battleships in protecting aircraft carriers during World War II.

The USS South Dakota (SSN 790) is a fast-attack submarine. Construction began in 2013, and the keel was put in place in 2016, and she joined the fleet in 2018. The ship is nuclear-powered, capable of launching torpedoes at other ships and missiles at ground targets. It is described as the world's most technologically advanced submarine.[140]

Cecil Harris: Distinguished Navy Pilot

Cecil Harris grew up on a farm near Cresbard and became one of the greatest Navy pilots of WW II. He was born in 1916 and graduated from Cresbard High School in 1934. After graduation he went to Northern State Teachers College for one year. He left to teach at Onaka, located on Highway 20, a few miles west of his hometown. It was there he met Eva who would become his wife. Cecil wanted to complete his college degree and returned to school in 1940. At Northern he took a civilian pilot training course. The course led to enlistment in the U.S. Naval Reserve in 1941. One year later he had completed his training and earned his wings.

In 1942 Cecil was assigned to the escort carrier USS Suwannee. Planes from the carrier supported the invasion of North Africa, known as Operation Torch. In August of 1944 he was transferred to the aircraft carrier USS Intrepid. On the Intrepid he was part of VF-18 "Fighting 18."[141] The fighter plane he flew was a (F6F) Wildcat. Because of his experience and flying ability, the squadron commander put Cecil in charge of training pilots who lacked experience. He taught them new dog-fighting techniques. One of those was to attack the enemy head on. Another was to slow down, pull up, and let the enemy fly by, then attack from behind.[142]

His willingness to risk his own safety to protect and save his fellow pilots is part of his great legacy. The Japanese were always on the lookout for planes that had been damaged. On one occasion Cecil went back to protect a damaged plane. Two Japanese planes were ready to finish off the American when Cecil arrived and shot both of them down, allowing the pilot to return to the Intrepid. After returning from another mission, his plane was being refueled and rearmed. Cecil saw two kamikaze planes approaching the ship. He turned his plane and destroyed the Japanese planes before they could crash into the carrier. Another act of bravery involved more than fourteen planes. They were returning from a mission as dusk was approaching, and they were low on fuel. One option was to crash-land in the ocean and hope they would be rescued or find the carrier. Cecil asked to find the carrier and was given permission to do so. Cecil located the ship, and all the planes landed safely.[143]

Cecil was a hero, but did not brag about what he had done and wanted to avoid the public spotlight. Upon his return to Cresbard after the war, a crowd had gathered at the railroad station. He made his exit on the other side of the train to avoid the crowd.[144]

Cecil has been honored in several ways. The USS Intrepid is harbored in New York City. A replica of his F6F Wildcat with twenty-four rising Sun insignias is on the deck.[145] The USS Yorktown is harbored in Mount Pleasant, South Carolina, near Charleston. The area is known as Patriots Point. The Carrier Hall of Fame is located on one of the lower decks. A plaque is dedicated to Cecil Harris, a captain, USN Reserve, WW II ace pilot with twenty-four kills. Cecil was awarded the Navy Cross; the only military award above it is the Congressional Medal of Honor. Additional medals he received were the Silver Star with a second gold star, the Distinguished Flying Cross with two stars, and the Air Medal with two stars.[146]

South Dakota has honored Cecil in several ways. He became a member of the South Dakota Hall of Fame in 1994. The South Dakota Aviation Hall of Fame welcomed him as a member in 2008. The eighty-mile section of South Dakota Highway 20 between U. S. Highways 83 and 281 was named the Cecil E. Harris Memorial Highway in 2009.[147] In 2014 a bronze statue of Cecil was dedicated on the campus of his alma mater, Northern State University.[148]

In recent years several people have been pursuing the proposition of Cecil Harris being awarded the Congressional Medal of Honor. Ken Schroeder of Rapid City and Jerry Krueger of Aberdeen have been the leaders in this movement. The biggest roadblock is that an individual must have been nominated within three years of their service. As of 2018 the award had not been granted.[149]

A final tribute to his ability and good luck is that over a period of eighty-one days and forty-four missions in late 1944, he shot down twenty-four Japanese planes, and his plane did not have a bullet hole in it. Cecil passed away in 1981 and was buried at Arlington National Cemetery.[150]

A South Dakota Volunteer

Captain Robert "Duke" Hedman was from Webster. He served in China before the U.S. was officially in the war. Robert was the only member of the American Volunteer Group to become an ace in one day when he shot down four bombers. He was awarded the Distinguished Flying Cross. Robert passed away in 1995.[151]

The 8th and 15th Air Forces

American bomber crews had the most dangerous job in the war. In October of 1943, less than one out of four Eighth Air Force crew members could expect to complete his tour of duty, twenty-five missions. The 8th suffered 26,000 fatal casualties in the war, more casualties than the entire U.S. Marine Corps.[152] The 8th flew disastrous missions to Schweinfurt and Regensburg, Germany. They lost sixty bombers and nearly 600 men.[153]

The Fifteenth Air Force was in operation from November of 1943 to the end of the war in May of 1945. Their bases were in Foggia, Italy.[154] During their period of operation, the 15th was part of the strategy to prevent the Axis countries from using their main source of oil at Ploesti, Romania. They destroyed enemy communications and continually bombed plants producing a variety of materials and weapons.[155] Several missions were flown to Ploesti resulting in heavy losses. The raids on Schweinfurt and Regensburg also resulted in heavy losses. Schweinfurt was a target as ball-bearings were produced there, and they were needed in all moving equipment. Airplanes were produced at Regensburg.[156] At Blechhammer in Silesia the Germans were producing synthetic fuel from coal. This source of fuel was important to them. This location became an important target for the 15th.[157]

The cost of the raids was high in men and planes. A total of 67,441 airmen were sent to Italy. By May 20, 1945, 2,703 had died, 2,553 had been wounded, 8,007 were missing, and 4,352 had become POWs. The percent of loss was twenty-six, which was very high.[158]

Most of the losses suffered by both the 8th and 15th were the result of two factors, enemy fighter planes and flak. The German antiaircraft guns fired canisters/shells set to explode at the altitude the planes were flying. When the shells exploded, they sent flak/shrapnel in all directions. The shrapnel was jagged pieces of metal that tore into planes and men. The planes could not change direction and had to fly through it.[159]

South Dakotans with Twenty Missions or More Before They Died in Service to Their Country

William Bauer was born in October of 1920 in Yankton. He entered active service in December of 1942. William was a crew member on a B-17 bomber. The magic number to qualify for leave to go home was fifty missions. He had completed forty-eight. His wife's birthday was in November. He had volunteered for extra missions as he wanted to be back for her birthday. On September

12th his plane was shot down over Germany. William and his wife Darlene had a young son and daughter. The remains of all crew members were buried as a group in Zachary Taylor National Cemetery in Louisville, Kentucky.[160]

Ernest Block was born in Webster. He joined the Army Air Corps in 1943 and was trained at Biggs Field in Amarillo and at Laredo, Texas. He was sent to England and joined the 701st Bomber Squadron, 445th Bomber Group. He was a top-turret gunner. Ernest had completed forty-eight missions when his plane was shot down over Hollen, Germany, in February of 1945. His body was not recovered. He is listed on the Tablets of the Missing at Henri-Chapelle American Cemetery in Belgium. Ernest was awarded the Purple Heart.[161]

Alfred Brammer, Jr. graduated from Belle Fourche High School and attended Black Hills State Teachers College in Spearfish. He enlisted in the Army Air Corps in April of 1942. Alfred earned his wings at Cal Aero near Los Angeles. Overseas he was with the 337th Bombardment Squadron, 96th Bombardment Group. Alfred was a co-pilot on a B-17E Flying Fortress. He was on his twenty-third mission when he perished over Berlin. His body was returned to Belle Fourche for burial.[162]

Bruce Brooks graduated from Platte High School in 1938. He was studying chemical engineering at the University of Iowa and left in his junior year to enlist in the Army Air Corps. Bruce earned his wings at Williams Field in Arizona. In 1943 he was sent to North Africa where he flew several missions. From there he went to Sicily and then to Italy. He was the pilot of a A20 Havoc strafing plane. Bruce had completed more than forty-five missions when his plane was shot down over Italy. He left behind his widow, Donna, and an infant son, Bruce Craig Brooks.[163]

Donald Burke had ten siblings. He graduated from Colome High School in 1940. His training took place in Texas and Idaho. Donald was with the 491st Bomber Group-854th Bomb Squad in England. He was trained to be a bombardier and an aerial gunner. He completed sixty-six missions over Germany as part of the crew in a B-24 bomber. His plane was shot down on a mission over Frankfurt, Germany, in November of 1944. He was awarded the Purple Heart. Donald was buried in Ardennes American Cemetery near Liege, Belgium.[164]

John Conde was born in 1920. His first assignment was to the Aleutians. He was decorated twice while serving there. His next deployment was to England. John had completed twenty-one missions and was the radio operator on the "Double Trouble." His last mission was cancelled while his plane was in the air. The pilot continued to fly to give his navigator more practice. Nobody knows why, but during the flight, the plane hit the ground, became airborne again, and then crashed. Twelve 500-pound bombs exploded on impact, and all crew members perished. It was June 8, 1944. John was awarded the Purple Heart.[165]

Robert Crosswait graduated from Woonsocket High School. He served in the Civilian Conservation Corps in the Black Hills. Robert attended the South Dakota School of Mines and Technology before enlisting in the 109th Engineers. During training at Camp Claiborne, he transferred to the Army Air Corps. After earning his wings, he was sent to the Pacific Theater. His first assignment was to a bomber squadron, but he transferred to a P-38 fighter squadron. Robert had completed thirty-five missions when he was shot down over New Guinea. He is listed on the Tablets of the Missing at Manila American Cemetery. Robert was awarded the Purple Heart.[166]

Stanley Dahlman was born in Roberts County in 1921. He had six brothers and one sister. He joined the Army Air Corps in 1942 and was sent to England. He flew fifty-seven missions. Stanley was a crew member on a B-17 Flying Fortress that was shot down over Regensburg, Germany, on August 17, 1943. Between fifty-two and fifty-nine bombers did not return from the mission. Stanley was awarded the Purple Heart and Air Medal. Stanley was buried at the Bethania Cemetery in Rosholt.[167]

Kenneth Ernster was born in 1921 and graduated from Bonilla High School in Beadle County in 1940. He joined the Army Air Corps in 1942. His training took place in Oklahoma. He served in the European Theatre. Kenneth was the belly gunner on a B-17 bomber. He had completed thirty-two missions which qualified him to go home, but the paper work had not been completed. He was obligated to go on another mission, his last. His plane was shot down over Germany in July of 1944. His remains were returned to the U.S. in 1949 and buried in the Bonilla cemetery. He was awarded the Air Medal and oak-leaf cluster.[168]

Hollis Foster was born at Wakonda in Clay County. In January of 1941 he enlisted in the Army and was sent to Port Darwin, Australia, in December of that year. He was trained as a gunner and became a member of the Fifth Air Force. After completing sixteen missions in Australia, New Guinea, and the Pacific, he came home on a 21-day furlough. After more training he was sent to England. Hollis was the top turret gunner on a A-20 bomber. He was on his twenty-fifth mission when his plane was shot down over France. In 1952 his remains were returned to St. Louis. Hollis was awarded the Purple Heart.[169]

John Gagnon graduated from Yankton High School in 1938. His first military duty was with the Army in Alaska. He transferred to the Army Air Corps in December of 1942. John earned his wings and became a member of the 717th Bomber Squadron in the 15th Air Force. He was the navigator on a bomber and had completed twenty-five missions. He died on a mission over Germany. John was buried in Sicily-Rome American Cemetery, Nettuno, Italy. He was awarded the Purple Heart.[170]

Victor Gentzler was attending the School of Mines and Technology prior to enlisting. After receiving his wings in 1942, he was stationed in North Africa, England, Sicily, and Italy. He flew fifty-eight missions from those locations. In October of 1944, he was sent to France. He was the pilot of a P-51 Mustang and went on reconnaissance missions. This was his second tour of duty, and he completed twenty-eight more missions. Victor died on a mission over Germany in March of 1945. The war ended in May. He received the Silver Star and four oak-leaf clusters. His brother, Robert, was also in the military. Victor's brother-in-law died in battle.[171]

Roland Hann was born in 1921 on a farm near Winner. After graduating from Winner High School, he enrolled at St. Ambrose College in Davenport, Iowa. He took the CPT course and earned his license. He joined the Army Air Corps Reserve in 1942. Upon being called to active duty in 1943, his training took him to bases in Texas and Oklahoma. He earned his wings and became a second lieutenant. He went on for further training and became the pilot of a B-24 bomber. Roland and his crew left for Italy in June of 1944. Hahn was on his thirty-first mission when his plane was shot down over Mariabor, Yugoslavia. He was awarded the Air Medal with two oak-leaf clusters, the Purple Heart, and President's Citation. Roland was buried in Florence American Cemetery.[172]

Urban Kurtenbach was born in 1923 and graduated from Parkston High School in 1941. He entered the Army Air Corps in 1943. Training took him to Florida, Texas, Utah, Colorado, and

Kansas. Urban had completed over twenty-five missions when his B-24 crashed on takeoff. The bombs they had on board all exploded when the plane crashed. Several crew members died in the explosion. His remains were returned to Parkston in 1949. He was awarded the Purple Heart and the Air Medal with one oakleaf cluster.[173]

William Lown was born in 1915 and graduated from Spearfish High School. He went on to graduate from the School of Mines and Colorado School of Mines. Before entering the service, he was employed as a metallurgical engineer. William entered the service and became a second lieutenant. He flew a P-40 fighter plane in the South Pacific Theater. From his first mission, October of 1942, until his last on January 2, 1944, he flew over one hundred and eighty-eight combat missions. William is listed on Tablets of the Missing at Manila American Cemetery He was awarded the Distinguished Flying Cross, a Purple Heart, and the Air Medal with oakleaf clusters.[174]

James Lynch was born in 1920. James and his younger brother owned and operated a gas station known as the Lynch Brothers Station in Sioux Falls. He joined the Army Air Corps. He began basic training began in 1941 and training continued in Texas and Florida. He was an engineer on a B-24 bomber. James was on his forty-eighth mission when his plane was shot down. He had been scheduled to go home after two more missions. His body was never recovered.[175]

Maurice Pershing graduated from Aberdeen High School in 1934. Maurice and Caroline Smaltz were married on November 30, 1940. He joined the Army Air Corps and trained to be a tail gunner. Maurice was stationed in England. The planes were cold on long missions, and he asked Caroline to send him wool socks to keep his feet warm. He had only three flights left before he would have been eligible to return home. He died on February 22, 1944. Maurice did not see his baby daughter, Barbara Lee, who had been born on February 9, 1944.[176]

Lynn Peterson was born at Stratford in Brown County in 1918. After graduating from Frederich High School, he attended Northern State College and Pasadena Junior College in California. Lynn joined the Army Air Corps in 1942. In April of 1943 he married Evelyn Angerhofer of Pasadena. He did his basic training in California and advanced training in Arizona. He piloted a B-24 bomber and was stationed in England. Lynn had completed twenty-three missions. On March 18, 1944, his plane was on a mission over Friedichshafen, Germany, when it was attacked by a large group of enemy fighter planes. In the attack the tail and waist gunners were killed, and two engines were put out of commission. Lynn and his co-pilot kept the plane under control while six crew members parachuted to safety. They were not able to parachute in time and died in the plane crash. Lynn's body was returned to Frederick for burial. He was awarded the Distinguished Flying Cross, a Purple Heart, the Air Medal, and three oak-leaf clusters. It was a costly mission as twenty-eight planes left and only seven made it back to England.[177]

Charles Pittman was born in Meade County. He graduated from Black Hills State Teachers College in 1941. Charles took flying lessons while he was attending college. He earned his wings and was assigned to the China-India-Burma Theater. He was a crew member on a B-24 Liberator bomber. On a mission in April of 1944 the plane was hit by enemy fire killing the pilot. Charles took control of the plane and got it to an altitude so that some of the crew could parachute out. He died when the plane crashed. The wreckage of the plane was discovered in 1949. The remains of the crew were returned to the U.S. and buried in a group grave at Arlington

National Cemetery. Charles was awarded the Distinguished Flying Cross for flying combat missions out of India totaling more than two hundred hours.[178]

Richard Rensch was from Madison. He was drafted into the Army Air Corps and trained to be a pilot. He was engaged and sent his fiancé an engagement ring in the mail. The stamp cost 3 cents. Richard was with the 8th Air Force in England. His unit flew fighter protection for B-17 bombers. As a pilot of a P-51 Mustang, he flew over thirty combat missions. Richard died in an airplane crash. He was buried in Cam- bridge American Cemetery in England. He was awarded the Distinguished Flying Cross. His brother Patrick was also in the Army Air Corps.[179]

Michael Schreier was born in Dell Rapids in 1921. He enlisted in the Army Air Corps in 1942. Training took place in Texas and California. He was promoted to staff sergeant and was the flight engineer on bombing and reconnaissance missions in the Pacific. Michael had completed over forty-five missions when he lost his life in the South Pacific in 1944. His final resting place was in Dell Rapids on July 3, 1948.[180]

Ralph Sehnert was born in Isabel in Dewey County in 1918. The family moved to Clark County where Ralph was a farmer. He entered the service in October of 1941. Ralph trained at Shepard Field in Wichita Falls, Texas, and became an instructor there. His next assignment was in February of 1944 when he became a gunner on a Liberator bomber. Ralph's thirty- seventh mission was his last. His plane was shot down over Friedrichshafen, Germany. No parachutes were seen exiting the plane.[181]

Robert Shay was born in Mt. Vernon and graduated from Letcher High School in 1940. He joined the Army Air Corps in 1942. Robert was a member of the 8th Air Force stationed in England. His position on a Liberator bomber was that of top turret gunner. Robert's plane was attacked by an enemy fighter plane, exploded, and crashed near Hersfeld, Germany. He had completed twenty-seven missions. Robert was awarded the Distinguished Flying Cross, an Air Medal, and four oak-leaf clusters.[182]

Warren Smith was born in Belle Fourche in August of 1919. He graduated from high school in 1937 and the School of Mines and Technology in 1941. During his last year of college he took the CPT course. Warren joined the military in January of 1943. His unit was part of the 8th Air Force. Warren was a co-pilot on a B-17 bomber and had completed over twenty missions when his plane was shot down over Cologne, Germany. He became a POW in 1945 and died from his wounds in a German camp. He left behind a wife and a daughter who had been born in 1943.[183]

Archie Snoddy was born in Hot Springs in August of 1919. He enlisted in the Army Air Corps in May of 1942 at Ft. Meade. In May of 1943 Archie was sent to Sioux Falls to train as a radio operator. His instructor was Corporal Ruth Mackay, who later became his wife. In 1944 he was assigned to a base in England. He had completed twenty-five missions when his B-17 was shot down over Germany in August of 1944. Archie and Ruth had been married in June of 1944.[184]

Albert Svarstad was born in Brown County in 1917 and joined the military in 1942. Albert was trained to be a fighter pilot at several locations through- out the U.S. He was stationed on the aircraft carrier USS Hoggatt Bay. He flew missions to the Ryukyu Islands and in the vicinity of Okinawa. Albert flew over fifty missions between May 17 and June 12,1945. On June 21 as he was returning from a mission, the wings on his plane folded, and he was not able to land on the carrier. He was awarded the Distinguished Flying Cross, the Air Medal, and two gold stars. There is a stone in

Albert's memory in Scandinavian Cemetery, and his uniform can be seen at the museum in Britton, S.D.[185]

Harvey Swenson was from Aberdeen. He joined the Army National Guard there. Harvey was with the quartermaster division of the 109 Engineers. He was at Camp Claiborne in Louisiana when he accepted an offer to join the Army Air Corps. He went to OCS and on to training to fly a B-17 bomber and later a B-29. Harvey was stationed in the Mariana Islands and flew bombing missions over Japan. He had flown twenty missions when his plane was shot down and ditched in the ocean. The Navy picked up six of the crew and Harvey's body. He was buried at sea. Harvey is listed on the Tablets of the Missing at Honolulu Memorial in Hawaii. He was awarded the Distinguished Flying Cross and a Purple Heart.[186]

Clifford Walters was born in Fort Pierre. He enlisted in the National Guard in Brookings in June of 1940. Clifford entered the service in 1941. He was honorably discharged in 1943 to accept a commission. Clifford was assigned to a Fighter Group in the 8th Air Force. He was promoted to first lieutenant and then to captain after flying sixty-four missions in Europe. Clifford was on a mission over Peru when his plane was reported missing in July of 1946. The official report was that he died in the vicinity of the Gulf of Panama. His plane was never found. Clifford was awarded the Distinguished Flying Cross.[187]

Harold Walth was born on a farm near Hosmer in Edmunds County in 1920. He was attending Northern State College and joined the National Guard to help pay for his tuition. Harold was teaching in a rural school when he was called to active duty after Pearl Harbor. His National Guard unit went to Ft. Ord in California for field artillery training. He was recruited by the Army Air Force, and they trained him to pilot a B-24 bomber. He was sent to India. His plane and crew flew missions over the Himalaya mountains. They bombed Japanese shipping along the coast of China. One danger on each mission was that the wings of the plane would ice up when they went over the mountains. After completing fifty missions he was scheduled to go home, but a replacement did not come to relieve him. His plane was returning on his fifty-third mission but could not gain enough altitude to get over the mountains and crashed into the side of a mountain. The cause could have been icing on the wings. The Chinese found the plane in January of 1944. His body was returned to Aberdeen and buried in Riverside Cemetery. He was awarded the Distinguished Flying Cross, a Purple Heart, and the Air Medal.[188]

Lloyd Weins was born in Platte. He started high school in Platte and graduated from Washington High School in Sioux Falls in 1940 and went to Augustana College. He joined the Army Air Corps in 1942 and became the pilot of a P-38 Lightning fighter plane. His unit was on duty during D-Day. Lloyd had completed twenty-six missions when he died in combat over France in July of 1944. He was buried in Normandy American Cemetery. Lloyd was awarded the Air Medal with three oak-leaf clusters.[189]

Morton Westby graduated from Stratford High School in Brown County in 1935 and attended Northern State College. He joined the Army Air Corps at Ft. Snelling in April of 1942. He became a pilot and flew a B-24 Liberator bomber. Morton was on his forty-eighth mission when his plane was shot down over the oil fields in Romania. He had been scheduled to go home after this mission.[190]

Eugene Westphal was born in September of 1921 at Onida. He had one brother and seven sisters. Eugene joined the Army in 1942. He trained to be an airplane mechanic at several bases throughout the U.S. Eugene was stationed at Mahan Bari Field in the Upper Assam Valley in India. He was a mechanic on a C-46 transport plane. Supplies were flown from the base over the Himalaya mountains to the front at Kumming, China. Eugene did not return from his forty-third mission in June of 1944. The plane crashed somewhere in the Himalaya mountains.[191]

Henry Williams was from Bennett County. He entered military service and was sent to Fort Leavenworth in Kansas. His next assignment was to Scott Field in Illinois where he was trained to be a radio operator and gunner on heavy bombers. His overseas assignment was to the Pacific with the 13th Air Force. Henry completed fifty missions in less than a year. He was authorized to go home and was waiting for the paper work. To occupy his time he joined the crew of a C-47 transport plane flying to Australia. He was the radio operator. Tragically, the plane encountered bad weather and ran out of fuel. Henry stayed at the radio sending SOS messages until it was time to bail out. The plane crashed near Bathurst, Australia. Henry's body was not recovered. It was assumed that his parachute did not open. All the other crew members were picked up. 54 He was awarded the Purple Heart. Henry is listed on the Tablets of the Missing at Manila American Cemetery.[192]

Leo Wilson was from Arlington. Leo and his wife, Midge, had one son. He joined the Army Air Corps and was stationed in England. He flew twenty- four missions in a B-17 bomber. His plane was shot down over the Mediterranean Sea. Leo had not learned how to swim, and his body was not found.[193]

Ferdinand Karstens was born in Elkton in 1923 and graduated from high school in 1941. He joined the Army Air Corps. His training took him to Nebraska, Colorado, Texas, and Utah. He became a top turret gunner on a bomber. Ferdinand was stationed in Italy. He flew over eighty-five missions from a base in Italy. His bomber was on a mission over the oil fields in Polesti, Romania, when they flew into a heavy field of flak that damaged the plane.

The crew bailed out over Yugoslavia. When the plane crashed, it exploded, and a piece of the plane hit Ferdinand, causing his death. He was reinterred in Elkton in 1949.[194]

John Skoba was born in Webster in 1923. He joined the Army Air Corps in 1943. John earned his wings and was sent overseas. He was with the 15th Air Force B-17 Flying Fortress Squadron. The 15th was stationed in Italy. John had flown twenty-five missions. His plane was returning from a mission over Austria when it was shot down. He was buried in Switzerland, but returned to the Webster cemetery in 1949. He left behind his widow, Eriene, and daughter, Roseanne Beth.[195]

Many Missions Flown Before Returning to the United States

Technical Sergeant Charles Conner was from Sioux Falls. He was the waist gunner on a B-24 Liberator named the Wash's Tub. He flew seventy- three missions over North Africa and Europe. The crew was credited with shooting down twenty-two enemy planes. They were awarded the Distinguished Flying Cross for participating in the famous bombing of the Polesti oil fields.[196]

Wendell Hanson was born in Sioux Falls in 1919. He graduated from Washington High School in 1937 and attended Augustana College one year. He transferred to the University of Texas in Austin. Wendell was a student there three years and needed only a few hours of class work to fulfill his graduation requirement when war clouds appeared.

His draft notice came in the mail. He did not want to be drafted, as that would not give him any options to select the branch of the service he wanted to be in. Wendell enlisted in the Army in September of 1941. He transferred to the Army Air Corps in January of 1942. His interest in flying began at a young age. A barnstorming pilot landed his bi-plane in Sioux Falls. Wendell was six when his father took his sons up for a ride. He held one son on each knee. Wendell was sixteen when he took his next airplane ride in a Ford tri-motor plane.

Wendell's Air Corps training started in 1942 and continued through 1943. He learned everything from weather conditions to cloud formations that would have an impact on flying an airplane. A typical day included flight training and ground school training. Wendell trained to fly various types of aircraft. Training was held at Fort Sam Houston in San Antonio, Texas. After completing his training, he was awarded his wings and a commission.

He was assigned to the 341st Bomb Group, 22nd Bomb Squadron. Wendell and his unit were sent to India. In 1944 they were stationed in China. During his time in China, he was under the command of General Clair Chennault. Chennault had become famous for organizing and commanding the American Volunteer Group, The Flying Tigers, from 1941 to 1942. Later they were incorporated into the Army Air Corps.

In 1943 Wendell's unit became part of the 14th Air Force. He flew missions to the Gulf of Tonkin and northern Thailand. His unit was on a mission to attack an air base in Thailand. Their target was Japanese planes on the ground. They went in at a low level to shell the target. The planes were loaded with fuel and ordinance and exploded. Wendell's plane was damaged from the explosions. It made it back to the base but had to crash land. On another mission his plane was damaged from antiaircraft fire, resulting in a second crash landing. His third crash landing was due to engine trouble. Wendell is proud that through all of these crash landings he did not lose a crew member.

After completing fifty missions, he was given the option to continue flying or return to the US. He chose to return and did so in

April of 1944. He was stationed at Blackland Air Base near Waco, Texas. His assignment was to teach returning pilots how to instruct cadets in the art of air combat.

Wendell left active duty in November of 1945 and became a reserve officer. As a reserve officer, he continued his training to keep up-to-date on the newest aircraft. He stayed in the reserves until 1965. He had been promoted to captain and after the war became a lieutenant colonel. Wendell was awarded the Air Medal with four oak-leaf clusters, China's Liberation Medal, and the Distinguished Flying Cross.

Wendell and his wife, Helen, had five children. He was in the real estate business in Sioux Falls for many years. Helen taught biology at Washington High School.[197]

Morris Magnuson was born in 1921 in Bon Homme County. He joined the Army Air Corps after Pearl Harbor. His training took him to California and Arizona. He became the pilot of a P-47 Thunderbolt fighter plane. Morris was stationed in England, Belgium, and France. His group was assigned to work with and protect the ground troops. They bombed and strafed gun emplacements, destroyed bridges, railroad cars, and locomotives. He was on his one-hundred-eighth mission when he was shot down over Germany in March of 1945. He became a POW. Morris was promoted to lieutenant colonel. He was awarded The Distinguished Flying Cross, a Purple Heart, and the French Croix Guerre. In May of 2006 the French honored him with the Legion of Honor, the highest award the French can bestow on an individual. Morris returned to college after the war. He was employed by the Brandon School District as principal and superintendent for many years. Morris passed away on August 28, 2010, at age 89.[198]

Howard Muchow was born in 1923 in Sioux Falls. He attended the School of Mines, South Dakota State College,

Washington University in St. Louis, and Northrop Aeronautical in California. He enlisted in the Army Air Corps in 1942. He became the pilot of a B-17 bomber. Howard served in Europe from 1944 to 1945 and completed thirty-five missions. During those missions he lost his original crew and was shot down twice over Germany. He returned to the U.S. in 1945. Howard was a founding member of the South Dakota Air National Guard and was inducted into the S.D. Aviation Hall of Fame. He wrote a book *Forever Yours—If I Make it Home Alive.* It is a collection of stories about his tour of duty as a pilot and the love letters he sent home to his new bride. Howard passed away on May 6, 2003, at age 80.[199]

George McGovern was born in the Wesleyan Methodist parsonage in Avon where his father was the Methodist minister. The year was 1922. He had two sisters and a brother. George was five when Lindbergh made his solo flight, and George put him on a pedestal.[200] George and his father were avid pheasant hunters. On one of their outings they encountered a farmer who had just gotten a check from the stockyards for all the pigs he had sold that year. The check was not enough to pay for hauling the pigs to market. Dust clouds, grasshoppers, low prices, and bank closures told the bleak story of the farm economy in the late 1920's and 1930's.[201]

George's family moved to Mitchell, and Dakota Wesleyan was close to his home. He began his freshman year in 1940. The school was willing to offer a course in Civilian Pilot Training (CPT) if ten students enrolled. George's classmate, Norman Ray, wanted to learn how to fly. He recruited enough students, one of whom was George, and the course was offered. After eight hours of flight time George was qualified to solo.[202]

Shortly after Pearl Harbor, George and other students from the CPT course decided to drive to Omaha and enlist in the Army or Navy. They borrowed cars from the school's president and dean. In

Omaha the Army Air Corps offered a free lunch of roast beef, mashed potatoes and gravy worth seventy-five cents. They enlisted.[203]

Eleanor Stegeberg, whose hometown was Woonsocket, was also attending Dakota Wesleyan. George and Eleanor had debated against each other in high school. She had won the debate, but they still got engaged.[204] In 1943 George received his orders to report for active duty. He had seventy-two hours to get to Jefferson Barracks in St. Louis. A train took him to Ft. Snelling, Minnesota, where he became a buck private. From there he rode a train to Jefferson Barracks. The barracks were not well-built and were very cold. Basic training consisted of marching, learning how to shoot a rifle and pistol, and more marching. After completing basic training, he was sent to Southern Illinois Normal University for five months of testing and ground school training. George's next assignment was to the air base in San Antonio. He and others stayed there until the military had built facilities for flight training. The next stop was Muskogee, Oklahoma, for flight training.[205] Because of his flight training in the CPT program, the twelve weeks of training went smoothly.[206] More training took place in Coffeyville, Kansas. After basic schools came advanced school in Pampa, Texas. At Pampa, George learned to fly a twin engine plane. It was here that George received his wings. His wife, Eleanor, pinned them on. They had been married in 1943, and she had followed him from base to base.

George and Eleanor went to Liberal, Kansas, where George learned how to fly a B-24 bomber. From Liberal they went to Lincoln, Nebraska. George's last stop in the U.S. was at Camp Patrick Henry near Norfolk, Virginia.[207] The overseas destination for George and his crew was the Adriatic side of Italy. They were transported on a captured German passenger ship. The ship held 4,000 men and took close to a month to make the trip. In Italy they became part of the Fifteenth Air Force and were stationed in Foggia.[208]

Inexperienced pilots were assigned to fly their first five missions as a co-pilot with an experienced pilot. This was military policy. George's first mission was on November 11,1944, which at that time was known as Armistice Day. The planes were going to fly at 20,000 feet or higher. The temperature was predicted to be between 20 and 50 degrees below. To prepare for the cold the crew put on heavy winter underwear, long wool socks, and a wool uniform. Next to go on was a leather jacket and leather trousers, both lined with sheepskin and, lastly, sheepskin-lined boots. Their gloves were lined with silk. The pilot and co-pilot were issued Colt .45 pistols with a shoulder holster. A backpack held their parachutes. Flak jackets were carried on the plane. Flak jackets become mandatory after the disastrous raid on Polesti. On his first mission George learned the deadly consequences of flak. One pilot in his group died when a piece of flak, flying metal with jagged edges, took the top of his head off.[209]

Every B-24 in Italy had a name painted on it. Some had nose art, usually of young women. George flew a different plane on each mission. Regardless of the name painted on the plane, George called all planes he flew the Dakota Queen in honor of Eleanor.[210] Every plane had a ground crew. They did a tremendous job of repairing planes and getting them ready to fly another mission. A ground crew did not have a way of keeping their weekly allotment of beer cold. The beer was put on a plane that flew at 20,000 feet or higher in cold temperatures. The beer would cool and be ready for consumption if and when the plane returned.

After completing five missions as a co-pilot, George assembled his own crew and made his first flight as a pilot. It was December 6, and the target was the railroad yards at Graz, Austria.

Clouds obscured the target, and the entire formation turned and headed back to base. All planes dropped their bomb loads over the Adriatic. They could not land with the bombs on board.[211] George's second mission was the railroad yards in Linz, Austria. The Germans were moving men and equipment through Linz to the eastern and western fronts. The flak was heavy. A large piece came through the windshield and landed between George and his co-pilot, Lieutenant Ralph "Bill" Rounds. Had it hit either one of them, they would have died.[212]

On December 17 the target was an oil refinery at Odertal, Germany. As McGovern's plane was proceeding down the runway for takeoff, a tire blew out. He decided to go ahead with the mission. On returning, he landed the plane with the tire blown. His skill in the landing brought a recommendation for the Distinguished Flying Cross.[213]

In January of 1945, Sam Adams, a close friend of George's, died when his plane was destroyed by flak. They had shared a tent for several weeks and the loss was hard on George.[214] On a mission over Austria the last bomb was stuck in the bomb rack, and when it was finally freed, it hit a farmhouse at 12:00 p.m. Knowing that farmers ate at that time, George was shook up about it. The scene stayed with him for many years.[215] In 1985 the Austrian government was doing a documentary on Austria and WW II. George was lecturing at the University of Innsbruck and agreed to be interviewed for the documentary. He was asked if he had any regrets about his missions over Austria. He discussed the mission described above. After the documentary was shown on Austrian television, the station got a call from an Austrian farmer. He was sure the bomb McGovern described had hit his farm. He went on to say that they had seen the bomber coming and left the house to seek shelter in a ditch. Nobody was hurt. The station called George and told him the farmer's story. McGovern was relieved beyond words.[216]

George completed thirty-five missions over Germany, Austria, Italy, and Czechoslovakia and was qualified to go home. George returned to college after the war to finish his undergraduate degree and pursue a Ph.D. George's first child, a girl, had been born when he was in Italy. George passed away in 2012.

Myles L. Walter was born in 1918. His home town was Fedora. He enlisted in the Army Air Corps in 1943. Myles and George McGovern were in the same squadron during their training at Pampa Air Field in Pampa, Texas, Myles received his wings and was commissioned a second lieutenant. He was sent to Virginia and then shipped overseas.

Myles was stationed in northern Africa and was the pilot of a B-24 bomber. His unit flew missions over northern Italy and Romania. Their main target in Romania was the oil fields of Ploesti. He flew twenty-five missions and was promoted to captain. Myles was offered another promotion if he would continue to fly more missions, but declined the offer. Myles returned to the U.S. and was stationed in Victorville, California. He trained pilots until he was discharged in 1945.

Myles returned to Fedora and went to work with his brother on the family farm. His next job was at the International Harvester dealership in Canova, and later he purchased the dealership. He sold the dealership in 1962 and then farmed for many years. Myles served on the school board in Canova several years and was an avid golfer.

Myles and Frances Bennett of Fedora were married on August 21, 1943, in Pampa, Texas. Frances had been an elementary teacher in Franklin, South Dakota, before becoming a stay-at-home mom with two daughters to raise. Myles passed away in 1981 and Frances in 1993.[217]

Hilary Cole was from Tyndall. He was born in 1920 and enlisted the Army Air Corps in October of 1941. He trained at Coleman Field in Texas and became the pilot of an A-20 bomber. On D-Day he was on a mission to Argenton, France. They were assigned to attack the 25th Panzer Division. As his plane flew over Normandy, he observed the death and destruction on the beaches.

Hilary completed sixty-five missions, including nine with England's Royal Force. He felt that luck had been with him. Hilary and another pilot had flipped a coin to determine who would go on an afternoon mission. The other pilot lost the flip and was killed when his plane was shot down. Hilary returned from one mission with the instrument panel destroyed and the tires shredded from flak but the plane made it back to England.

Hilary was awarded the Distinguished Flying Cross and the Air Medal with twelve bronze oak-leaf clusters. Five of his brothers—Cletus, Firman, Vitalis, Nester, and John—served in WW II, and all returned to the U.S. Hilary passed away in March of 2019, at age 98.[218] He was buried at Black Hills National Cemetery.

Delmar Claussen was born on November 16, 1924. He graduated from Washington High School in Sioux Falls and enlisted in the Army Air Force as an aviation cadet. Delmar completed his training and was commissioned a lieutenant. He became a crew member on a B-17 bomber. Delmar was sent to England and completed thirty-one missions over Europe. He survived four B-17 crash landings. The planes had been damaged from antiaircraft fire. He was awarded the Air Medal with four oak-leaf clusters. On one of his missions he was injured from a burst of flak and had to bail out. He was awarded the Purple Heat for this action.

Delmar was honorable discharged and returned to South Dakota. He joined the 175th Fighter Squadron of the South Dakota Air National Guard. Delmar was employed by major aerospace companies. He worked with teams to research and develop devices that were sent into space and returned.

Delmar and Beverly Kittelson were married on July 28, 1946 at Romsdal Lutheran Church in rural Hudson, South Dakota. Beverly passed away in 2018. Delmar passed away in May of 2020 at age 95. He was buried in Romsdal Lutheran Church Cemetery.[219]

Nick Gjelsvik and his brother Matt immigrated from Norway in 1906. Immigration officials informed them that Gjelsvik was too hard to pronounce. Their family farm in Norway was Thune and their last name became Thune. Harold was born to Nick and Maude on December 28, 1919. The family had settled in Murdo and worked in a hardware store.

Harold was an outstanding basketball player. The 1937 basketball team played in the State B tournament but lost in the championship game. Their bragging rights were bolstered as Harold was named the tournament's most valuable player. Harold began his college basketball career at the junior college in Hibbing, Minnesota. He transferred to the University of Minnesota and in 1942 was the teams' most valuable player. He graduated in 1942 and joined the Navy.

Harold completed his primary training at Wold-Chamberlain Airport in Minneapolis. He was sent to Corpus Christi, Texas for advanced training and learned how to fly small planes. His next destination was Melbourne, Florida. The purpose of operational training was to teach him how to fly the planes he would fly in combat. He completed the training and was sent to San Diego. He was assigned to a squadron of Hellcat fighter planes. His squadron was assigned to the aircraft carrier USS Intrepid.

Cecil Harris, from Cresbard, was Harold's flight officer on the Intrepid and Harold was his assistant. Cecil taught Harold and other pilots new combat maneuvers. Cecil was a disciplinarian and Harold respected him for that. Harold and Cecil played on a softball team. Cecil pitched and Harold caught. When Cecil got married Harold was his best man. Harold had gotten married earlier.

In a combat mission over Formosa Harold shot down four Japanese planes and Cecil also shot down four. Harold was awarded the Distinguished Flying Cross. Harold had a close encounter with death on the island of Peleliu. As his plane was about to take off a tire blew out and the plane caught on fire. The rest of the squadron thought he was dead and left on the mission. Harold suffered some burns. Harold was in combat for fourteen months and flew more than twenty missions.

Harold and his wife Yvonne Patricia "Pat" returned to Murdo and worked in the family hardware business. Harold began a teaching and coaching career in 1963. He was voted into the South Dakota Sports Hall of Fame and the South Dakota High School Basketball Hall of Fame. Harold and Pat had five children. Pat passed away in 2012. Harold passed away on Saturday, August 15, 2020 at age 100.[220]

A Light-hearted Prank During Wartime

Lon Jackman was born in 1923. His father worked for the railroad. They moved to Edgemont where Lon graduated from high school in 1941. Lon was commissioned a second lieutenant at Walla Walla Air Station in Washington. He was a member of the 303 Heavy Bomber Squadron known as "Hells Angel." The unit was assigned to duty in England. Before leaving, Lon was the pilot on a B-17 named "G.I. Sheets"; his plane, along with three others, buzzed the first game of the 1943 World Series at Yankee Stadium. The Yankees were playing the St. Louis Cardinals. A reporter stated that "an Army bomber roared over Yankee Stadium so low that Slats Martin could have fielded it." Upon landing at Presque Isle Airfield in Maine, the pilots were confined to their quarters while court-martial papers were being prepared.

They were held only a few days. Fines of $75.00 each were assessed, and they were released. Bomber crews were needed in Europe. Lon flew five missions as a co-pilot with First Lieutenant Robert Sheets. After the fifth mission the plane had been damaged beyond repair and could not be flown again. Lon was assigned as co-pilot on Alexander Alex's bomber. On the first mission with the new crew, antiaircraft fire destroyed one engine, and then an enemy fighter attacked the plane. Most of the crew bailed out. The plane crashed near Bremen, Germany, and Lon was the only crew member to die in the crash. His body was recovered in December of 1943 and buried by locals. After the war Lon was reinterred at Netherlands American Cemetery in Margraten Netherlands, near Aachen, Germany. Lon was awarded a Purple Heart and the Air Medal.[221]

South Dakota and the WASP program

The Women Airforce Service Pilots (WASP) organization was created on August 5, 1943. The women were federal civil service employees and did not have any military benefits. The purpose of the program was to free male pilots for combat duty. Over 25,000 women applied, 1,830 were accepted, and 1,074 completed the training. New recruits had to complete the same primary, basic, and advance training courses as male Army Air Corps pilots. They were not trained in combat maneuvers. Each trainee logged about 1,400 flying hours. They flew fighters and bombers from factories to the East and West coast. From there the planes were either flown or shipped to combat areas. They flew a total of sixty million miles. Some of the women trained male pilots.[222]

Ola Mildred Rexroat was an Oglala Sioux from the Pine Ridge Reservation. She was the only Native American in the program. Ola was born in 1917. She graduated from the University of New Mexico with a B.A. degree in Art in 1939. As a WASP she had the dangerous job of towing targets for aerial gunnery students. The male pilots were learning how to fly and practice shooting at a moving target. Her awards included the Congressional Gold Medal and induction into the S.D. Aviation Hall of Fame in 2007. At the time of her passing in 2017, Ola was a resident at the Veteran's Home in Hot Springs.[223]

Helen Josephine Anderson was born in Marvin in Grant County in 1918. She graduated from Summit High School in 1936. While attending South Dakota State College, she took a CAA flying course. The instructor said she was one of the best students. She graduated from SDSC in 1940. In 1942 she graduated from the University of Illinois library school. She married Lieutenant Robert Severson in 1942. When he was sent overseas, she returned to Urbana, Illinois, and became co-manager of the airport. While he was on military duty, she took further training and became a WASP. Helen was on a training mission with two other women when their plane crashed north of Big Springs, Texas, in September of 1943.[224] Robert had trained to fly light airplanes and be an artillery spotter. He was on a mission along the French and German border when his plane was shot down in 1944.[225]

Helen and Robert were buried in Greenwood Cemetery in Brookings. For sixty years there was no flag or foot stone denoting her service. Her family had tried for years to have Helen recognized as a veteran. WASPs had been granted Veteran's status in 1977. Tammy Schroeder, the American Legion Commander from Grant County, took up the cause. She helped the family prepare and file the official paper work. When approval came, Brookings Monument Company donated Helen's veteran's marker. Helen's marker was dedicated in 2007, with rifle fire, the folding of an American flag that was given to her sister Neoma, and an air force fly over.[226]

When the war ended, so did the WASP program. A PBS Home Video "Fly Girls" is an excellent history of the program. It is part of the series "The American Experience." The National Museum of the Mighty Eighth Air Force is located in Pooler, Georgia, about ten miles from Savannah where the 8th was commissioned in 1942 at Savannah Army Air Base. One exhibit is a tribute to the "Fly Girls."

CHAPTER 4

Families Who Sent Sons & Daughters to War

Brothers and Sisters Who Served

Harold Bankert was born in Bancroft in Kingsbury County. He was twenty-four when he enlisted. His training took place at several locations. He was sent to North Africa. Harold was injured in a tank battle but returned to duty. He died later in combat. His brothers Boyd and Ward were in the military. His sister Zetta was an instructor at the Sioux Falls Air Base radio school. Harold's wife, Alice, was in the WAAC.[227]

Howard Beck graduated from Lake Preston High School in 1931 and entered the military in 1941. He trained in Tennessee and Georgia. He was a member of an artillery battalion that was attached to the 10th Armored Division. His death occurred on December 23, 1944, during the Battle of the Bulge. He was buried in Belgium. In 1949 he was reinterred in Luxembourg American Cemetery. He was awarded the Purple Heart. His brother Merwin served in the Navy. His sister Helen Marie was a lieutenant in the Navy Nurses Corps.[228]

Leonard Blacksmith was born in 1921 in Charles Mix County. He was inducted into active duty at Ft. Snelling in 1942. Leonard was sent to fight in the European Theatre. He was in combat in France when he lost his life. The date was July 11, 1944.

Leonard's family was of Sioux heritage. Five of his brothers served in the military: Clement, Walter, and Sylvester served in the Navy, Stanford served in the Army Air Corps, and Edward served in the Army. His sister Vera Mae was a Marine.[229]

Norman Bondurant was born in 1921 in Buffalo Gap in Custer County. He joined the Navy in 1943 and trained in Virginia and California. Norman was a member of the Fourth Marine Division. He was a machinist's mate and died in combat when American forces were attacking Iwo Jima. He was buried at sea in February of 1945. Norman was awarded the Purple Heart. He is listed on the Tablets of the Missing at Honolulu Memorial in Hawaii. His brother Joe served in Europe and returned home as did his sister Helen who was stationed in the Philippines.[230]

Lester Dansky was born in 1916. He enlisted in the Army Air Corps in 1942. Lester earned his wings and was commissioned a second lieutenant. His sister pinned on his wings. He was assigned to the 353rd fighter squadron group. Lester perished on a bombing mission over France in August of 1943. His mother received his Air Medal and Purple Heart. Lester's two brothers were also lieutenants in the Air Corps. His sister Irene served in the WAVES.[231]

Albert Delker was living in Faith in Meade County when he was drafted. His sister Verna became an Army nurse at the same time, and his sister Irene was a WAVE. His brother Robert was in the Marines, while brothers Dean and Dale were in the Army. Albert was sent to Europe in May of 1944. He was attached to the 60th Infantry Regiment of the 9th Infantry Division. His unit was fighting at St.-Lo, France, where he died in combat. His remains were returned in 1949 and buried in Black Hills National Cemetery.[232]

Julian Hamre was born on the family farm north of Willow Lake. He entered the military in June of 1941. He trained at several bases. Julian shipped out of Camp Rob in California for overseas duty. He was a member of the 63rd Infantry Battalion. Julian fought on New Guinea and was part of a unit that helped retake the Philippines. He was on the island of Luzon when a sniper's bullet took his life. It was February 25, 1945. His body was returned and buried in Pleasant Lutheran Cemetery near Vienna, South Dakota. His brothers Melvin, Albert, and Norman were in the service. Julian's sister Anna was a first lieutenant in the nurse corps.[233]

Cecil Meyer was born on the family farm in Bennett County in 1922. He earned a teaching certificate from Southern State Teachers College in Springfield. Cecil taught in a rural school near Cody, Nebraska. He was a good teacher, and the students enjoyed his classroom. Cecil enlisted in October of 1942 and was promoted to sergeant. He was sent overseas in November of 1944 and was part of the 42nd Infantry Rain- bow Division. His unit was fighting a German force near Hagenau, France. They were low on ammunition. Despite exploding mortar shells, artillery, and rifle fire, Cecil supplied ammunition to his fellow soldiers. Caught in the open with ammunition in hand, he was cut down by enemy fire. It was January 25,1945. His unit withstood the attack. The war in Europe ended in May of the same year. He was awarded the Silver Star. Cecil's brother Charles was a hospital corpsman in the Navy. His sister Ellen served as an Army nurse.[234]

Roger Miller was born on the family farm northwest of Ramona in Lake County. He graduated from South Dakota State College with a degree in mechanical engineering. Roger enlisted in the Navy and was sent overseas. He was in charge of harbor installations in Scotland and France. His next assignment put him on a patrol boat where he was an engineering officer. He lost his life on the boat. His parents did not receive any details regarding his death. Roger was buried in a military cemetery in France. His sister Geraldine was in the Army Nurse Corps. She was stationed on

Guadalcanal in the Solomon Islands. He was the only son of Mr. and Mrs. Andrew Miller.[235]

Harold Overski was from Nunda in Lake County. After basic training he was assigned to the 358th Infantry Regiment of the 9th Infantry Division. His unit landed in France on June 16, 1944. Harold died in combat on July 23, 1944. He was buried in Normandy American Cemetery, St. Laurent-Usr-Mer, France. His brother John was sent to the South Pacific. His sister Mildred was a captain in the Army Nurse Corps.[236]

Ernest Rose was born in Athol in Spink County. After enlisting in the Army, he was sent to Ireland for training. He was a member of a Field Artillery Battalion. The unit saw action in North Africa, Sicily, and Italy. He died in combat in Italy. His body was returned to Athol for burial. His two brothers Albert and Henry were in the military. Ernest's sister Beth was a WAVE.[237]

Roy Samp graduated from Ipswich High School in 1936. He was sent to Ft. McClellan, Alabama, for basic training and went overseas in August of 1944. Roy was a member of the 320th Engineer's Battalion, 95th Infantry Division. On December 14, 1944, his unit was checking the streets of Saarlautern, Germany, for mines. A sniper's bullet took his life that day. He was buried in Luxembourg American Cemetery, Luxembourg City. His brother Howard was in the Army. His sister was in the WAVES.[238]

Willard Schwant graduated from Winner High School in 1936 and Huron College in 1940. He enlisted in the Naval Air Corps Reserves and was sent to training in Oakland, California. His combat missions were flown out of Trinidad. Willard flew a PMB. His plane attacked and sank a German submarine, but disappeared. His brother Cleo was in the Navy. His sister Elna was a lieutenant in the Army Nurse Corps, and Leona was a lieutenant with a Medical Detachment.[239]

Nathan Young graduated from Aberdeen Central High School in 1936. He took pilot training in Santa Ana, California, and Hobbs, New Mexico. After receiving his wings, he was sent to England. He was the pilot of a B-17 Flying Fortress. Nathan died on a mission in March of 1944. His brother Harold was with the Navy in the South Pacific. His sister Ruth was a WAC. He was buried in Ardennes American Cemetery near Liege, Belgium.[240]

South Dakota Nurses in WW II

Twin sisters Evangelyn and Evelyn Halverson were born on the family farm east of Toronto in Deuel County. They graduated from Toronto High School in 1940 and the Sioux Valley School of Nursing in 1943. Evangelyn worked at Sioux Valley hospital and at the hospital in Hendricks, Minnesota, before joining the Army Nurse Corps. She was sent to Camp Carson, Colorado, for basic training. Her final assignment was at Bushell General Hospital, Brigham City, Utah, in October of 1945. Evelyn was stationed at the same hospital. The sisters had picked up two Soldier patients from the train in Ogden. They were involved in a head-on crash near Ogden on April 24, 1946. Evangelyn and one patient died in the wreck. A cause for the accident was never determined. Evelyn was seriously injured and was hospitalized for several months. The second patient was injured, but survived. Evangelyn's funeral was held in Toronto. She was laid to rest with full military honors.[241] Her parents were buried beside her. Evelyn married Raymond Paula in December of 1951. They had two children. Evelyn passed away in December of 2009.

Marcella LeBeau is an enrolled member of the Cheyenne River Sioux Tribe. She served with the Army Nurse Corps and was stationed at a hospital in Minister, England. Marcella was twenty-four. Marcella and other nurses were on duty to treat the first casualties from the landing on D-Day. After D-Day the Allies began to push the Germans back to Germany. Nurses were always on duty to treat the wounded from small battles and the multitude of casualties from the Battle of the Bulge. Her assignments found her serving in hospitals in Belgium and France. For her service in Northern France, the Ardennes, and the Rhineland, Marcella was awarded three service stars. She considered it a privilege to care for the wounded. Marcella received the Chevalier de la Legion d'Honneur from the French government. It is their highest civilian honor.[242] Marcella was inducted into the South Dakota Hall of Fame in 2006.

Margie Camper was born in Sioux Falls and graduated from Washington High School in 1938. After completing nurse's training at San Diego County General Hospital, she became an Army nurse. Her first assignment was for two years at Camp Cook in California. In 1944 she was sent to New Caledonia where she served nine months. Her next assignment was to a general hospital in Assam, India. Margie was returning from leave in Calcutta when she died in a plane crash. Lieutenant Camper was buried in Honolulu Military Cemetery. Her sister Catherine was an Army nurse who served in Europe.[243]

Anna Dolezal was born in Burke and graduated from White River High School in 1939. Anna had always wanted to be a nurse. She pursued her goal at St. Joseph's Hospital in Mitchell and completed her training in 1943. Her training continued at Camp Carson in Colorado where she was commissioned a second lieutenant. She was sent to Winter General Hospital in Topeka, Kansas. Anna died of heart failure at the hospital where she had been working. Anna's final resting place is in the White River cemetery. Anna was buried with full military honors.[244]

Helen Raecke was born in Brown County. She was a nurse at Lutheran Deaconess Hospital in Chicago before she enlisted in the Army Nurse Corps in 1944. Helen was sent to Camp Carson in Colorado for basic training. Her overseas duty was with the 139th Evacuation Hospital serving in France, Germany, and Austria. Her last assignment was in Ebensee, Austria, at a concentration camp. There were 3,000 sick inmates left in the camp. She described them as living skeletons.

After completing her assignment in Austria, Helen was granted leave and returned home. Her next station was in Camp Butler, North Carolina. Helen had always loved to ride horses and did so whenever she had time. Her scrapbook was full of riding stories. Helen was riding when a stirrup broke on her English saddle. She died from the injuries suffered in the fall. Her body was returned to Groton Union Cemetery for burial. She was buried with full military honors. Helen's twin sisters, Laverne and Lorraine, were in a nursing program at the time of her death.[245]

Ernestine Koranda was born in Lesterville near Yankton. She took her nurses training in St. Paul. Ernestine was working in Detroit, Michigan, when she joined the Army Nurse Corps as a reserve. As part of her training she went on maneuvers in Illinois, Arkansas, and Louisiana. Her overseas assignment took her to Townsville, Queensland, Australia. The wounded were brought in from New Guinea and several other Pacific islands. On December 19, 1943, she was on a plane to Sydney. She was to wed her fiance Bob Middleton. The plane had been in the air for an hour when engine problems caused it to crash. Everybody on the plane perished. She was buried in Australia. After the war her remains were returned to the U.S. for burial. Ernestine received a final honor when a hospital ship was named after her.[246]

Mary Rose Harrington was from Elk Point, and Eldene Paige was from Edgemont and grew up in southern California. Throughout their years as prisoners of the Japanese, Mary Rose and Eldene were part of a group that became known as the "Twelve Anchors"; only one was not a Navy nurse. Most of them were in their mid-twenties when the war broke out.[247]

Cavity Naval Base was south of Manila on the island of Luzon in the Philippines. The attack on the base came on December 10, 1941. The Japanese bombers left a path of destruction.[248] As soon as they could, Corpsmen began delivering the injured to the hospital. Nurses began to treat dislocations, head injuries, and places where limbs used to be. They first tried to stop the bleeding and then gave shots of morphine for the pain. Wounded civilians were also brought to the hospital. The reality of war became more apparent as patients died and had to be moved to the morgue.[249]

The nurses were transferred to Santa Scholastic, a former women's college that had become a hospital.[250] The nurses became prisoners of war. They accepted their fate and continued on with their responsibilities as if it was just another day. The Japanese took their utility knives and flashlights, along with personal items including watches, rings, and pens. Margaret "Peg" Nash opened a jar of cold cream, removed her engagement ring from her clothing trunk, and pushed it deep into the cream.[251]

In March of 1942 the nurses were transferred to Santo Tomas, a POW camp south of Manila. When the nurses arrived, there were already three thousand inmates in the prison. Living quarters were cramped. All the prisoners had to stand in line for food and water. The wait to use a bathroom was especially long as the main building had only six bathrooms for twenty-one hundred people. There was no privacy; a sign read, "If you Want Privacy, Close Your Eyes." The nurses were forced to take group showers.[252]

The Japanese guards were sadistic. Three inmates were accused of trying to escape. They were beaten for several hours, and two days later they were shot and buried. Young Philippines were beaten on a regular basis and some were executed.[253]

By 1943 conditions at Santo Tomas were gradually getting worse. Only two meals a day were served, and worms were a part of the breakfast cereal. Bedbugs and lice were a constant torment. In May the nurses agreed to go to Los Banos which was also south of Manila. Upon arriving at the camp, they discovered that the surgical unit was devoid of equipment. There were no beds in the wards and no supplies for the nurses to use.[254]

In the fall of 1944 Sadaaki Konishi cut food rations by 20% and later cut them even further. At the same time vegetables were left to rot in the fields. The nurses, along with the other inmates, were suffering and losing weight. The nurses had to take in their uniforms.[255]

In December of 1944 American POWs at Palawan Prison Camp were massacred.[256] The massacre caused the Army to discuss plans to rescue POWS at other camps. The first rescue took place at Cabanatuan on Luzon. Plans for rescue at Bilibid Prison and Santo Tomas were discussed. Los Banos was low on the priority list at that time. The inmates at Los Banos were finally rescued in February of 1945. A total of 2,147 American and Allied POWS were freed.[257]

Sadaaki Konishi was captured in the Philippines and put on trial for starving inmates and killing local residents. He was found guilty and was executed on April 30, 1949.[258]

All twelve of "The Anchors" survived and returned to the U.S. They were awarded Bronze Stars for serving in a combat zone.

Mary Rose Harrington and Robert Merrill were married on April 13, 1945. He had also been a prisoner at Los Banos. They had four children. Mary continued her nursing career as a Red Cross volunteer with blood mobiles and by giving polio shots. She passed away in 1999 at age 85.

Eldene Paige returned to her family farm near Paradise, California. She lived with and cared for her mother. She died in 2004 at age 90. Eldene was the last of the twelve anchors to die.[259]

Families Who Lost Their Only Child in WW II

Richard Craig was the only child of Richard and Gladys. He graduated from Valley Springs High School in 1941. Richard enlisted in the Navy and was sent to the Great Lakes Naval Training Center at Great Lakes, Illinois, for boot training. He was assigned to a destroyer, the USS Shea. The destroyer was on duty during the invasion of Okinawa. A bomb struck the ship killing Richard and 34 other sailors.[260]

Robert Knorr was the only child of Herman and Lilly. He graduated from Marion High School and South Dakota State College with a degree in pharmacy. Robert's unit was fighting the Japanese on the island of Cebu in the Philippines where he was killed by enemy fire. The family received official notice of his death in May of 1945. The specific date of his death was not given.[261]

Clarence Kukral was the only child of Eugene and Sophia. He worked on the family farm prior to enlisting in the Marine Corps. After basic training he was sent to Guadalcanal in the Solomon Islands. Clarence was struck down by a Japanese sniper. His parents learned about his death over the radio. It was difficult for them to deal with the loss. Their farm house had eight rooms, but they shut off most of the home and lived in the kitchen and one bedroom.[262]

Wayne Larson was the only child of Harold and Mayme. He enlisted in the Army Air Corps in December of 1941. He became the pilot of a B-17. Wayne was sent to Germany in November of 1943. On January 30, 1944, his B-17 collided in mid-air with another B-17. Fourteen crew members from the two planes died in the collision. Wayne was among those who perished. Only eight could be identified. All fourteen crew members were buried in individual graves in Community Cemetery in Otze, Germany, on February 2, 1944.[263]

John was the only child of Dr. and Mrs. J.W. Lewis. He attended the University of Chicago two years and then enlisted in the Army Air Corps. John took his flight school training in Texas. In August of 1941 John's parents and his fiancée attended the commissioning ceremony to observe John receiving his wings and becoming a second lieutenant. Following the commissioning John and Mildred were married in a chapel on the air base. John's first assignment was to Hamilton Field, San Diego. Mildred went with him. At Hamilton Field John flew a P-40 fighter plane. The landing gear on the P-40's was defective. Pilots had to crash land or bail out. The problem got fixed. John's last overseas assignment was to French New Caledonia. John was taking off on a mission, but his plane did not gain enough altitude and crashed into a mountain. His final resting place is at Punch Bowl National Cemetery in Honolulu.[264]

Donald Pearson was the only child of Mr. and Mrs. Walfred Pearson. His father was a station agent for the Chicago & Northwestern Railroad. The family lived in Deadwood where Donald graduated from high school. Donald enlisted in the Marine Corps in October of 1943. He was a member of the 22nd Marine Regiment, 6th Marine Division. He was killed in action on May 13, 1945, on Okinawa. His body was not recovered. Donald is listed on the Tablets of the Missing at Honolulu Memorial.[265]

Joseph Schnee was the only child of Joseph and Jennie. After Pearl Harbor Joseph wanted to volunteer but was not old enough. He needed his father's approval which was granted. After basic training he was assigned to the USS American Legion. Joseph died in an accident aboard ship. His final resting place is at Fort Snelling in Minnesota.[266]

Orville Sethne was the only child of John and Mabel. He entered the military in July of 1944 and was sent overseas in January of 1945. In France Orville was with the 7th Army. He was in combat for the first time when he died on March 16, 1945. Orville is buried at Lorraine American Cemetery, St. Avold, France.[267]

Robert Siddons was the only child of Glenn and Ruth. He attended the University of Kansas two years and then accepted an appointment to the Naval Academy in Annapolis, Maryland. Robert participated in sports and ranked high academically in his class. He died in an accident at the Academy. His family was not informed of any details about the accident.[268]

Lennis Smith was the only child of Calvin and Helen. He graduated from Belle Fourche High School in 1937 and worked at various jobs before entering the military. Lennis and his wife Marion had three children. Lennis was sent to the Pacific with the 382nd Infantry, 96th Division. He died in combat on Okinawa in May of 1945. His remains were returned and buried in Spearfish cemetery.[269]

James Taylor was the only child of James and Elizabeth. After graduating from high school he worked in Mobridge before entering the Navy in 1942. James was trained to maintain the arresting gear on an aircraft carrier. He died from an accident that occurred on ship. It is not known what actually happened, but it is assumed that a cable broke and struck him. He died instantly and was buried at sea. He is listed on the Tablets of the Missing at Honolulu Memorial.[270]

Vincent Taylor was the only child of Bert and Coral. He was in the Army Air Corps and trained to be a pilot. Vincent was promoted through the ranks and became a captain. He was sent overseas in March of 1944. Vincent died on a mission in December of 1944.[271]

Ned Van Osdel was Eunice Fillion's only child. He worked at the air base in Sioux Falls and joined the military in March of 1943. Ned became an airplane mechanic. He had an appendicitis attack and entered the Balboa Naval Hospital in San Diego. Ned did not survive the attack. He was buried in Mission Hill cemetery.[272]

Henry Watkins was the only child of Ramsey and Grace. Henry worked on the family ranch before entering military service. At age seventeen he needed parental permission to enter military duty. Henry was in the Army and stationed on Okinawa. He died in combat on May 22, 1945.[273]

Allen Watson was born in Marion in Turner County to Thomas and Nancy. He farmed in the Canistota area, where he lived with his wife, Gertrude, and their daughter. Allen entered the military in 1942 and was trained at Ft. Snelling. He was sent overseas in 1942. Allen died in combat on Luzon on February 13,1945. He is buried in Manila American Cemetery. Allen was survived by his mother, wife, and daughter.[274]

Jacob Woods was the only child of John and Esther. He married Virginia Robertson in 1940. They had three children. One died in infancy. Jacob was working for local farmers when he was drafted in November of 1943. Jacob's army unit was fighting in Germany when he was killed in combat in March of 1945. Jacob was buried at Veteran's Cemetery in Devil's Lake, North Dakota.[275]

Families Who Lost Their Only Son in WW II

James and Alice Allen had three children: Melvin, Joyce, and Marlene. Melvin was born in Kimball. Melvin and his wife, Lucille, had two children. He enlisted in the Army and was trained at Fort Leavenworth, Kansas. He was sent to Okinawa with the 27th Infantry Division. Melvin died in combat on April 21, 1945. His remains were returned and buried in Memorial Park in Sioux City, Iowa.[276]

Glen and Marie Allen had three children: Robert, Donna, and Shirley. Robert graduated from high school in Rapid City. After graduation he joined the Army and was trained at Ft. Hood, Texas. He was sent to Okinawa where he died in combat on June 22, 1945.[277]

Charles Barnard was born to William and Anna on the family farm in Charles Mix County. He enlisted in the Navy in February of 1942. Charles was serving on the USS Morrison off the coast of Okinawa. On May 5, 1945, Japanese kamikaze planes crashed into the ship causing it to sink. His remains were returned and buried in ZCBJ Cemetery near Wagner.[278]

John and Bertha Benson had five children: Weldon, Carol, Marian, Paulette, and Delphine. Weldon was born in New Effington in Roberts County. He graduated from Peever High School in 1944. Weldon joined the military in September of 1944 and trained at Camp Hood in Texas. Weldon was sent overseas in January of 1945. He was fighting on Okinawa when he was wounded. Weldon was in a field hospital when he died on June 17th. He would have been nineteen on June 21st. His body was returned and buried at Ft. Snelling National Cemetery.[279]

Harold and Mary Jane Berg had two children, Lyman and Betty. Lyman was born in Aberdeen and graduated from Aberdeen Central High School. He attended Northern State College two years. He transferred to the School of Mines and Technology before entering the military. He joined the Marines and was trained in Georgia and Texas. Lyman earned his wings and commission in Pensacola, Florida. He was stationed at several bases before he was sent overseas in February of 1945. Lyman was piloting a torpedo dive bomber when he was shot down over Okinawa.

Lyman was declared missing in action on April 29th. Lyman is listed on the Tablets of the Missing at Honolulu Memorial.[280]

Frank Walter and Viola Cahoy had three children: Frank Wayne, Mabel, and Hagretta. Frank Wayne was born in Fairfax in Gregory County. He attended the University of South Dakota prior to entering the military. He was sent overseas in August of 1944 with the 101st Infantry Regiment of the 26th Division. He was killed in Luxembourg on December 30th.[281]

Edwin and Zena Carlson had two children, Zane and Lois. Zane earned his wings at Luke Field, Arizona, and was stationed in Italy. He was re- turning from a bombing mission in his P-47 Thunderbolt when he spotted a convoy of German trucks. On their first strafing pass he and his wing-man set one truck on fire. On their second pass Zane was hit by an anti-aircraft shell. He bailed out but was too low for the parachute to open; he died on impact. After the war, his remains were returned and buried in the family plot at New Sweden Cemetery near Holmquist in Day County.[282]

Alvin and Josie Christensen had two children. Kermit was from Egan in Moody County. He was drafted into the Army. After basic training at Camp Hood, Texas, he was sent overseas in February of 1945. He joined the 96th Division on Okinawa. Kermit was killed in combat on June 16, 1945. In 1949 his remains were returned and buried in Flandreau cemetery.[283]

James and Tena Faiferlick had two children. Walter was born in Nunda in Lake County. The year was 1911. He graduated from Madison High School. He worked for his father and then the Farmers & Merchants Co-Op. Walter would not have been required to serve as he was over the draft age and was responsible for his parents' support. He did volunteer in 1943 and was trained at Camp

Roberts in California. After further training in the Pacific he was assigned to the 105th Infantry Regiment, 27th Infantry Division. He was sent to Okinawa. His unit went into combat on April 18th. Walter was killed the next day. His remains were returned in 1949 and buried in Graceland Cemetery in Madison.[284]

Peter and Stephanie DeMuynck had eight children. Henry was the oldest and was followed by seven sisters: Mathilda, Margaret, Marie, Emma, Mary, Emily, and Leona. Stephanie died after the birth of her seventh daughter, Leona, in March of 1942. Henry enlisted in the Navy in 1942. He was trained at two locations before being sent to Corry Field in Pensacola, Florida. He was not feeling well and entered the Naval Hospital where he died on January 21, 1943. The cause of death was an abscess on his brain. His body was returned and buried in the Catholic cemetery in Pipestone, Minnesota. Henry was buried beside his mother and two infant sisters.[285]

Ernest and Minnie Eisnach had four children. Lloyd had an older sister, Zola, and two younger sisters, Florence and Delores. Lloyd volunteered for the Army in May of 1941. He was trained at two locations before attending Officers Candidate School at Fort Benning, Georgia. Upon graduation from OCS he was commissioned a second lieutenant. He went overseas in September of 1942 and was stationed in France. Lloyd died on October 26, 1944, when a road mine exploded. His body was returned to Estelline for burial. Lloyd left behind his widow, Mariem.[286]

Joseph and Anna Gabriel had three children: Harold, Betty Jo, and Deanna. Harold graduated from South Dakota State College in 1942 and joined the Army in November of that year. He was sent overseas in in December of 1943. Harold was attached to the 709th Amphibious Tank Battalion. The official letter to his mother stated that Harold had died in combat on the island of Saipan in the

Mariana Islands. Harold is buried in National Memorial Cemetery in Honolulu.[287]

Jacob and Sabina Gottlob had six children: John, Cecelia, Florence, Leona, Geneva, and Mildred, John trained in Kansas and went overseas in September of 1943. He was on duty in Belgium when a sniper's bullet took his life. It was ironic that John, who was of German descent, was killed by a German. John was buried in Belgium.[288]

Enoch and Florence Hickman had two children, Marion and Doris. Marion graduated from Letcher High School. He worked with his father on the family farm prior to joining the Marines. He trained at Parris Island, South Carolina, and Camp LeJeune, North Carolina. Marion was attached to the 6th Marine Division and sent to Okinawa in December of 1944. He had volunteered to drive a truck to the front lines but died in action before he reached his objective. His body was returned in 1949 and buried in the Legion Plot of Graceland Cemetery in Mitchell.[289]

Ralph and Garnet Hockridge had two children, Doris and Ralph Jr. Doris was in the United States Coast Guard Women's Reserve, SPARS. Ralph Jr. was in the infantry and serving in France. He died in combat in France on July 2, 1944.[290]

Carleton Hoyer was born to Edward and Emma in Sioux Falls. He graduated-ed from Washington High School and joined the military in March of 1942. His training took place at several locations. In April of 1944 he was sent overseas. His unit was fighting in France when he died in combat on August 5, 1944. His remains were returned in 1948 and reinterred at Mount Pleasant Cemetery in Sioux Falls.[291]

Joe and Anna Kleinsasser had three children. Arnold was born on a farm near Yale in Beadle County. He went to high school for one year and was drafted into the Army in 1944. He completed basic training at Camp Hood, Texas. His last assignment was to Okinawa. A sniper took his life on June 10, 1945. His body was returned in 1949 and buried in Bethel Church Cemetery.[292]

Mr. and Mrs. J. J. Peacock had two children. Donald was born in 1908. He grew up on the family farm south of Watauga in Corson County. After graduating from high school, he farmed with his parents. He left the farm to join the service. After basic training he was part of a medical unit that was attached to an infantry unit on Luzon. Donald died in combat on February 1, 1945. His remains were returned and buried at Fort Snelling National Cemetery.[293]

James M. and Alta Rano had four children. James Daryl was born in Rapid City. He worked at the Air Base in Rapid City prior to entering the military. He joined the Navy at Farragut, Idaho, and trained in Faring, Texas. In 1944 he was sent to the Pacific on the USS Mannert L. Abele. The ship was patrolling off the coast of Okinawa when it was sunk. The ship sank quickly, taking about one-fourth of the officers and crew with it. James is listed on the Tablets of the Missing at Honolulu Memorial.[294]

Emma Romig had three children. Philip graduated from Wessington Springs High School in 1937. He was drafted in November of 1942. After basic training in California, he was assigned to the 6th Armored Division. It was a tank corps made famous by General George Patton. The division was in several major battles in Europe. Philip was in combat in Germany when he was hit by shrapnel. He died on April 2, 1945. His remains were returned and buried in the cemetery in Alpena, South Dakota.[295]

Walter and Lillian Ruby had four children: Donald, Florence, Blanche, and Doris. Donald enlisted in the Army. After basic training he was sent to France, where he died in combat. Donald was buried in the Epinal American Cemetery near Epinal, France.[296]

Arthur and Vivian Schleher had three children. Paul enlisted in the Navy in 1937. After basic training, he served on several ships from 1937 to 1941. Paul's last assignment before being discharged in October of 1941 was on the USS Nevada. He re-enlisted and was called to active duty after Pearl Harbor. In March of 1942 he was assigned to the USS Aaron Ward. The ship was stationed off the coast of Guadalcanal. Its main responsibility was to guard transport ships. On November 12, 1942, a sea battle between American and Japanese forces began. The USS Aaron Ward took nine direct hits, and Paul died as a result of one of those direct hits.[297]

Floyd Smit was born to Mr. and Mrs. Ben Smit. He grew up on the family farm near Lennox and graduated from Lennox High School. Floyd was drafted in February of 1942 and trained at several locations. He was sent to the Pacific and stationed on New Guinea. Floyd died in combat. Floyd's remains were returned in 1949 and buried at Lennox.[298]

Albert and Julia Sorenson had eight children: Henry, Gladys, Clarice, Irene, Sadie, Ellen, Evelyn, and Joan. Henry graduated from Roslyn High School in 1938 and joined the South Dakota National Guard. He was attending South Dakota State College when he was drafted and sent to Camp Claiborne, Louisiana. Henry's first overseas assignment was in Tunisia with the 34th Division. One responsibility of his unit was repairing and building roads, essential for the movement of troops and supplies. The unit was also assigned to locate and remove land mines that had been placed by Germans. Enemy aircraft were attacking Henry's half- track squad when he was wounded and died in November of 1943. Henry was buried in a U.S. Military Cemetery in Carano, Italy. His remains were returned in 1948 and buried at Fron Lutheran Cemetery.[299]

Marvin and Isabelle Stellmacher had two children, Marlowe and Beverly. Marlowe was born in Gary in Deuel County. After high school he enlisted in the Navy. His first assignment was on the USS Reno. The Reno was part of the fleet that fought the Japanese in the Battle of Leyte Gulf. The battle took place during the latter part of October 1944. It was one of the major sea battles of WW II. Marlowe died in November of 1944 when a Japanese torpedo stuck the USS Reno. He was buried at sea. There is a marker in his honor in American Cemetery in Manila.[300]

Dr. Herbert and Ada Stevens had two children, Warren and Eileen. Warren graduated from Aberdeen Central High School and the University of South Dakota. His intention was to attend law school. Warren was in the ROTC program and after Officers Candidate School became a second lieutenant. He was stationed in France and was part of a unit that was assigned to clear mines after the Germans had retreated. A mine exploded, killing two men under his command. Warren and another soldier went out to bring their fallen comrades back. On their return they stepped on a mine, and Warren died on November 3, 1944. Warren was buried in Epinal American Cemetery near Epinal, France.[301]

Gustave and Elizabeth Sturm had two children, George and Charlotte. George graduated from Aberdeen Central High School. He was attending Officers Candidate School in Texas when he was sent overseas. George was sent to Europe in September of 1944. His unit was in Germany when he died in combat on March 15, 1945. He was buried in Henri-Chapelle American Cemetery in Henri-Chapelle, Belgium.[302]

Winston was born to Mr. and Mrs. Ed Toomey. He attended Northern State College and played on the football team. Winston enlisted in the Army Air Corps. His plane was on a mission over Germany when he was wounded, but he stayed at his post and made sure all the bombs were released. He died before the plane returned to base. Winston was buried in Cambridge American Cemetery near Cambridge, England.[303]

George and Marcelle Trotman had two children. Their son, George, graduated from Rapid City High School in 1942. He was underage and needed his parents' permission to join the military. He became a paratrooper and was sent overseas in October of 1943. George was stationed in England. He was part of the D-Day invasion on June 6, 1944. George died in the flooded fields of Normandy. He was buried in Cambridge American Cemetery near Cambridge, England.[304]

Donald Tuttle had one sister, Beverly. He joined the National Guard Band during his senior year in high school. He graduated from Letcher High School in 1938 and enrolled at South Dakota State College where he joined the band. Donald was called to active duty in 1940 and was assigned the 147th Field Artillery Band. After completing Officer Candidate School he was commissioned a second lieutenant. He became a member of the "Red Arrow" Division. Donald was on patrol in New Guinea when he was reported as missing in action in July of 1944. He is listed on the Tablets of the Missing at Manila American Cemetery.[305]

Emil and Clare Ulmer had four children: Erwin, Ada, Leona, and Irene. Both parents died at a young age. Erwin was thirteen years older than Irene and became her legal guardian. Erwin was drafted and became a tank driver. He was sent overseas in 1943. His unit fought in North Africa and then moved on to Italy. They were fighting north of Rome in December of 1943 when his tank drove over a land mine and Erwin died from the explosion. In 1948 his remains were returned and buried in Menno cemetery, Menno, South Dakota.[306]

Camiel and Edith Vande Boss had two children, Robert and Erma. Robert enlisted in the Army Air Corps. He was trained as a mechanic and sent to Patterson Field in Colorado Springs. Robert and his crew were moving an airplane into a hangar when an accident occurred. He died from the accident. His remains were returned and buried in Graceland Cemetery in Mitchell.[307]

Joel and Rhoda Vaughan had three children, Orel, Beva, and Pearl. Orel joined the military in July of 1942. His unit was in combat in Luxembourg where he died from machine gun fire. It was late January of 1945. Orel was buried in Luxembourg American Cemetery.[308]

Mr. and Mrs. Lyle Vaughters had five children: Kenneth, Isabel, Cita Mae, Lila Rae, and Lois. Kenneth was born in Avon in Bon Homme County. Kenneth was thirty-one when he was drafted in November of 1942. He served in New Guinea and Leyte. Kenneth came down with hepatitis. He died on Leyte and was buried there.[309]

Fred and Irma Voelker had five children: Charles, Mercedes, Irma, Dorothy, and Darlene. Charles joined the military in March of 1942 and went overseas in January of 1944. He was stationed in France where he was part of a Tank Destroyer Battalion. Charles died in combat on August 17, 1944. He fell on a fellow soldier and sacrificed his own life in the process.[310]

Peter and Katherine Volz had two children. Francis joined the military in March of 1942. He trained at several locations and was sent overseas in June of 1944. Francis was stationed in France and was a member of the 116th Infantry Regiment. Francis died in combat in France on July 31, 1944. His remains were returned after the war and buried in Fort Snelling National Cemetery.[311]

James and Theresa Vosika had four children. John served in the CCC before enlisting in the Army. He trained at two locations and was sent over- seas in November of 1942. John's first assignment was to Africa and then on to Italy. While serving as a Ranger, John's unit was outnumbered, and the enemy annihilated his group. John died on February 27, 1944. He was buried at Ft. Snelling National Cemetery.[312]

Carl and Elisabeth Waldow had two children. August was born in 1910 on the family farm near Willow Lake in Clark County. He was drafted in 1941 and trained at Fort Leonard Wood in Missouri and Luis Obispo in California. He fought on New Guinea and then was sent to Luzon. August was standing guard on a bridge when he was injured. He was sent to a hospital ship where he died on May 5, 1945. His body was returned and buried in Bethlehem Lutheran Cemetery in Willow Lake.[313]

Gustva and Sylvia Wallquist had two children. After joining the military in March of 1942, Forrest was transferred to the Enlisted Reserve Army Corps. He was sent overseas in August of 1943 and was a member of the 135th Infantry Regiment, 34th Infantry Division. Forrest died in combat near Marsanello, Italy. His remains were returned and buried in Grand Valley Cemetery.[314]

Mr. and Mrs. Gordon Waters had two children, Veloris and Lavonne. Veloris joined the South Dakota National Guard in January of 1940 and trained at Camp Claiborne, Louisiana. Overseas, he fought at Anzio and in the Mt. Cassino area. Veloris died in Italy from shrapnel wounds on June 26, 1944.[315]

Edward and Elizabeth Watznauer had three children— Angelo, Lillian, and a married daughter, Mrs. Edmund Goudy. Angelo was born in 1913 and joined the Army in May of 1942. He trained in Texas and Wisconsin. He was sent to Ireland and then on to England. Angelo was part of the force that invaded France. He died in combat on February 21, 1944. His final resting place is in St. Anthony Cemetery in rural Artesian.[316]

William and Mary Weddell had two children, Cyril and Ruby. Cyril was sent to Europe in 1945 and was in the 291st Infantry. His unit was fighting near Dorsten, Germany. He was putting down communication wires for his battalion when he died. The jeep he was using drove over a land mine. Cyril is buried in Netherlands American Cemetery in Margarten, Holland.[317]

Mr. and Mrs. Edwin West had two children. Thomas joined the South Dakota National Guard, 109th Engineers. He transferred to the Army Air Corps in 1942. He trained at several bases and earned his wings at Lawrenceville, Illinois. In April of 1943 he was sent to a B-24 school. He trained in Pueblo, Colorado, with the crew he flew with until his final mission. Thomas and his crew were sent to Torretta Field in Italy. Their last mission was to the Odertal Oil Refinery when their plane was hit by fire from enemy aircraft. The plane exploded near Muglitz, Germany. Czechoslovakian partisans found his body and the bodies of five other crew members. They were buried in Troubky, Czechoslovakia.[318]

Amelia Wilson had two children. Her son, Andrew, was trained at several locations and then sent overseas to the Hawaiian Islands. He was part of the force that invaded Leyte. He was wounded there and returned to action. His unit invaded Okinawa. In the official letter to his mother Andrew was praised for his bravery on Okinawa. He disregarded his own safety and under enemy fire crawled to get morphine to a wounded soldier. He died while returning to his position. In May of 1949 Andrew's body was returned and buried in Lakeview Cemetery in Clear Lake, South Dakota.[319]

Mike and Rebecca Wollman had five children. Albert entered military service in June of 1941. He was trained at several locations. Albert served in the Hawaiian Islands and in New Guinea. His last assignment was on the island of Luzon where he died in combat. A granite obelisk at the Huron Public Library contains his name.[320]

Clifford and Catherine Woods had three children. Lyle enlisted in the Army Air Corps. He was trained at two locations and sent overseas. Lyle was the top turret gunner on a B-17 bomber. His plane was shot down over the English Channel. Lyle's body was not recovered. There is a marker for him in Ardennes American Cemetery near Liege, Belgium.[321]

Mr. and Mrs. Ferdinand Wulff had two children. Orville was in the Army Air Corps and was stationed in England. He was a crew member on a B-24 bomber. His plane was on a bombing mission when enemy fire knocked out two of their engines, and after losing another engine, the plane crashed into a range of hills. The crew was buried in England. Orville's final resting place is in Fort Snelling National Cemetery.[322]

Two Brothers Went to War and One Returned

Isaac Allum was born in Gregory and went to school in Herrick. He volunteered for the Navy doing his senior year of high school. Issac was attending Sioux Falls College when he was called to active duty. He was trained at the U.S. Naval Training Station at Great Lakes, Illinois, to be a hospital corpsman. Isaac was assigned to the USS Newberry. Marines from the ship were landing on Iwo Jima. Isaac went ashore to help with the wounded. He responded to a cry for help and did not return. His body was never found. Isaac is listed on the Tablets of the Missing at National Cemetery in Honolulu. He was awarded the Purple Heart. His brother Kermit was a Marine.[323]

Kenneth and Alfred Bakkie were born on a farm near Tulare. Because of the drought and depression they joined the CCC and worked in the Pierre area. They joined the Army in 1940. After completing their training, they were sent to North Africa. Kenneth and Alfred were on patrol when Kenneth stepped on a land mine.

His final resting place is at Fort Snelling National Cemetery in Minneapolis.[324]

Dale Barrows was born in Aurora County. He graduated from Stickney High School and Yankton College. He enlisted in the Naval Air Corps in 1942. After earning his wings, he was sent to the South Pacific. According to the official report, Dale was attacking Japanese ships in Kobe Harbor when his plane went down. His body washed ashore in Kobe Harbor on March 19, 1945. His body was returned and buried in Dudley Cemetery in Aurora County. His brother John was also in the Navy.[325]

Cecil Beardemphl was born in Ashton in Spink County. The year was 1919. Cecil married Jean Gifford in 1942. Cecil and his brother Cody enlisted together in 1942. After training they were sent to Europe. Cecil went to Italy and Cody to London. Cecil died in combat in September of 1944. He was buried in a cemetery near Florence, Italy. His remains were returned to Ashton in 1949 and buried in the family plot.[326]

Edmund Bowar was born in 1921 in Dimock in Hutchinson County. He had two brothers and four sisters. Edmund was drafted in 1942 and trained in Kansas. He was sent to England and then to France and to Belgium. His last stop was Germany where he died in combat. His brother Vincent was in the military.[327]

Maxwell Bowling was from Clearfield in Tripp County. He enlisted in the Army in November of 1941. Maxwell was with an Armored Division in France when he died in combat. His brother Robert was in the Navy.[328]

Robert Carnie IV worked for the South Dakota Game, Fish, and Parks Department in Woonsocket prior to joining the military. His wife, Marie Lavold, was from Redfield. They had one son, Robert Carnie V. Robert entered military service in 1943 and became a pilot. He flew a P-51 "Mustang" fighter plane. Robert and other pilots were protecting American bombers on their way to enemy targets in Romania. Several enemy fighters were approaching the bombers when Robert made contact with them. Robert and his leader worked together and destroyed five enemy fighters. As he continued the attack, his plane was involved in an accident and crashed. He was awarded the Distinguished Flying Cross, Air Medal, and four oak-leaf clusters. His brother Edwin was also in the Army Air Force.[329]

Lorenzo Collins was born in 1926 in Dixon in Tripp County. He was inducted at Ft. Snelling in 1944. Lorenzo became a member of the 8th Armored Division and shipped out on January 31, 1945. He was fighting in Germany when he was killed on March 5, 1945. The war ended in May of that year. His brother Vernon was stationed in England.[330]

Harold Denison was from Vermillion. He trained at several locations and became a crew member on a B-24 Liberator. His plane flew out of Guadalcanal on a mission to Bouganville Island in the Solomon Islands. The plane disappeared on the return trip. Many years later his family received his medals. Harold is listed on the Tablets of the Missing at Manila American Cemetery. Harold's brother Steven also served in the South Pacific.[331]

Robert Devers was from Huron. He enlisted in the National Guard. Robert became part of the 109th Engineers. He was sent to Camp Claiborne and then on to several other locations for more training. Robert was transferred to the 132nd Engineers and sent to the Pacific. His unit was part of the invasion force at Guam and Leyte. Robert was in combat on Le Shima in April of 1945. A fellow Soldier had been killed, and Robert died in an attempt to retrieve the body. His brother Forest was also in the military.[332]

Gerald Flynn was from Elk Point. Gerald and his brother Morris enlisted in the Marines together. After basic training Gerald was sent overseas. He died in combat on Guadalcanal. His final resting place is in National Cemetery of the Pacific in Honolulu. He was awarded the Purple Heart.[333]

Donald Fox was born in 1918 and grew up in Harding County. He worked on the family ranch until he was drafted in 1942. He trained in California and Hawaii. He was sent to the Solomon Islands where he was in combat for twenty-two months. After spending leave time in New Zealand and New Caledonia, he was sent to Luzon in the Philippines in 1944. Donald was on scout duty for his platoon when he was killed. His youngest brother, Lloyd, had also served in the Philippines.[334]

Vernon Frey was born in Burke. He enlisted in the Navy in March of 1944. Vernon was sent overseas in September of 1944. His ship was near the Bataan Peninsula when it was sunk by Japanese torpedoes. His brother Elmer was also in the Navy.[335]

Galen Gass was from Brandt in Deuel County. He joined the military in April of 1942 and was sent overseas in July of 1943. He was on New Guinea when he came down with dermatitis, known to the Soldiers as Jungle Rot. He recovered and was sent back to his unit. The disease reoccurred. He also came down with diphtheria. Galen was sent to a hospital in San Francisco where he died on March 23, 1945. His brother Chester was also in the military.[336]

Nicholas Gebhart was born in Faulkton. He enlisted in the Army in 1940. After basic training he was assigned to the 3rd Infantry Division. His unit fought in North Africa, Sicily, and Salerno, Italy. Nicholas died in action at the Volturno River north of Naples on October 14, 1943, the expiration date of his enlistment. The Italian Campaign has been described as the "Forgotten Front"; the 3rd Division suffered the most casualties of any unit in WW II. Nicholas was buried in Watertown. His brother George was in the Army.[337]

Delbert Gerlach was born in Newell and graduated from high school in Rapid City. He wanted to be a pilot and joined the Navy. Delbert trained in Iowa City and received his wings in 1943. His overseas assignment was on the USS Lunga Point. He piloted a torpedo bomber. Delbert was promoted to Lieutenant Junior Grade. He flew missions to Leyte Gulf and Iwo Jima. On March 25, 1945, he was on a spotting mission for Marine Corps artillery when he was shot down. The battle of Iwo Jima was raging. His remains were returned to the U.S. for burial. His brother Charles was in the Navy.[338]

Maurice Goblirsch graduated from Gary High School in 1944. Shortly after graduation he was drafted. He was sent overseas in November of 1944. Maurice died in combat in France. He was buried in Lorraine American Cemetery at St. Avold, France. His brother Leonard served in Europe.[339]

James Hagerty graduated from high school in Aberdeen and attended Northern State College, South Dakota State College, and the University of North Dakota. James was a civil engineer with the State Highway Commission before entering the military. Jane Hurst became his bride in 1942. He joined the Army but transferred to the Army Air Corps. James earned his wings, a commission, and then was sent overseas in 1943. He received a Silver Star for completing a difficult mission over Gasmata, New Britain. It was a bombing in which large oil fires were started in enemy installations. They encountered opposition from the enemy. James died in action in the Pacific on November 11, 1943. A brother was serving in the Navy.[340]

Raymond Harrington was born in Wagner. He left high school to join the Army. Raymond perished on Okinawa. After the war his remains were returned to Wagner. His brother Harold was also in the military.[341]

Charles Hartman was from Gettysburg. He enlisted in the 11th Cavalry, but it was disbanded. His last assignment was as a radio operator on a B-17 bomber. His plane flew reconnaissance missions out of Townsville, Australia. They were looking for Japanese submarines and surface ships. His plane did not return from a mission in August of 1942. Charles is remembered on a cross in Black Hills National Cemetery. His brother William served in the military.[342]

Merlin Henke was born in 1921 in Union County. He had four brothers and one sister. Merlin married Lucille Knecht in 1943, and they had one son, Raymond. Merlin enlisted in the Army. His training took him to several camps. Merlin was assigned to the 28th Regiment of the 8th Division. His brother Kenneth was also in the infantry. Merlin died in combat on September 5, 1944. He received the Purple Heart. Merlin was buried in Brittany American Cemetery near St. James, France.[343]

Maurice Henrichen Jr. was born in Gann Valley in Buffalo County. He graduated from Gann Valley High School and in 1942 enlisted in the Army. He was fighting in Luxembourg during the Battle of the Bulge when he was killed. Maurice was buried in Henri-Chapelle American Cemetery in Belgium. His brother George served in the military and was a POW for several months.[344]

Allan Holtquist was born in 1918 in Grant County. He graduated from Milbank High School in 1936. Allan joined the CCC and worked in the Black Hills a year. He had joined the Minnesota National Guard, which was called to active duty in 1941. After basic training in Louisiana the unit was sent overseas in 1942. They were sent to Scotland for more training. The unit was part of the invasion of North Africa in November of 1942. After Africa they went on to Sicily and then Italy. They were fighting at Cassino, Italy, when

Allan was hit by artillery fire and died. It was February 6, 1944. His brother Kenneth was in the same unit but survived the war.[345]

Eugene Holzworth was from Eureka. He entered military service at Fort Snelling on March 26, 1941. His brother Edwin joined shortly after Eugene. Eugene shipped out for Europe in January of 1944. The brothers managed to meet once during the war. Eugene was part of the 125th Reconnaissance Squadron and had been on duty three years when he died in action on August 19, 1944. He was in France. Eugene was awarded the Purple Heart, European Theatre Ribbon, and a Good Conduct Medal.[346]

Walter Isley was born in 1919 in Yankton. Both of his parents had died by 1935. Walter and his siblings were raised in Platte by an aunt and uncle. Walter enrolled at Augustana College in 1937 and took a course in aeronautical training. He was drafted in January of 1941. He was trained at several fields, earned his wings and a commission. Walter was on a training mission when his bomber crashed at Lake Apopka, Florida, on January 18, 1942. His body was not recovered. His brother Morris was in the Army.[347]

Howard Ives was born in Andover in Day County. He started his military duty in February of 1942. Howard was sent overseas in April of 1943. He died in combat near Paestum, Italy. Howard's brother Dean was in the Army Air Corps.[348]

Twin brothers Clifford and Clayton Jacobson were born in 1917 in Flandreau and graduated from high school in 1935. Clifford was inducted into the Army at Fort Snelling. He was trained to be a mechanic. After completing training he came home on furlough before being sent to Europe. Clifford was stationed in Belgium, and Clayton was in Luxembourg. They both got passes and spent some time together. Clifford was in Germany when he died in combat on March 30, 1945.[349]

Herbert Joachim was from Greenway in McPherson County. After basic training he was sent to the South Pacific in 1942. As a member of the 358th Port Battalion he perished following an explosion and fire on a base in 1943. Herbert was buried in National Cemetery of the Pacific in Honolulu. One of his brothers was also in the service.[350]

Ludwig Krein was born in 1925 in Hot Springs and graduated from high school in 1943. He had six brothers and sisters. Ludwig was drafted in 1943. He trained in Florida before going overseas in July of 1944. He was part of the 3rd Infantry Division. His unit fought in Italy and France. Ludwig and his brother Walter were both in Epinal, France, at the same time but did not know it until later. Ludwig was in France when he died in combat from a shell fragment to the chest on January 24, 1945. He was nineteen. Ludwig was awarded the Purple Heart and was buried in Epinal American Cemetery in Epinal, France.[351]

Walter Lakeman was born in 1916 and graduated from Brookings High School. He enlisted in 1941. Training started at Ft. Snelling and continued in Tennessee and Kentucky. He became a medic and joined the 83rd Infantry Division. His brother Ray was in the 82nd Airborne Division. The two divisions both fought in the Battle of the Bulge. Waltersaw action in the hedgerows of Normandy in July of 1944. He was on the front lines and aided the wounded while facing enemy fire. January of 1945 found him in Belgium during the Battle of the Bulge. He died on the 10th from a mortar wound to the chest. Walter was buried in Henri-Chapelle American Cemetery in Belgium. He was awarded the Purple Heart, Silver Star, and several other medals.[352]

Lloyd Larson was born in 1918. He had six brothers and sisters. Lloyd and his brother Merle enlisted together. His advanced training was with an armored unit. In 1943 he was sent to England.

After D-Day he went to France. He was wounded by a German sniper in September of 1944. He received a Purple Heart, recovered, and returned to the front lines. He was killed in combat on November 17, 1944. His brother was a German POW at the time. Lloyd was returned to the U.S. for burial.[353]

Harry Laustrup was born in Rapid City in 1918. He was attached to a signal corps unit in Italy. Harry fell from a moving military vehicle and died from a skull fracture on July 28, 1944. His brother Paul was serving in New Guinea.[354]

Benjamin Lucas was born in Sioux Falls. He first reported for duty in Kansas and then was sent to Fort Knox, Kentucky, for more training. Benjamin was assigned to the 894th Tank Destroyer Battalion. The unit was sent to North Africa and then to Italy. Benjamin died in combat near Nettuno, Italy. He was buried in Sicily-Rome American Cemetery near Nettuno. He was awarded the Purple Heart. He left behind his widow, Dorothy. His brother Albert was serving in England.[355]

Thomas Lyon had twelve brothers and sisters. His first assignment was with the Army Air Corps in 1943. He transferred to the infantry as he felt that he was needed more there. Thomas and Shirlee Bloodgood were married in June of 1944. His unit left the U.S. in November of 1944. They landed in Europe as the Battle of the Bulge was raging. Thomas died from wounds sustained in battle. The date was March 28, 1945. He was buried in Lorraine American Cemetery at St. Avold, France. He left behind his widow, Shirlee, and an infant daughter who was born three months after her father's death. His brother William was a Navy officer.[356]

Walter Mager was born on the family farm near Rockham in Faulk County. He enlisted in the Army; his brother Melvin had joined the Army Air Corps. Walter loved horses and signed up to be in the Cavalry but did not see a horse in the military. He was very thoughtful and sent money home every month to his mother. His first overseas duty was in Ireland in 1942 and then to Africa. Walter's unit was in position to defend a town against a possible tank attack when German bombers attacked his position. He fired his .50 caliber machine gun at the bombers. A bomb exploded near Walter, causing a fatal wound. He was awarded the Silver Star for his bravery. His parents requested that Walter be returned to Redfield for burial.[357]

Howard Marquardt was born in Badger in Kingsbury County. He graduated from Arlington High School in 1934 and served in the CCC. Howard became interested in flying and joined the Army Air Corps. He was sent to Hickam Field in Hawaii and trained to be a mechanic. Howard was wounded during the Japanese attack on Pearl Harbor. He recovered and was sent to Maui Island with his unit. On Maui he did patrol duty and flew reconnaissance missions. Howard was wounded during the Battle of Midway. He was the flight engineer on a B-17 bomber when it crashed in 1942. His brother Lloyd was in the service.[358]

Elmer Maunu was born in June of 1924 in Brown County. He was sent to Ft. Snelling for induction into the Army. It was April of 1944, and he was nineteen. After completing training he was assigned to the 148th Infantry Regiment and sent to the Pacific. In 1945 American troops were in combat to retake the Philippines. Elmer died in the fighting on Luzon. It was April 25, 1945. He was awarded the Purple Heart. His brother Lester also served in WW II.[359]

Lyle Mosteller was born in 1919 in Hughes County. After Pearl Harbor Lyle and his brother Larry enlisted in the Navy. Lyle trained in San Diego. Lyle served on the USS Smith in the South Pacific and perished in the Battle of Santa Cruz. The ship was hit by torpedoes and a kamikaze plane. He was awarded the Purple Heart and the WW II Victory Medal. Lyle is listed on the Tablets of the Missing at Manila American Cemetery.[360]

Samuel Noring, Jr. was born in 1921. He graduated from Gregory High School in 1939. Samuel attended college in Sioux City, Iowa, and held a government job in Aberdeen. He enlisted in the Army in 1942. After basic training he was sent to France. Samuel died in combat on August, 3, 1944. His body was returned and buried in Fort Snelling National Cemetery. His brother Harold was in the Naval Reserve.[361]

Roger Parlee was born in Huron in 1919. He was in the National Guard and left when the unit was activated in 1939. He transferred to the 139th Engineers. His unit was engaged in combat north of Leghorn, Italy. He died from an anti-tank mine. His brother Wendall was also in the military.[362]

Marlin Peterson was born in 1914 on a farm south of Webster. There were fourteen children in the family. He was drafted in 1941. After training in Missouri, Tennessee, and California he was sent to New Guinea in 1944. American troops invaded Luzon in January of 1945. Marlin was wounded in the fighting and after recovering was sent back into battle. He was wounded a second time in July but this time by friendly fire. Marlin was in the General Hospital on Leyte until September when he was flown to California. His condition got worse, and he died on October 4, 1945. The family plot in the Hosanger Cemetery south of Webster is his final resting place. His brother Orville continued to serve in the Sixth Division.

The division had been in combat for 112 straight days, which was longer than any unit in the Pacific.[363]

Edward Plihal was born in Tyndall and graduated from Tyndall High School in 1939. Edward attended Southern State Teachers College and South Dakota State College. He enlisted in the Army in 1942. Edward was commissioned a second lieutenant during college. His training took place at several locations. Edward's last assignment took him to Camp Hood in Texas. He was an instructor in the tank destroyer school. Edward came down with meningitis and died in Texas. He was buried at Bohemian National Cemetery near Tyndall. His brother Joe was serving in England.[364]

Laurence Radlinger was born in Tea. He was drafted in 1941 at the age of twenty-six. Laurence and Merle Johnson had been married in 1938. They had a daughter, Marlene. He was sent overseas in June of 1944. Laurence was assigned to the 2047th Aviation Fire Fighting Platoon. He died fighting a fire. Laurence was buried in Epinal American Cemetery near Epinal, France. He was awarded the Purple Heart. His brother Frank was in the service.[365]

Milton Reisenweber was born in Marshall County in 1921. He was stationed in Paris. He died in a pedestrian accident when he was run over by a jeep. Milton was buried in the Britton Cemetery. His brother Mervin had joined the Army Air Corps.[366]

Alvin Roeber was born in Tulare. He joined the service in 1942. He was home on furlough in 1944 and did not survive emergency surgery. Alvin was buried in St. John's Cemetery in rural Tulare. His brother Walter was serving in Europe at the time.[367]

Eugene Sanders was born in Aberdeen. He graduated from Aberdeen Central High School in 1941 and enlisted in the Navy. He went overseas on the USS Helena. The ship was on patrol in the Kula Gulf in the Solomon Islands. Shells from Japanese ships hit the Helena, causing it to sink. Eugene's body was never recovered. His brother Steve was in the Army Air Corps.[368]

Alfred Schutt was from Edgemont. Alfred and his brother Roy joined the National Guard in 1940 and were sent to Camp Claiborne. The brothers were in the same unit. They fought in North Africa and Italy. In December of 1944 Roy went home on furlough.

Alfred was wounded in battle and died in April of 1945. The war ended in May. Alfred was buried in Florence American Cemetery near Florence, Italy. He was awarded the Purple Heart.[369]

Charley Simek was born in Tyndall. Charley and his brother John joined the service at the same time. They trained together and took the same boat to England. The brothers were separated on D-Day. John did not see Charley again. Charley was with the 357th Infantry Regiment when he was killed in battle on June 22, 1944. He was buried in Normandy American Cemetery.[370]

Lewis Sisson graduated from Belle Fourche High School in 1933. He earned his bachelor's and master's degrees from South Dakota State College. Lewis taught in the high schools at Wall and Custer. He was in a doctorate program at Purdue University when he was called to active duty. He was with an airborne unit before transferring to the Army Air Corps. He was sent to India in 1944 where he taught Indian pilots. Lewis was sent to combat duty in Burma. His P-38 fighter plane was shot down over Burma. He was behind Japanese lines. Several weeks later his plane was located, but the cockpit was empty. He left behind his widow, Majorie, two daughters, Eleanor, age 5, and Dorothy, age 1. Lewis is listed on the Tablets of the Missing at Manila American Cemetery. He was awarded the Purple Heart. One of his brothers was also in the military.[371]

Donald Smith was from Aberdeen. He enlisted in the Army in 1944. Donald was sent to Ft. McClellan, Alabama, for basic training. His brother Robert was stationed in New Orleans. Donald was sent to Europe in November of 1944. He lost his life in the English Channel. His body was not recovered. He was awarded the Purple Heart.[372]

Leonard Smith was nineteen when he enlisted in the Navy. He was sent to Great Lakes, Illinois, for boot training. Leonard was on the USS Neosho during the Battle of the Coral Sea. His ship was sunk during the battle. Leonard's body was not recovered. His brother Milan Kenneth was in the Army Air Corps.[373]

Gerald Stambaugh was born on a farm near Oacoma in Lyman County. He graduated from Chamberlain High School in 1940. Gerald graduated from the Army Air Force Pilot School in Stockton Field in California. He was awarded his wings and was sent to Sioux City, Iowa, for further training on a B-17 bomber. Gerald was assigned to the 8th Air Force and was stationed in England. His plane and another plane collided on a mission over England. Gerald was buried in Iowa National Cemetery in Cacique. His brother Dwain was in the military.[374]

Jacob Stolz, Jr. was born in Tyndall. Jacob and Marie Marzolf were married in 1938. They had two daughters, Betty Marie and Katherine May. Jacob began his military service in October of 1941. He was sent to Hawaii, then later to the Southwest Pacific area, and then to New Guinea. He was part of an infantry unit. His unit was in combat on Leyte Island in the Philippines when Jacob was killed. Jacob was buried in Manila American Cemetery. His brother Edwin was also in the Philippines.[375]

Murl Swayze joined the Army in July of 1944. He was in the 145th Infantry. The unit was sent to the Philippines. Murl died in combat on Luzon in the Philippines in April of 1945. His brother Ervin was in the Navy.[376]

Robert Swigert was born in Oelrichs in Fall River County. He enlisted in the Marines and went to basic training in San Diego. Robert was sent overseas with an infantry unit. He fought at Guadalcanal and lastly on the beach at Tarawa. It was November of 1943. His body was not recovered. There is a gravesite marker for him at Black Hills National Cemetery. His brother Chet was also in the military.[377]

Jay Timmerman was born in Platte and graduated from high school in 1937. He was drafted at the age of 28. After basic training he was sent to North Africa. He died in combat in February of 1943. After the war his remains were returned to the U.S. for burial. He was awarded the Purple Heart. One of his brothers was in the military.[378]

Arthur Ulfers, Jr. was born on a farm near Chancellor and graduated from Chancellor High School in 1941. Arthur enlisted in the Army and was trained to be a mechanic at a base in Texas. His brother Leo was sent to New Orleans. They never saw each other again. Arthur transferred to the Army Air Corps and earned his wings at Turner Field in Georgia. He was stationed at Morris Field in North Carolina. Arthur died in a plane accident near the field. Leo was a pilot in the 8th Air Force stationed in England.[379]

Wendell Vallin was from Huron. He enlisted in April of 1941 and was sent to Camp Claiborne, Louisiana, for basic training. Wendell was assigned to the 34th Division and went overseas in 1942. He fought in the African and Italian Campaigns. Wendell died in combat in Northern Italy on May 23, 1942. He was buried in Sicily-Rome American Cemetery near Nettuno, Italy. His brother Ervin served in New Guinea.[380]

Nice Verhoek was number five in a family of ten children. He grew up in the Toronto area and as a young man worked for local farmers. After basic training in 1941, he was sent to England. Nice was a member of the 24th Cavalry Reconnaissance Squadron. His unit was engaging a German force when he was hit by shrapnel. Nice died two days later on March 6, 1945. He was buried in Henri-Chapelle American Cemetery.[381] His brother Garret also served in the military.

Vincent Villagecentre was born in Corson County. He enlisted in the Army in September of 1941. Vincent was in a tank unit in the 2nd Armored Division. He fought in North Africa, Sicily, and France. His unit was in combat during the Battle of the Bulge. He died in Belgium in January of 1945. His brother Alex served in the Pacific Theater and died in combat during the Korean War.[382]

Norman Vogel was born in rural Parkston. He had eight brothers and sisters. Norman graduated from Tripp High School in 1943. He was drafted by the Marines. After basic training and a furlough home, he was sent to the South Pacific. He was a member of the First Marine Division. During the fighting on Okinawa he carried wounded Soldiers back to a medic station. He died in combat on the island. His body was returned and buried in Grace Hill Cemetery, Tripp. His brother Herbert was in the service.[383]

Roy Waddell was born in Henry in Codington County. He had nine brothers and sisters. Roy volunteered for military duty. He was on a ship bound for Japan when it was torpedoed by the Japanese. Roy rescued several Soldiers from the cold water but later came down with pneumonia. Because of the pneumonia and other complications, Roy died. He was buried in Alaska and years later was reinterred at Fort Snelling. His brother Robert served in the military.[384]

Charles Walker was born in 1918 in Chamberlain. He joined the Army in July of 1942 and became a member of the 60th Infantry. Charles was sent to Africa where his unit fought in the Tunisian Campaign. His unit was part of the invasion force that landed in Sicily. They were assigned as part of the invasion force landing in France. Charles was wounded in France and died on June 15, 1944. His brother James was in the Naval Reserves.[385]

Kenneth Wallenstein was from De Smet. He was drafted by the Army. Kenneth died on Christmas Eve in 1944. He was a passenger in an army transport plane that crashed into a mountain.

Kenneth was buried in Bryant, South Dakota. His brother Harold was also in the military.[386]

Charles Weber was born in Bridgewater and graduated from high school in 1935. He enlisted in the Army. After basic training he joined an armored regiment. He was sent to Indiantown Gap, Pennsylvania. Charles was on a training maneuver when an explosion occurred. A piece of shrapnel struck him in the chest, and he died instantly. Charles was buried in St. Stephen's Catholic Cemetery. His brother Joseph served in the Army.[387]

Sylvester Weyh was born in Waubay. He was drafted in May of 1944 and sent overseas in November of 1944. He was in the 19th Infantry that was stationed in Germany. Sylvester died in combat in Germany in February of 1945. He was awarded the Purple Heart. His body was returned to Waubay for burial. His brother Robert was also stationed in Germany.[388]

Wesley Wilcox was born in Rapid City. Wesley and his twin brother, Ashley, joined the military together. They were together through basic training and on a furlough home. They both went overseas to Okinawa. Wesley died there on May 17, 1945. His remains were returned to the U.S. and buried at Black Hills National Cemetery.[389]

Thomas Winterberg was from Hot Springs. He enlisted in the Army in May of 1942. Because of an old foot injury he was an instructor at Camp Walters in Texas for over a year. He was sent overseas and was in combat in Belgium. He was taken prisoner and sent to a prison camp in East Germany. Thomas had been wounded and came down with yellow jaundice. Thomas and other prisoners were on a forced march when he died. His body was returned and buried in Evergreen Cemetery in Hot Springs. His brother Jim was in the Army.[390]

John Fanset was born in Watertown and graduated from high school in 1943. He joined the military in 1943. John was trained at Ft. Benning, Georgia, and sent overseas with the 376th Infantry Regiment of the 94th Division. John was under the command of General Patton. John died in combat in Germany on January 15, 1945. He is buried in Luxembourg American Cemetery. His brother served in the Army.[391]

Three Brothers Went to War and Two Returned

Albertus Altfillisch was born in Faith and graduated from high school in Rapid City. He was serving in the Pacific when he perished. Albertus was a crew member on a Grumman Avenger. The Avenger was a torpedo bomber that flew off an aircraft carrier. His plane was attacking enemy shipping near the port of Rabaul on the island of New Britain. The plane was shot down, and his body was not recovered. There are markers at a cemetery in Hawaii and at Black Hills National Cemetery in his honor. Two of his brothers, Luke and Michael, were also in the military.[392]

Sherman Ames entered military duty in March of 1941. Sherman and June Lange were married in October of 1943. He trained at several locations before he was sent to England. Sherman was a tank commander in an armored unit. He was on a reconnaissance mission when he was wounded. He died from his wounds on August 2, 1944. His brother Robert was a tail gunner in the Army Air Corps, and his brother Dean was in the Navy.[393]

Harley Beck was born in Madison in 1921. He entered military service in 1941 and was a member of the 109th Engineers. Harley served in Ireland, North Africa, and Italy. He was on the Anzio beachhead putting down communication cable for his unit when he was killed on March 6, 1944. Harley was buried in a private grave in Italy. His brothers Leslie and Lloyd were in the service.[394]

Charles Blount joined the Army in June of 1941. In April of 1942 Charles and Virginia Foster were married. He was sent overseas as part of the 33rd Armored Regiment. Charles was fighting in France when he was killed in the line of duty. It was July of 1944. He was buried at Normandy American Cemetery. Charles was awarded the Purple Heart. His brother Lawrence was in the Army, and his brother Delmar was in the Navy.[395]

John Burke was born in Roswell in Miner County. He grew up in Sioux Falls and graduated from high school in 1939. John worked at the *Argus Leader* until he entered the Army in 1943. He went overseas in 1944. John was scouting targets for the artillery when he was killed. His brother Robert was stationed in Florida, and his brother Eugene was stationed in California.[396]

James Hackett was born in Rapid City. He attended the University of Colorado for a short period of time. James and Clarabeth Gentler were married in April of 1943. Their three children were Richard and twins, James and Judith. James was sent overseas with the 513th Parachute Infantry Regiment in January of 1945. He was in combat in Germany where he was wounded and died. His brothers Edward and William were in the Army Air Corps.[397]

Russell Hackett was from Bruce in Brookings County. He was a Marine and fought in the Battle of Guam. Russell was wounded and died on a hospital ship. He was buried at sea. Russell is listed on the Tablets of the Missing in the Honolulu Memorial. He was awarded the Purple Heart. His brothers Robert and Murro were also in the military.[398]

Francis Hein was born in 1922 in Lake County. Prior to entering the military, he worked for his father in De Smet. His induction was held at Ft. Snelling in 1944. Francis was a member of an infantry division in Germany. The citation from the office of

President Harry Truman stated that Francis had died on February 23, 1945. His brothers Lloyd and Oscar were serving in Europe.[399]

Maxwell Huffman and June Ballmes were married in December of 1940. They had two children, Kay and Gary. Maxwell was commissioned a lieutenant at Ft. Knox, Kentucky, and sent overseas in November of 1944. Maxwell was the commander of Able Company of the 761st Tank Battalion. In a battle they destroyed ten pill-boxes, twenty machine gun positions, one self-propelled gun, and killed ten Germans. Maxwell was wounded by a sniper and died five days later on March 25, 1945. They were in France. Maxwell was buried in Lorraine American Cemetery, St. Avold, France. Two of his brothers were also in the military.[400]

Richard Ivers was born in Ideal in Tripp County. He was sent to Germany in February of 1945. He died in combat. Richard was buried in Lorraine American Cemetery, St. Avold, France. His brothers Jack and A.G. were in the service.[401]

Joseph Jandel was born in Faulk County in 1916. He had four brothers and five sisters. He worked on local farms and at a CCC camp before enlisting in the Army in 1940. He trained in Washington state and California. In August of 1942 he married Rita Fehlman. They had one daughter, Jolene. Joseph never got to see her. He was sent to Africa and then to Sicily. The Allies had made a major landing on the beaches of Salerno, Italy. After securing the beachhead from the Germans, the Germans still held the hills around the beachhead. Joseph's commander needed a volunteer to lead forty men to attack a hill position. Joseph volunteered and was killed in the attack on October 16, 1943. In 1949 his remains were returned and buried in St. Mary's Cemetery in Zell. His brothers Edward and Clem also served in the military.[402]

Wesley Johnson was born in Sisseton. He had four brothers and six sisters. Wesley was drafted in 1941. He was trained at several locations on the West Coast. Wesley shipped out of Camp Roberts in California to the Pacific. He was in the 184th Infantry Regiment. Wesley and his brother Arnold spent some time together in Hawaii. He fought in New Guinea, Attu in the Aleutian Islands, the Marshall Islands, and Leyte. Wesley was fighting in Leyte when he was wounded but returned to duty. He was sent to Okinawa and was at a machine position when a Japanese soldier threw a hand grenade into Wesley's foxhole. He was wounded and received aid from a medic but died the next day en route to a hospital. His remains were returned and buried in Goodwill Cemetery in Sisseton. He was awarded the Purple Heart. His brothers Arnold and Glen served in WW II. His brothers Curtis and Ronald served in the Korean War, along with his sister Arlene.[403]

Richard Kausch was born in Watertown. He enlisted in 1942 and was sent to Sioux Falls for radio training. His next stop was gunnery training at the air base in Kingman, Arizona. After several other training stops he was sent overseas in October of 1943. Richard was the radio operator and bombardier on a B-17 bomber. His plane was shot down over Holland. He was buried in Netherlands American Cemetery near Margarten, Netherlands. He was awarded the Purple Heart. His brother William was stationed in Italy, and his brother Ernest was stationed in St. Louis.[404]

John Kerper was born in Sturgis. He entered the military in January of 1942. John was training in San Diego when he met Sue McCormick, who was in the WAVES. They were married on April 25, 1943. John was sent overseas in January of 1944. He died instantly on March 7, 1945, when he was hit by a mortar shell. He was on Iwo Jima. His final resting place is at Punch Bowl National Cemetery in Honolulu. John's two brothers James and Richard were in the service at the same time as John.[405]

Philbert Kjelden graduated from White High School in 1944. He joined the military the same year. His last training was at Camp Blanding in Florida. Philbert died on Christmas day in 1944 when the plane he was on crashed near Harrisburg, Pennsylvania. Another Brookings county Soldier also died in the crash. They were on their way home for Christmas. Philbert was buried in Singsaas Cemetery in Hendricks, Minnesota. His brothers Clifford and Orville served in the military.[406]

Harold Kruck was born in Sioux Falls in 1918. He was inducted into the military in 1941. Harold was trained to be a paratrooper. He was sent overseas in November of 1944. Harold died in action on January 7, 1945. His brothers Ralph and Donald were stationed in the South Pacific. Harold and Gertrude Woodall had been married in 1944.[407]

George Larson was born in Bryant in Hamlin County. His basic training was at Camp Hood in Texas. He shipped out of San Francisco to Hawaii. George was in the infantry, and his unit was in combat on Okinawa. As they were attacking a machine gun position, George was struck and killed. His body was returned and buried at St. Mary's Cemetery. He was awarded the Purple Heart. His brothers Bernard and Stanley were also in the military.[408]

Milo Mathieson was born in Ramona in Lake County. He had four sisters and nine brothers. Milo and Anna Rose Casanova were married in 1942. They had a daughter, Marlene Marie. Milo joined the Army in February of 1942 and was in combat in France. He was wounded on July 11th and died on the 19th. His final resting place is in Graceland Cemetery in Madison. His brothers Clarence and Harold were in the military.[409]

Robert McLaughlin was from Wessington Springs in Jerauld County. He graduated from high school in 1938 and married Edna Speck the same year. They had two children, Lyle and Shirley.

Robert was drafted in 1944. He was in combat in Germany and was wounded. He was moved to an Army hospital in France. He died from blood clots in his lungs and legs. Robert was buried in a U.S. Military Cemetery in France. Two of his brothers served in the military.[410]

Marshall McNickle was born in 1918 in Doland. His father was a victim of the flu epidemic shortly after Marshall's birth. He entered military service in 1942 and was assigned to a bomber group. He was sent overseas in 1943 and served in the India-Burma Theatre. Marshall's plane crashed in a flight over India in 1944. He is buried in National Cemetery of Pacific in Honolulu. Marshall's twin brothers Marvin and Melvin served in the military.[411]

Liquor Miles was born in 1898 in Yankton. He was drafted in 1942 at the age of 44. He was trained to be a mechanic and was stationed in Italy. Liquor was with other troops on a night mission to repair damaged equipment. The truck was driving under blackout conditions. It went over a cliff, and Liquor died the next day from his injuries. He was buried in Italy, and four years later his remains were reinterred at Fort Snelling. Two of his brothers served in the military. He left behind his former wife and a daughter.[412]

Leonard Neugebauer was born in 1918 in Douglas County. He had four brothers and three sisters. Leonard had farmed and worked in a CCC camp prior to entering the military. He was sent overseas in August of 1942 and was stationed in Sicily. He was attached to the 36th Field Artillery. Leonard died in combat on August 3, 1943. Leonard was buried in the family plot at the Lutheran Church cemetery in rural Dimock. His brothers Ralph and Norbert also served in the military.[413]

Leland Nielson was born in Yankton County. He volunteered in June of 1944 and after basic training was assigned to the 24th Infantry as a rifleman. His first overseas duty was on Leyte

Island. Leland was on the island of Mindanao when he was struck by a sniper's bullet and died the next day. His body was returned and buried at Bethlehem Cemetery, Irene, South Dakota. His brothers Orlyn and James were in the service.[414]

Fred Otto was born on the family farm near Menno in 1918. He was drafted in 1941. His first combat was on Attu in the Aleutian Islands. His unit was sent to Kwajalein Island in the Pacific. Fred was killed by a Japanese sniper. His final resting place is the Menno cemetery. His brothers Helmuth and Felix were in the military.[415]

Neil Peters was born in Madison in 1921. After graduating from Yankton College he joined the Army Air Corps. He was sent to Bombardier School in Deming, New Mexico. Neil was on a training mission when two planes collided. He was one of five cadets who died in the collision. His body was returned to Viborg where the funeral was held. His brothers Robert and Paul were in the Army.[416]

John Raderschadt was born in Watertown. He had three brothers and five sisters. John and Shirley Waits were married in February of 1941. They had one son, John. John joined the National Guard in 1940. He was sent to Camp Claiborne in 1941. John was assigned to the 34th Signal Company. He served in North Ireland and North Africa from February of 1942 to October of 1943. John returned to the U.S. and was a patient at McCloskey General Hospital in Temple, Texas. He died on January 29, 1944. His brother James was with the Army in Italy, and his brother William was in the Army stationed in South Carolina.[417]

Robert Raker and his twin brother Herbert were from Scotland. Robert was sent overseas in May of 1944. The family did not receive an official report detailing how Robert had died. They only knew that he died in France. His brother Herbert was in the Army Air Corps, and his brother Donald was in the Army.[418]

James Shoop was born in St. Lawrence in Hand County. He enlisted in the Army Air Corps. James had a variety of jobs before he entered training as an Aviation Cadet. He was sent overseas as part of the 9th Air Force. James was a crew member on a B-26 bomber. His plane was over France when it was hit by antiaircraft fire. All bombs on board exploded. James was buried in France as an "unknown soldier." The U.S. Graves Registration identified James by his estimated height and the size of the shoe found in the grave. His final resting place is in Normandy American Cemetery overlooking Omaha Beach. He was awarded the Purple Heart. His brothers Frank and Herbert were also in the military.[419]

Stanley Thomas was born in rural Ziebach County near Dupree. He had eight siblings. Stanley entered the military in June of 1944 after graduating from high school. He went to Ft. Knox, Kentucky, for basic training. Stanley was home on furlough and was best man at his sister Jean's wedding. He fought in Italy, then was sent to France. Stanley was with the 397th Infantry Regiment. They were fighting in Germany when Stanley was killed on April 4, 1945. The war ended in May. He was buried in Lorraine American Cemetery near St. Avold, France. Two of his brothers were in the Navy.[420]

Four Brothers Went to War and Three Returned

Gerhard Biberdorf was from Henry in Codington County. He joined the CCC and worked in the Black Hills. Gerhard was drafted into the Army in 1941. After basic training he was assigned to the 30th Infantry Regiment of the 3rd Division. Gerhard fought in North Africa and Sicily. He died in the attack on Anzio beachhead. It was June of 1944. He was returned in 1948 and buried in Black Hills National Cemetery. Gerhard's brother Raymond was in the Army Air Corps serving in Italy. They were together for three days before Gerhard was killed. Gerhard's brother Carl was in the Navy during WW II and the Korean War, John was in the Navy in WW II and the Korean War, Bernard was in the Army during the Korean War.[421]

Thomas Bradbury was born in Howard. The birth took place in his grandmother's home. He was one of twelve children. Thomas enlisted in the Navy at age 16 because his three brothers—Stewart, Everett, and Theophilus—were already in the service. His basic training was at Camp Farragut, Idaho. He was assigned to the aircraft carrier USS Liscome Bay and went overseas. It was on patrol in the South Pacific when it was torpedoed by a Japanese submarine. He was buried at sea. Thomas is listed on the Tablets of the Missing at the Honolulu Memorial. There is a marker for him in Black Hills National Cemetery. He was awarded the Purple Heart.[422]

Eugene Burdock graduated from Lemmon High School. He entered the Army in June of 1941. Eugene first served in the Pacific Theatre. He went on to Officers Candidate School and became a second lieutenant. Later he was promoted to first lieutenant. He was sent to Europe in October of 1944. Eugene was with the 311th Infantry Regiment. The unit was fighting in Scheuren, Germany, when he was killed. Eugene was buried at Netherlands American Cemetery in Margraten, Netherlands. He was awarded the Purple Heart. His brother Robert was in the Army, Jack was in the Merchant Marine, and James was in the Navy. Eugene left behind his widow, Viola.[423]

Herbert Chase was from Miner County. After basic training he was assigned to the military police force at a prisoner of war camp at Camp Polk, Louisiana. Herbert was on duty when he died from a gunshot wound. His body was returned to Fedora for burial. Three of his brothers were serving overseas.[424]

Clifford Garry was from Bridgewater and graduated from high school in 1939. He enlisted in the Navy. Clifford served on several ships, and his last assignment was on the USS LST 342. The ship was on patrol in the Solomon Sea when it was torpedoed, and Clifford perished in the explosion. His brother Edmund was in the Army Air Corps, Ralph was in the Army serving in Europe, and Vernon was in the Navy.[425]

Kenneth Hardy graduated from Deadwood High School in 1938. He worked at Homestake Mine prior to entering the military in 1942. Kenneth joined the Army Air Corps and became a pilot of a B-25 bomber. He was assigned to a base in India. His missions required his plane to fly over the Himalayas to bomb Japanese installations. Kenneth's last mission was on February 26, 1944, when his plane was shot down. There were no survivors, and the plane was never found. Kenneth is listed on the Tablets of the Missing at Manila American Cemetery. He was awarded the Distinguished Flying Cross and the Purple Heart. His three brothers were also in the service.[426]

Robert Jenks was from Huron. He joined the Marine Corps Reserve in 1942. Robert took basic training in San Diego and was sent overseas in April of 1943. He was assigned to a mortar unit in the Second Marine Division. The battle for control of Tarawa started on November 20, 1943. The Marines faced a determined Japanese force. Coral reefs prevented the landing boats from reaching the beach, and they became easy targets for the Japanese. In spite of the obstacles and opposition, the landing was a success. On the third day of battle Robert died in combat. It was his first battle. Tarawa was a bloody battle. Over three days 6,000 Soldiers died in an area the size of the Pentagon and its parking lots. Robert was awarded the Purple Heart and the Asiatic-Pacific Campaign. The Second Marine

Division received the Presidential Unit Citation. Brothers Joseph and James were in the Marines, and Arthur was in the Army.[427]

Thomas Kramer was born in Moody County. He had nine siblings. They all grew up on the family farm. Thomas was working at the Moore Shipyard in California when he enlisted in the Marine Corps. He trained at Camp Elliott in California and was sent to the Pacific in 1944. His first combat was on Peleliu. In his book *Brotherhood of Heroes,* Bill Sloan describes the fighting on Peleliu as the bloodiest battle of WW II. The 1st, 5th, and 7th Marine Divisions invaded the island on September 15, 1944. From September 15th to October 15th the 1st division alone suffered 6,500 casualties. The total casualties for the battle were 2,336 killed and 8,450 wounded. After Peleliu he was sent to Okinawa in 1945 where he died on May 4th. His brothers Edward, Louis, and George were also in the service.[428]

Allen Merrill of Potter County entered the service in 1941 and served in the Army. He had four brothers and three sisters. The government reported that he died in a German prison camp in January of 1945. His brother Charles was in the Marines, Robert was wounded in the Pacific, and Donald also served in the military.[429]

Francis Mullenix was born in Sioux Falls. He enlisted in the Army in 1941. Francis went to Europe and served in the infantry. He was fighting in Western Germany when he died in combat. All three of his brothers served in the military.[430]

Niels Nielsen was born in Yankton. He attended Yankton College one year. Niels joined the service as an Aviation cadet and earned his wings. He was stationed in England and was the pilot of a B-24 Flying Fortress. His plane was shot down over Germany on October 3, 1944. Niels was buried at Netherlands American Cemetery. He was awarded the Purple Heart. His brothers Roy and

Howard were in the Army Air Corps, and Willard was in the Navy.[431]

Carl Peterson was born in 1911 near Reliance in Lyman County. He joined a family of four sisters and six brothers. Carl graduated from high school in 1929. He worked for farmers in the area before enlisting in 1942. After basic training he was sent to the Pacific in 1943. Carl was on a troop ship in the Solomon Islands when it was torpedoed. The north shore of Guadalcanal was searched, but his body was not found. His brothers Verse, Lyle, and Walter were in the service at the time of his death.[432]

Alan Plasma was born on the family farm near Springfield in Bon Homme County. He enlisted in the Navy and was sent overseas in October of 1944. Allen was a crew member on the USS New Mexico that was engaged in the Battle of Okinawa. A Japanese kamikaze plane crashed into the ship on May 12, 1945. Alan and over 170 crew members were killed. His remains were returned and buried in the Springfield cemetery. He was awarded the Purple Heart. Three of his brothers served in WW II: Andrew was in the Philippines, John was in Italy, and David was in Germany.[433]

Willard Rediger was born in Hand County. He had twelve siblings. Willard joined the Army in 1944. He was assigned to an infantry unit and went overseas in January of 1945. His unit was engaged in combat on Okinawa. They were fighting on Shuri Hill when he was killed by machine gun fire. His final resting place is in Punch Bowl National Cemetery in Honolulu. He was awarded the Purple Heart. His brothers Walter, Cliff, and Clyde also served in WW II.[434]

Thomas Rundle grew up in Lead with three brothers and two sisters. He joined the military in March of 1943. After training at Fort Benning, Georgia, he was sent to Germany. He was a member of the 66th Infantry, 12th Armored Division under General George

Patton. Thomas and his unit were leading an attack into Germany. They got caught in a trap; most of the one hundred fifty men did not survive. Thomas was among those who perished. His final resting place is Epinal American Cemetery, Epinal, France. He left behind his widow, Wilma, and baby boy he never saw. All three of his brothers served in the military.[435]

Ralph Sedelmeier had seven siblings. He graduated from Centerville High School in 1927. Ralph entered military service in December of 1942. He shipped out in March of 1944. His first stop was in Ireland, and later he was sent to England. His unit took part in the invasion of Normandy. He was with an infantry unit and died in France. The official date of his death was July 26, 1944. The family did not receive any specific details about his death. Ralph was buried in Normandy American Cemetery. Three of his brothers served in the military.[436]

Joe Stangle was born in Rapid City and went to Rapid City Central High School. He joined the Navy in April of 1944. Joe was a fireman on the USS Drexler. The ship was on patrol near Okinawa. Two kamikaze planes hit the ship causing it to sink. Joe was among the 159 sailors who died in the attack. He is listed on the Tablets of the Missing at Honolulu Memorial. There is also a marker for him in Black Hills National Cemetery. He was awarded the Purple Heart. He left behind his widow, Mary, and their three children, Michael, Jo Ellen, and Mary Alice. Three of his brothers were also in the military.[437]

Kenneth Thompson was born in 1908 and grew up in Dell Rapids. He studied theology at a school in Pennsylvania and became a Baptist minister. Kenneth and Ruth Boyum were married in 1933. Five daughters were born to this union. Kenneth joined the Army and provided spiritual help to troops on the front lines. He came down with malaria and typhus causing his death in March of 1943.

Kenneth was serving on an island off the coast of Australia. All three of his brothers served in the military.[438]

Ferdinand Willuweit was born in Quinn in Pennington County. He had seven brothers and one sister. Ferdinand grew up on the family ranch. He was drafted in 1943. Ferdinand was in France on November 30, 1944, when he died in combat. His brothers Alvin, Chris, and William were also in the service.[439]

Nick Zerr was born in Aberdeen. He was a Navy Seabee serving on New Guinea in the South Pacific. Nick was reported as missing in action on November 14, 1945. It was assumed that he was on his way home and that the plane went down between New Guinea and the Philippines. No traces of the plane were found. On March 14, 1946, Mrs. Lois Zerr received the following information. A fingerprint check revealed that her husband, Nick Zerr, had been buried in the military cemetery on Leyte Island in the Philippines. His remains were returned and buried locally. Nick's brothers Pius, Joe, and Tuffy also served in the military.[440]

Five Brothers Went to War and Four Returned

Levi LeBeau was born in 1920 at the Cheyenne Agency in South Dakota. Prior to the military he owned and managed his own cattle ranch. Levi joined the service in October of 1942 and was sent overseas in June of 1944. Levi was assigned to the 381st Regiment stationed in the Pacific. His first combat was on Leyte Island. Levi's unit was part of the invasion force that landed on Okinawa. The 96th Division, of which his regiment was a part, suffered over 10,000 casualties in the fighting on Okinawa. A Presidential Unit Citation was awarded to the division. Levi was wounded on Okinawa and then transferred to Guam for treatment where he died on May 29, 1945. His remains were returned and buried on the Cheyenne River Reservation. He was awarded the Purple Heart. Four of his brothers served in the military.[441]

Elmer Halverson was born in 1917 on the family farm north of McIntosh. He was one of eleven children. Their mother died in 1931, and they had to take care of themselves. Elmer enlisted in the Navy in 1940 and became a radio operator. He was serving on the USS Edsall in 1942 when it was attacked by a Japanese ship. The ship and crew were never found. His brothers Bennie, Alfred, Roscoe, and Donald also served in the military. There is a memorial plaque dedicated to Elmer in the McIntosh cemetery.[442]

Russell Moore was born in Brookings and graduated from high school in Rapid City. He joined the Army Air Corps in 1943. After completing his training, he received his wings and a commission. In Europe he was the bombardier on a B-24. His plane flew aerial operational missions. Russell died in service to his country in June of 1944. He was awarded the Air Medal. His brothers Francis, Marvin, Merwyne, and Kenneth were also in the service.[443]

Orville Peterson was born in Astoria in Deuel County. He had seven siblings. Orville was a member of the 91st Infantry Division. He died in combat in Europe. His body was returned and buried in the Astoria cemetery. His brothers Ernest, Raymond, LeRoy, and Richard all served in WW II.[444]

Marvin Scheibe was born in Columbia in Brown County. He had six brothers and four sisters. Marvin graduated from Westport High School and attended Northern State College prior to enlisting in the Navy. He was a crew member on the YO-159 when it was sunk near Pentecost Island in the New Hebrides. He left a widow and son. Four of his brothers served in the military.[445]

Roy Tuttle was born in 1912. He was one of thirteen children. Roy graduated from high school in 1929. He worked at a variety of jobs before enlisting in the Army. He was discharged from the Army but was called back into service in 1941. His training took place in Missouri and Georgia. Roy was assigned to the 82nd Airborne Division. He made combat jumps in North Africa, Sicily, and the Rhineland. Roy's unit fought in the Holland Campaign known as "Operation Market Garden." He died in combat on October 4, 1944. His body was returned and buried in the Geddes cemetery. He was awarded the Silver Star and Purple Heart. His brothers Lyle, Leslie, Robert, and John Jr. served in the military.[446]

Charles Vice was born in Kadoka. He had five siblings. Their parents died when they were young. Charles enlisted in the Army Air Corps in February of 1944. Later he was transferred to the 104th Infantry Regiment, 26th Infantry Division. His unit was fighting in northern France when he died in combat. He is buried in Lorraine American Cemetery, St. Avold, France. Charles was awarded the Purple Heart. He left behind his widow, Joyce, and a son. Four of his brothers served in the military.[447]

Six Brothers Went to War and Five Returned

Herbert Brandt was born in Parker. He enlisted in the Marine Corps in 1943 and completed boot camp in San Diego. He became a member of the 4th Marine Infantry Division. In February of 1944 he was wounded while fighting on Namur Island. He recovered and rejoined his unit. The invasion of Saipan, located in the Marianas Islands, began on June 14, 1944. Herbert died in combat on Saipan on July 4, 1944. He had five brothers who also served in the Marine Corps.[448]

Robert Hahn was born in 1921. He lived in Sioux Falls several years prior to entering military service. Robert joined the Iowa National Guard and was in the infantry. He died in combat in

Italy in September of 1943. Five of his brothers were serving at the time of his death.[449]

Ralph Obermire was born in Armour in Douglas County. He joined the Army and was sent overseas in 1943. Ralph was a member of a tank battalion and died in combat in Italy. His brothers Jacob, Mathias, Leonard, Harvey, and Clarence served in the military.[450]

Wilbert Wittenhagen was born in Ethan in Davison County. He had twelve siblings. Of the nine boys, six served in the military. Wilbert joined the service in June of 1943. After basic training at Camp Roberts in California, he was sent to the Pacific in December of 1943. He fought in New Zealand and then went to Luzon. He died in combat on February 5, 1945. His remains were returned and buried in American Legion Cemetery in Mitchell.[451]

Seven Brothers Went to War and Six Returned

Richard Bertram and six of his brothers served in the military. Only one brother did not serve. He also had six sisters. Richard entered the service in June of 1944 and did his basic training at Fort Leonard Wood in Missouri. On Okinawa he was with the 382nd Infantry Regiment of the 96th Infantry Division. Richard was wounded on April 10th and sent to a hospital ship where he died. He was buried at sea. Richard is listed on the Tablets of the Missing at Manila American Cemetery.[452]

Albert Vielhauer was born near Hosmer in Edmunds County. He had seven brothers. In 1940 he enlisted in the Army. Six of his older brothers were already in the service. In 1945 American forces were fighting to take the island of Luzon in the Philippines. Albert died taking the island on January 20, 1945.[453]

Eight Brothers Went to War and Seven Returned

Paul Kirchmeier was born in 1917. He had seven brothers and four sisters. Paul's training took him to several locations. He was a member of the 3rd Infantry Division. He died in combat in Germany on April 18, 1945. The war ended the next month. He left behind his widow, Lillian, and a two- year-old daughter, Stephanie. His seven brothers were also in the service.[454]

A Family Who Sent Multiple Members to War

Donald Adams was born in Plankinton. He enlisted in the CCC and worked in the Black Hills and Marshall, Missouri. Donald joined the Army in 1942 and went to Fort Benning, Georgia, for basic training. After further training to be a paratrooper, he was assigned to the 82nd Airborne Division. His unit participated in the invasion of Italy and Normandy on D-Day. His last jump took place in September of 1944. His unit played a major role in "Operation Market Garden" in Holland. Donald's final resting place is in Fort Snelling. All of his brothers served in the military.[455]

A Mother's Story

Donald Jerred was born in Gregory. He attended two years of high school in Custer. Donald enlisted in the Army Air Corps in 1943. He trained in California and Florida. He earned his wings and was sent overseas in 1943. Donald was a crew member on a B-24 bomber and was on his 19th mission near Berlin when the plane was shot down by enemy fighters. He died in the crash. Carl Hartquist was the pilot. He survived and wrote Mrs. Jerred a complimentary letter about Donald. Mrs. Jerred wanted to know where Donald had been buried. She received a letter stating that Donald and two others had been buried near a local church. A second letter informed her that he had been exhumed and buried in an American cemetery in Belgium. Mrs. Jerred requested that Donald's remains be returned. His final resting place is the family plot in Custer cemetery. He was awarded the Air Medal, oak-leaf clusters, and the Purple Heart. Mrs. Jerred's three sons and a son-in-law served in the military.[456]

Families Who Lost Multiple Members in WW II

Donald and John were the sons of Clement and Ora Bell. Donald was in the Army Air Corps and served in Europe as a glider plane pilot. He landed his glider in Germany and was killed by enemy gun fire. He is buried in Netherlands American Cemetery in Margraten, Holland. John was in the Navy and stationed on the USS Houston. It was sunk by the Japanese during the Battle of the Java Sea in February of 1942. His body was not recovered. John is listed on the Tablets of the Missing at Manila American Cemetery.[457]

Martin and Sigurd were the sons of Elisabeth Bjertness. Martin was in the Army and died in combat on Okinawa in May of 1945. Sigurd joined the Navy. He was on a landing craft in the Gulf of Leyte when it was struck by a kamikaze plane. His body was not recovered.[458]

Ernest and Harold were the sons of Thomas and Lillian Delany. The brothers had thirteen siblings. Ernest was in the Army and died in combat in Germany. Harold died in combat in France. They are buried beside each other in Normandy American Cemetery. Their brother Wilbur was also in the Army, and James was in the Navy.[459]

Jacob and John were the sons of Joseph and Mary DeRungs. Jacob was with a tank unit. He died during the Battle of the Bulge, December 30, 1944. John died in the fighting on Okinawa. Their brother Louis was stationed in Germany, Florin was in France, and Leo was in Italy. Two of their sisters were nurses.[460]

Erle and Philip were the sons of Peter and Clara Gillenberg. Erle was a crew member on the aircraft carrier USS Franklin. It was supporting the invasion of Okinawa when kamikaze planes struck. The explosions caused the ship to sink. Erle's body was not found. He is listed on the Tablets of the Missing at Honolulu American Cemetery. Philip was commanding an antiaircraft gun crew in Belgium when he was wounded. He died in a hospital in Holland. Their names are listed on an obelisk in front of the Huron Public Library. The brothers were from Wolsey.[461]

Alan and Joseph were the sons of James and Rhoda Hayden. There were twelve children in the family. Alan was in the Army Air Corps. His plane crashed near Brooklet Field, Alabama. His body was returned to De Smet for burial. Joseph was also in the Army Air Corps. His unit was stationed on New Guinea. They bombed Japanese installations in the South Pacific. He perished in a midair collision with another bomber. His body was returned to DeSmet for burial. Alan and Joseph were both buried in the family plot.[462]

Earl and Martin were the sons of Ernest and Elizabeth Hofemann. The brothers were in the Army. Earl died in combat in France. His remains were returned to Tulare for burial. Martin's unit was engaged in intensive fighting in Italy when he was killed. His remains were returned and buried in Tulare.[463]

Melvin and Oscar were the sons of H.S. and Mary Ireland. Melvin was in the Army Air Corps. He was on his final training flight when his plane crashed near Ellsworth, Kansas. His body was returned to Martin for burial. Oscar was in the Army. He died in combat in Germany. After the war his remains were returned and buried in Martin Community Cemetery. He left behind his widow, Iris, and a daughter.[464]

Leonard and Walter were the sons of Charles and Amy Lee. Leonard and Walter were in the Army Air Corps. Leonard died in a training accident at Myrtle Beach, South Carolina, in November of 1941. Walter was returning from a mission when his plane crashed on landing in New Guinea and he died in the crash. Walter is buried in Manila American Cemetery. Two other brothers served in the military and returned home.[465]

Lloyd and Walter were the sons of Lawrence and Floribel Lewis. Lloyd was in the Navy serving in Manila. He became a POW and died of beriberi. He is buried in Manila American Cemetery. Walter was in the Army. He died in combat in Germany. Walter is buried in Henri-Chapelle American Cemetery in Belgium.[466]

Nelson and Thomas were the sons of Thomas and Lucy Linton. Nelson was in the Army and part of an antiaircraft battery. He was stationed in Italy when he died in combat. Nelson is buried in Sicily-Rome American Cemetery in Nettuno, Italy. Thomas was a crew member on the aircraft carrier USS Saratoga It was on patrol in the waters off Iwo Jima. In February of 1945 several Japanese planes made repeated attacks on the ship. Over 120 crew members died in the attacks. Thomas was lost at sea. He is listed on the Tablets of the Missing at Honolulu Memorial. There is a marker for him at Black Hills National Cemetery.[467]

James and Herbert Lyman were born in Lemmon. They grew up on a ranch in Corson County. James enlisted in the Army. He died in combat in Italy. Herbert was in the Army Air Corps. He died in France. They are buried beside each other in Brittany American Cemetery at St. James, France.[468]

Stanley and Vernon Martin were the sons of Mr. and Mrs. William Martin. Stanley was in the Army Air Corps. He was the radioman in the 91st Reconnaissance Squadron. He died during the fighting in North Africa. Stanley is buried in Sicily-Rome American

Cemetery in Nettuno, Italy. Vernon was in the Marines when the Philippines fell to the Japanese, and he became a POW. The official report stated that he died of dysentery. He is buried in Manila American Cemetery.[469]

Gene and Mark Minier were the sons of Earl and Marcia. Gene joined the South Dakota National Guard and in 1941 was sent to Camp Claiborne, Louisiana. He served in Tunisia and then Italy. Gene's unit was clearing mine fields for troop movement. A mine exploded taking his life. They were close to Anzio beach in Italy. Mark was in the Army Air Corps. He was sent overseas to Japan. His plane crashed in the ocean, and his body was never recovered.[470]

Jack and James were the sons of Mr. and Mrs. James Pardy. Jack was in the Merchant Marine and made two trips to Europe. He transferred to the Army Air Corps. After basic training he became a waist gunner on a B-29. His plane was returning from a test flight when the landing gear failed and the plane exploded. Jack died in the explosion. James joined the Army. He was overseas when he died in a motorcycle accident. James was buried in England.[471]

George Jr. and Robert were the sons of George and Alice Philip. George graduated from the Naval Academy in 1935. He served on two ships before being promoted to commander of the USS Twiggs. George experienced several battles in the Pacific. The USS Twiggs was on patrol near Okinawa when it was struck by a Japanese kamikaze plane. The ship sank, and George's body was not found. There is a memorial marker for him in Black Hills National Cemetery. He left behind his widow, Margaret, and two children. Robert was a ROTC member while attending college. After graduation he became a second lieutenant in the Army. He transferred to the Marine Corps. He became a Marine pilot and was sent to the Pacific. His plane went down in the ocean. Robert's body was not recovered. There is a memorial marker for him in Black

Hills National Cemetery. He left behind a widow, Alice, and a son.[472]

Carl and Randolph were the sons of John and Cleopatra Pickett. Carl was in the Army. He served in North Africa and Italy. Carl died during the invasion of Italy. Randolph was also in the Army. He was a member of an Antiaircraft Artillery Battalion. Randolph was serving on Goodenough Island in the Solomon Sea when he died in combat. He is buried in Manila American Cemetery.[473]

Emery and Marvin Risch were born into a family of ten. The total included two sets of twins. Their parents were Christian and Anna. Emery and Murray were twins. Emery joined the Army in 1937 and was honorably discharged in 1940. He re-enlisted in the Army Air Corps. Emery trained to be a bombardier-navigator. He was stationed in Italy. Emery's last position was that of tail gunner on a B-17 Flying Fortress. The plane crashed on take-off, and the bombs on board exploded. None of the individual remains could be identified. Emery's remains were buried with the other crew members. The crew was first buried in Italy. In 1949 the remains of the crew were reinterred in Zachary Taylor National Cemetery in Louisville, Kentucky. Marvin volunteered for the Army in August of 1944. He went overseas in January of 1945. Marvin was an infantryman and was attached to the 3rd Infantry Division. He was in combat in France when he died from an exploding artillery shell. Marvin's final resting place is in Fort Snelling.[474]

Lawrence and Royal were the sons of Theodore and Inez Rosheim. Lawrence joined the Marines in 1940 and was sent overseas in 1942. He died in combat in the Marshall Islands. Lawrence is buried in National Memorial Cemetery in Honolulu. Royal was in the Army Air Corps. He died in the Pacific and is also buried in National Memorial Cemetery.[475]

Thayne and Kendell were the sons of Lester and Flora Smith. Thayne enlisted in the Navy after graduating from Clark High School. He volunteered for submarine duty and became a crew member on the USS Shark. The Shark left Pearl Harbor in December of 1940 bound for Manila. The Shark went down in the South Pacific with all of its crew members on board. It was February of 1942. Kendall was drafted into the Army. His unit was fighting on Okinawa where he was wounded. He recovered and returned to his unit. Kendall died in combat on Okinawa on June 19, 1945. He was buried on Okinawa. At his parents' request his remains were returned and buried at Rose Hill Cemetery in March of 1949.[476]

Melton and Karl were the sons of Lee and Leota Wood. There were ten children in the family. Melton joined the Navy in 1943. The official letter stated that he died on a destroyer in April of 1945. His body was returned and buried in Greenwood Cemetery in Brookings. He left behind his widow, Darlene, and two children. Karl volunteered for the Navy after graduating from Brookings High School. He was stationed on the USS White Plains in the Pacific. Karl was both the radio operator and tail gunner on a Grumman Torpedo Fighter Bomber. His plane was attacking a Japanese battleship, and before it could release its bombs, the plane took a direct hit. He died in the explosion, and his body was not recovered. There is a headstone for him in Greenwood Cemetery.[477]

Herman and Edwin Wudel were the sons of Nathaniel and Dora. Herman joined the South Dakota National Guard and trained with the 147th Field Artillery. Overseas he was with the 119th Engineers Battalion. Herman was part of a demolition squad when he was wounded in action and died the next day. He was buried in Epinal American Cemetery in France. He left a widow, Esther, and a daughter. Edwin volunteered for the Army. He was in the infantry and died in combat on July 28, 1943. His unit was in the South Pacific.[478]

Eugene, Ordien, and LeRoy were the sons of Marmien and Albert Herr. Eugene enlisted in the Navy in 1943. He was stationed on a destroyer, the USS Johnson. A large American fleet and a large Japanese fleet fought in the Battle of Leyte Gulf. Hundreds of aircraft took part. The USS Johnson was engaged in battle against a superior Japanese force for three hours. Eugene was in the water for two days before succumbing to exhaustion. He was buried at sea. Ordien joined the military on December 19, 1941. He was in the Naval Air Force. He was stationed in the Pacific where he was wounded. After recovering, he transferred to a torpedo bombing squadron. Ordien died in a plane crash at sea. His body was returned and buried in Bethany Cemetery near Butler, South Dakota. LeRoy graduated from Northern State Teachers College and taught school for one year. In 1942 he enlisted in the Naval Air Force. His plane was on patrol over Catalina Island in the South Pacific when it crashed. He left his widow, Virginia, and a daughter who was born after LeRoy died. He was the third son of Marmien and Albert to die in two-and-one-half years.[479]

Francis, Louis, and Cletus were the sons of Frank and Victoria Meyer. Francis joined the Army Air Corps in May of 1942. He was on a training mission when his plane crashed near New Ajo, Arizona. Louis served with the Royal Canadian Air Force from 1941 to 1942 when he transferred to the Army Air Corps. He was stationed in Tunisia with a fighter squadron. Louis and his unit were returning from a mission when he was shot down by a German fighter. He is listed on the Tablets of the Missing at North African American Cemetery in Carthage, Tunisia. Cletus joined the Army Air Corps. He was stationed at Coolangatta, Queensland, Australia. Cletus was swimming when he drowned.[480]

PHOTOS

U.S. Air Force Brigadier General La Verne Saunders.
Saunders directed the first land-based attack on Japan in 1944.
(South Dakota Hall of Fame)

Above: Sargent Jim Hale. Below: Jim Hale flew many mission over the "Hump". Jim Hale in the sunglasses with one of his flight crews. (Paula Rogers' personal collection)

Captain Donald G. Smith was one of the pilots on the Dolittle Raid. (South Dakota Hall of Fame)

Lieutenant Commander John Waldron and his squadron made the ultimate sacrifice that helped win the Battle of Midway. (South Dakota Hall of Fame)

Captain Cecil Harris was a highly respected Navy pilot. (Wikipedia)

Cecil's plaque on the USS Yorktown. (Wikipedia)

Lieutenant Colonel Hilary Cole. Cole flew many missions over Europe. (Mrs. Vivian Cole's personal collection)

Captain Ola Mildred Rexroat served as a Women Airforce Service Pilot (WASP). (Wikipedia)

The Halverson twins were U.S. Army nurses. (Clear Lake Courier)

Lt. Evangelyn Halverson, Toronto, Killed in Car Crash; Twin Sister Seriously Hurt

EVANGELYN   EVELYN

Marcella LaBeau was an Army nurse who served in Europe. (Native Sun Times Today)

Kenneth Scissions
was known for his
ability to operate
behind enemy
lines.
(South Dakota
Magazine)

Staff Sergeant
Elmer Roth was on
a flight over the
USS Missouri as
the peace treaty
was being signed.
(Bev Hammrich's
personal
collection)

Clarence Wolf Guts, Lakota code talker. (South Dakota Magazine)

Sylvan Vigness and Dale Fields served in the U.S. Navy. Sylvan is pictured on the left and Dale on the right. (Doug Fields personal collection)

Master Sergeant Woodrow Wilson Keeble, Medal of Honor recipient. (Wikipedia)

Captain Arlo Olson, Medal of Honor recipient. Below: Olson's Headstone at Fort Snelling National Cemetery. (Wikipedia)

Dr. Robert Giebink, pictured on the right, served as an Army doctor in Europe. (Alexa Giebink's personal collection)

Sergeant Jack Thurman fought on Iwo Jima. (Jack Thurman's personal collection)

Russell White and Don Willey, Sicily-Rome American Cemetery. (Bree McCarthy's personal collection)

CHAPTER 5

Individual and Family Stories

Curt Eggers was eighteen when he left Renner and joined the Army. After six months of training, he attained the rank of private first class. He was promoted to corporal, then sergeant, and was a staff sergeant when he was sent overseas. His platoon was fighting near Remlingen, Germany, in late April of 1945. They had been assigned to make sure that there were no German Soldiers in the abandoned buildings. One of the buildings was a railroad station. To be on the safe side, Curt threw a hand grenade into the basement. After the explosion, three German Soldiers came out and became POWs. During combat Curt was promoted to platoon sergeant.

Curt was discharged in November of 1945, returned to the U.S., got married, and started to farm near Renner. Curt and his wife, Jean, had five children.

Forty-three years later Curt started to attend Army reunions. In 1994 he received a letter from Franz Fetter of Dallas, Texas. He had been a German Soldier. Franz said that if there was a reunion near Dallas, he would like to know about it and attend. A reunion was held in Dallas in 2001, and Franz attended. Curt and Franz struck up a conversion. Franz said that he had been captured by A Company, 114th Infantry, 44th Division on April 25th near Remlingen, Germany. Franz described how and where he was captured. Curt and Franz determined that Franz was one of the three German Soldiers who had emerged from the basement of the railroad station.

After the war Franz came to the U.S. and settled in Texas. Franz preferred to be called Mike in the U.S. Franz went to work for a dairy. He went on to learn the printing trade and run his own printing shop. Curt and Franz maintained their friendship many years. In 2002 Franz sent Curt a calendar. There was a different picture of them for each month.

In *The Curtis O. Eggers Story,* Curt writes about his time in the military and other events related to that time period.[481]

Kenneth Cuthbert Scissions was born in 1915 on a ranch south of Colome in Tripp County. He could trace his Lakota heritage back to his grandmother, Hannah Mule. Kenneth's family moved to Rapid City where his father was employed at the Warren-Lamb lumber company. Kenneth completed grades one through six at the Rapid City Indian School. At the beginning of seventh grade he transferred to public school.

During his senior year he had a disagreement with his basketball coach and did not return to school. He went to work at Warren-Lamb and put in ten-hour days. His job was shoveling sawdust into railroad cars. The Depression came, and he lost his job. Kenneth joined the CCC and worked near Hill City. At the end of the day trucks transported workers back to their base camp. Kenneth choose to return on foot. He ran over the rugged terrain and was relaxing at camp when the trucks arrived.

Melvin Cory and Kenneth met at the CCC camp. Melvin had a picture of his sister Evelyn. Kenneth looked at the picture and declared that he was going to marry the girl in the picture. His sanity was questioned. Kenneth and Evelyn met in the spring of 1937, and two weeks later they were married. Evelyn's parents learned of the marriage from an article in the Deadwood newspaper. Kenneth and his father built a one-room home in Rapid City for the newlyweds. Kenneth provided for the couple by hunting and fishing in the Black Hills, working at the CCC camp, and playing in a dance band. Dances were held in Hill City.

Kenneth joined the S.D. National Guard in 1936 and after basic training was assigned to the headquarters of the 109th Engineering Regiment in Rapid City. Three years later he re-enlisted. With war on the horizon after Germany invaded Poland in 1939, Kenneth and five other Soldiers from the 109th volunteered for federal service. LeRoy Anderson, Jerry Gorman, and Richard Griffin were from Sturgis; Bill Turner and Andrew Hjelvik were from Lead. Bill died in combat on December 17, 1943.

They were sent overseas and trained with British Commandos. The unit conducted raids in occupied Europe. The plan was that the Americans would rejoin their original unit when the U.S. entered the war. The group of six would use their combat experience to train troops arriving from the U.S. The U.S. Army Rangers were formed in 1942, and Kenneth applied for a transfer, but was turned down; they did not accept married men.

The Allies invaded North Africa in November of 1942. Kenneth's unit hit the beaches at Algiers, Tunisia. The Germans were in control of the airfield at Bizerte; Kenneth's unit was assigned to take the airfield, but was forced to retreat. Kenneth was in a squad that was to protect the Soldiers who were retreating, but his squad was attacked, and they had to fight for their own lives. Automatic rifle fire forced them to take cover and not try to advance. Kenneth suggested that the only way out was to go around the hill and surprise the Germans from behind. Twelve volunteers had to cross an open area to get to a creek bed, and when they got the creek bed, only five were left. They were halfway up the hill when another

Soldier was shot. Those who were left decided to retreat. Jerry Coleman and another Soldier retreated down the hill. Kenneth and Guy Wright of Oklahoma were in position to fire on the Germans as Jerry and another Soldier were retreating. They killed several Germans. This action lasted less than five minutes. Kenneth and the remaining members of the squad set out to return to their base, but had to avoid German Soldiers along the way. It took them four days to reach their base. Kenneth's greatest regret upon returning was that he had lost the picture of his wife and three-year-old daughter. Kenneth was awarded the Distinguished Service Cross for his bravery.

George Hecht and the Parents Institute published eighty-four issues of *True Comics* from April of 1941 through August of 1950. Super heroes were popular at the time, but Hecht and his editorial board thought that young people might also like stories that were factual and exciting. Kenneth's story of protecting the retreating soldiers was in one of the issues.

Kenneth went out on his own and engaged the Germans behind their lines. His success led the Germans to put out wanted posters throughout Tunisia. He became known as "Mustachio Commando" because of his handlebar mustache. Kenneth was sent to Anzio to aid the American invasion. He was assigned to go behind enemy lines and capture Germans to be interrogated. The Germans he captured were interrogated, but Kenneth did not always agree with his superiors on military strategy. One of his daughters related the story of his fighting. Her mother always knew when he was fighting as he left base as a sergeant and returned as a private.

Kenneth returned to the U.S. in the spring of 1945. Because of what he had been trained to do in combat, he was sent to a base in Texas for six weeks. Military officials thought he needed some time to adjust to civilian life. Kenneth became a conservation officer with the S.D. Game, Fish, and Parks Department and was a criminal investigator with the Bureau of Indian Affairs. In addition to the Distinguished Service Cross, Kenneth was awarded four Bronze Stars and a Purple Heart. Kenneth passed away in September of 1973.[482]

Baltus Fritzemeier: From Tractors to Tanks

Baltus Fritzemeier's hometown was Mt. Vernon. He was born in 1922 and grew up on the family farm. His family was of Dutch descent. He worked part-time for a local farmer. The farmer told him to use one tractor for plowing and a different one for cultivating corn. After that, Baltus was on his own. Little did he know that driving large equipment was in his future. He enlisted in the Army and was sent to Ft. Knox, Kentucky, for basic training. He trained further in Maryland.

Baltus was sent to France in 1942. It was during December, and the seas were rough. He was seasick most of the days and did not want to leave his bunk. One day an alarm went off warning them that a submarine had been spotted. An officer came around to make sure everybody had his life jacket on. Baltus didn't care if he had his on or not and told the officer so in no uncertain terms. He did say he got into a little trouble for the position he had taken.

Baltus was assigned to the 4th Armored Division under the command of General Patton. Within the division he was part of a mechanized unit in the 6th Cavalry made of tanks, half-tracks, and jeeps. Their duty was reconnaissance, and they used the tanks when they went on a mission. Each tank had a crew of five—the commander, a driver, an assistant driver, a loader, and a gunner. The tanks were Sherman M-1's; Baltus was the driver of tank #9. The reconnaissance unit went into an area to gather information about the strength of the enemy, including the number of troops, mechanized equipment, and artillery pieces. The information was passed on to the commanders who used it to help plan an attack.

On their first day of reconnaissance, Baltus was introduced to the tragedy of war. The loader of his tank was on an assignment and died when an artillery shell hit him.

As the Americans pushed across France and Germany, his unit had another assignment. After the main fighting force had driven the Germans out of a town, Baltus and his squadron came in to make sure all the enemy were gone and there weren't any snipers left. Snipers killed many Allied Soldiers in Europe and the Pacific. In their march across Europe, the Allied Soldiers liberated several POW camps that held ten to twenty prisoners. He still has vivid memories of the prisoners' poor physical condition. In one town in particular, Baltus recalled how mad the POWs were at the mayor of the town, blaming him for their poor physical condition. The American troops let the prisoners deal with the mayor in their own way.

As the squadron moved across Europe, they were hit by artillery fire three times. Fortunately, they did not suffer any causalities. From time to time they had slept under their tanks. Other times they stayed in German homes after the residents had been forced to leave. His squadron pushed into Belgium as the Battle of the Bulge was winding down. Patton and his tanks had helped save the day. A more important factor in the fighting was a change in the weather. The skies cleared, allowing the air force to destroy German tanks and other mechanized equipment.

Baltus was scheduled to go home, but the seas were rough. He did not want to risk experiencing the sea sickness he had on the way over. He was assigned to Special Services coaching basketball and softball. There was one tall player on the basketball team, and they won all eight games they played. He also did security at the

Brandenburg Gate, at that time part of the dividing line between East and West Germany.

Baltus returned to the U.S. in April of 1946. He had attained the rank of master sergeant and was awarded the Sharp Shooter Medal.

Baltus is listed on a plaque at the Washington Pavilion for teaching World Geography and coaching at Washington High School for over twenty years. His 1971 basketball team won the State A Championship. His wife, Miriam, is also listed on the plaque for teaching Spanish for over twenty years.[483]

Robert Goodhope

Robert Goodhope was born in September of 1923 in Hurley. He enlisted in the Navy in 1944 and completed basic training in Great Lakes, Illinois. After basic training he was assigned to the USS Santee. Robert worked in the General Communications center and was responsible for sending messages to other departments on the ship. Robert was on the same ship as Dale Fields of Egan. They became good friends and maintained their friendship after the war. The USS Santee served in the Pacific and refueled other ships in its combat unit. During the battle of Okinawa, planes from the ship engaged their Japanese opponents.

Robert was discharged in 1946. He went to Yankton College on the G.I. Bill. He taught at Geddes, Viborg, Wakonda, and Centerville. He served as High School Principal at Viborg and Centerville. Robert and his wife, Roberta, had five children. Robert retired in 1984 when his youngest graduated from high school.

I interviewed Robert in March of 2020. He was ninety-six.[484]

Don Crawford and Norman Thormodsgard of Canton: U.S. Navy: WW II

Don was born in 1924 and enlisted in the Navy in 1943. He was sent to the Naval Training Station in Farragut, Idaho, for basic training. He trained further in Los Angeles. Don was trained to be a radio operator. After training was completed, he was assigned to the USS Prince Georges whose designation was AP-165; it was changed later to AK-224. The USS Prince Georges was a cargo ship. The ship delivered troops and supplies throughout the Pacific.

The bloody battle of Tarawa in the Gilbert Islands lasted from November 20th to the 23rd, 1943. Don's ship delivered supplies to the Marines after they had taken the island. He did not go ashore but could see the devastation on the island. The ship also delivered supplies to troops on Makin Atoll in the Gilbert Islands, Kwajalein Atoll in the Marshall Islands, Saipan in the Marianas, and Iwo Jima in the Volcano Islands.

Don served in the Pacific two years and one day. During that time he returned only one time to the U.S. Don was discharged in 1945, and his rank at that time was Radioman 2nd Class. He said that he was not interested in reenlisting.

Don's sister, Delores Eleanor Crawford, married Norman Thormodsgaard in 1939. They had three children. Norman joined the Navy in 1944 and was sent to the Naval Training station at Camp Farragut, Idaho. He was home on leave in Canton when he first saw his newborn son, Norman Douglas. It was in early 1944.

Norman was trained to be a fireman and was assigned to the USS Colorado which was sent to the Pacific. The ship was engaged in the Battle of Leyte on November 27, 1944, when a Japanese aircraft crashed into the ship. Norman died from several wounds and loss of blood. He was buried in U.S. Air Force Cemetery in the

Philippines. His remains were returned to the U.S. in 1948 and laid to rest at Fort Snelling National Cemetery.[485]

Elmer Roth

Elmer Roth of Aberdeen enlisted in the U.S. Signal Corps at Ft. Snelling, Minnesota, in October, 1942. His first assignment was to attend radio school in Aberdeen for six months. He took three more months of training in Des Moines, Iowa.

In late 1943 he went into active service and transferred to the Army Air Corps. His plan was to become a pilot. Elmer was an Aviation Cadet at the University of Minnesota. He trained seven months and was ready for his solo flight when fate intervened. The President issued an order that all enlistees had to return to their previous branches. He was sent to Sioux Falls for a three-month refresher course in Air Force communications. His next assignment was Alamogordo in White Plains, New Mexico, for training on a B-29 Superfortress.

Elmer became a member of the 505th Bombardment Group, 313th Bombardment Wing of the 484th Squadron. The 505th was a unit in the Twentieth Air Force. Roth's crew was sent to Tinian in the Mariana Islands in the South Pacific. A large airfield with long runways had been built so the new B-29 Superfortresses could make bombing runs to Japan. Elmer was the radio operator for his crew. They flew eight missions and then were sent back to the states for "lead crew training." Upon returning, his crew was one of the lead planes on nine more missions over Japan.

Roth played a vital role in the rescue of the crew from a downed B-29 bomber. He was the radio operator on a B-29 known as "Lassie Too." His bomb group had made a raid on the Oita airfield in northern Kyushu. On their return flight to the home base on Tinian, the group was attacked by Japanese fighter planes. A bomber known as "Mary Ann" had lost power from two of its engines, and a third engine was not operating at full capacity. The pilot, Lieutenant Andrew Penn, and Master Sergeant Eugene Sorenson had been seriously wounded. Lieutenant Ralph Len took control of the plane. Another bomber under the command of Lieutenant John Bulmer fell out of formation to escort the "Mary Ann" back to Tinian. Len decided to fly to Okinawa instead.

Lieutenant John Corrick and his crew were on double duty that day. They were spotting B-29s that had crashed in the ocean and protecting a submarine in the area to pick up survivors. Corporal Roth overheard Len give the order to ditch the "Mary Ann." The "Mary Ann" and Bulmer's "Bad Medicine" were sighted off the coast of Kyushu. Elmer informed the submarine of their location and told Len to head for the sub but Len could not keep his plane airborne. The plane landed in choppy waters and sank in fifteen minutes. The submarine picked up ten of the eleven crew members. Some were in a life raft; others were wearing life jackets known as Mae Wests. Lieutenant Andrew Penn did not survive.

Elmer was part of a crew that made a historic flight.

The following is the crew's account of their flight over the USS Missouri. "Our plane flew over the battleship USS Missouri two times during the signing of the Peace Treaty with Japan. Our journey on September 2, 1945, began on the island of Tinian (our home base), in the Mariana Islands; we headed north to Japan, a distance of 1,400 miles.

When we reached Japan, we flew east of Tokyo, and made a left turn. We flew over the burned-out city of Tokyo, then took our turn flying over the signing occurring on the USS Missouri. Again, we made another left turn and headed back east and north of Tokyo, making another left turn to fly over the burned-out city, then back over the signing again. At that time we headed south for the long trip back to Tinian." Many B-29s and other planes flew over the signing. A show of power was exactly what General McArthur wanted on VJ Day.

Elmer was honorably discharged on December 10, 1945. He received the following decorations and commendations: American Theater, Asiatic Pacific Region, Air Medal with two bronze stars, WW II Victory Medal, Good Conduct Medal, Sharp Shooters Medal, and Expert Pistol Medal. Staff Sergeant Roth's uniform represents the Army Air Corp and is on display at the Pheasant Canteen in Aberdeen, South Dakota.[486]

Clifford Hullinger and the 109th Engineers

Clifford Hullinger was born in Vivian. He had seven brothers and sisters. His first job at eight years of age was driving the school bus. It was a horse-drawn cart. In time he moved up to a Model T Ford. While attending South Dakota State College, he joined the National Guard. By joining, he received $1.00 per week for drill duty. Clifford considered it "mad" money as he did not want to waste the money from home on what he considered riotous living.

Clifford was a member of the 109th Combat Engineers that was part of the 34th Infantry "Red Bull" National Guard Division. They were responsible for building bridges, constructing roads, setting mine fields. clearing enemy mine fields, and engaging in combat when needed. They were the first American unit sent overseas to North Africa and then to Italy. The unit was in combat over 500 days, no other division was in combat for a longer period of time. The unit suffered many casualties and was awarded numerous medals.

Clifford's Military Experiences

While attending SDSC the unit went to Rapid City for two weeks of spring camp. Most of his time was spent on KP duty. Summer camp in 1940 was held in Camp Ripley near Brainard, Minnesota. He was in his junior year when the unit was called up. They were sent to a new camp, Camp Claiborne, in Louisiana After Pearl Harbor they were moved to Camp Dix, New Jersey. The overseas destination of the 109th Combat Engineers in February of 1942 was Ireland. The unit was on the USS American Legion when a propellor shaft broke after the first day of their voyage. They were close to Halifax, Nova Scotia. German submarines were in the vicinity, and one fired three torpedoes, but missed the ship. A Canadian sub-chaser sank the submarine. They were towed to Halifax for repairs. After repairs were completed, the ship returned to Boston and left with another convoy. They reached their destination in May. In Ireland, the engineers practiced repairing bridges.

From Ireland they went to England and then on to Oran in North Africa and finally to Tunisia. The U.S. suffered a major defeat at Kasserine Pass. The 109th Engineers did succeed in building a road and finding another longer stretch of road allowing some American troops to withdraw. They received a commendation for their actions. After the battle, their mission was to dig up and disarm Italian mines and booby traps.

After the beachhead at Salerno had been secured, Cliff's unit was assigned to move up the Italian boot. The Volturno was a winding river and had to be crossed several times as the troops moved north. Bridges were a necessity as troops, tanks, motorized vehicles, and supplies could not be moved without them. In their first attempt to build a bridge across the river, they were driven back by German artillery fire. The engineers came up with a solution to the problem. They went back to the river at night and set up smoke pots to fog up the area. The Germans were convinced they were building a bridge under the cover of the smoke and shelled the area all night. Meanwhile the engineers had moved up the river and built a bridge free of artillery fire.

As the Germans retreated, they blew up every bridge and culvert to slow the Allied advance. In one stretch of fifteen miles engineers had to build eleven bypasses around blown bridges and culverts. After traffic was moving again, they went back and built bridges. Heavy rains created mud, making the challenge of building bridges even greater. As the engineers continued to build bypasses, bridges, and replace culverts, they took fire from German artillery, suffering casualties.

The Battle of Monte Cassino lasted from January 17th to May 18th of 1944. Monte Cassino was a historic abbey built on a mountain top. Because of its historic significance it was off-limits to artillery fire and bombs. Although the Allies were convinced the Germans were using the abbey as an observation post, their assessment was proven untrue. The Allies attacked the abbey four times and suffered 55,000 causalities. The Allies bombed the abbey.

Clifford's unit participated in the battle. The engineers put wooden box culverts in the Rapido river to allow for the movement of troops and equipment. Cliff and members of his unit witnessed the bombing of the abbey. They were not thinking about its historical significance, but rather the six weeks of mud, snow, and shelling they had endured. They were also thinking about the two thousand soldiers from their division who had been lost taking the mountain.

The unit continued to move north until the war was over. Cliff was on his way home on a B-17 bomber whose guns and bomb racks had been replaced by benches. The pilots were not happy about their duty. The co- pilot was falling asleep, so he changed places with Cliff. The pilot put the plane on automatic pilot and fell asleep. Cliff was comfortable in the co-pilot's until he saw another B-17 coming at them. It crossed in front of them, causing the pilot to wake up and stay awake until they reached their destination. After changing planes several times, he finally got to the U.S. He took a train from Miami to Minneapolis and another one to Vivian. The date was June 1945. After the Japanese surrendered, he was discharged in October 1945.

Clifford returned to SDSC and picked up where he had left off in the middle of his junior year, only five years later. He earned his bachelor of science and master's degree at SDSC and a Ph.D. at Purdue. The G.I. Bill helped make his education possible as it did for thousands of veterans. Clifford away August 4, 2017, at age 97.[487]

Members of the 109th Engineers Who Died in Service to Their Country

The following members of the 109th Engineers did their basic training at Camp Claiborne in Louisiana and died in service to their country. Robert Christensen,[488] Cleo LaFave,[489] Roger Loesch,[490] Leland Ortmayer,[491] and Wayne Satre had transferred to Company A and were stationed in North Africa. They were part of a crew clearing a road of land mines. The crew had picked up 450 mines when a live mine was thrown into the truck, causing an explosion. They all perished, along with other members of Company A.

Harry Daum had transferred to the Army Air Corps and received his wings. His assignment was to move a B-24 Liberator bomber to Africa. The plane hit a mountain near Fortaleza, Brazil. None of the crew members survived.[492]

Clair Grams enlisted in Company F, the 109th Engineer Combat Regiment, at age sixteen. After basic training at Camp

Claiborne, Clair left the 109th when he was transferred to flight school. He flew missions out of New Guinea. Clair piloted a C-47 cargo plane carrying troops and supplies. Clair was eligible to return to the U.S., and papers were being prepared There was a shortage of pilots, and Clair volunteered to be the co-pilot for a pilot on his first mission. The plane was loaded with a highly flammable substance. After their first take-off, they returned for repairs. The second take-off was successful, but they did not return on schedule. Natives reported that the plane had crashed into a mountain and burned. Searchers located the plane and returned the men's dog tags.[493]

Virgil O. Johnson joined Company A of the 109th Engineer Battalion. He was reassigned to Company B and then to Company D. He was very good at laying mines and communication wire between various units. Virgil was in Italy when he died on April 22, 1944, while performing his duties. His body was returned and buried in the city cemetery in Oldham, South Dakota.[494]

Elmer Maxvold was born in DeSmet. In 1941 he enlisted in the National Guard and became part of Company C with the 109th Engineers. He was sent to Italy. Elmer was driving a truck loaded with ammunition when it hit a land mine and exploded. He was buried in American Cemetery in Italy. His brother Donald was a Marine.[495]

Ben Owen was the commanding office of Company D, 84th Chemical Battalion when he died in combat on May 26, 1944. His unit was in Italy. A white cross at Fort Meade National Cemetery at Sturgis commemorates his service to his country. Ben was the only son of Ivan and Eula.[496]

Jack Pahl was born in Lead in 1921 and graduated from high school in 1940. He was in Company E of the National Guard from 1937 to 1941. Jack was called to active duty and assigned to the 109th Engineers, 34th Division. Jack trained at Camp Clairborne,

Louisiana, in New Jersey, and in Massachusetts. Jack was sent overseas in 1942. His first combat duty was in Africa during the Tunisian Campaign. His unit landed on the Anzio beachhead on March 22, 1944. Jack was trying to destroy a German machine gun emplacement when he was killed by a sniper. It was June 1, 1944. His final resting place is Bear Butte Cemetery in Sturgis.[497]

Russell White joined the National Guard in 1935. Russell and his wife, Fern, had three children, Bill, Joyce, and Jerry Jean. He was called to active duty in February of 1941 with the 109th Engineers. He completed basic training in Camp Clairborne, Louisiana. His first combat was in North Africa. His unit was sent to Italy. Russell died when he stepped on a land mine. It was November 9, 1943. He is buried in Sicily-Rome American Cemetery.[498]

William Turner was from Lead. He enlisted and became part of Company E, 109th Engineers, 34th Division. William was sent overseas and served in North Africa and Italy. He was wounded in combat and died in October of 1943. William was serving in Italy at the time of his death. William was buried in Sicily-Rome American Cemetery, Nuttuno, Italy. His brothers, Robert and Rodney, were also in the military.[499]

South Dakotans Who Were Honored by Having Ships Named After Them

Clement Anderson was born in Hitchcock. Because of the drought and Depression, he joined the CCC in 1938 and worked in the Black Hills. Clement was drafted in 1940 and in 1943 was sent to the South Pacific. His unit was on patrol when it was ambushed on January 31, 1944. He received the Silver Star for his bravery in the attack. The citation read as follows: "He crawled under heavy enemy fire to deliver machine gun ammunition and assist in operating the gun. When the enemy attacked the position with powerful offensive grenades, Private Anderson located the hidden enemy, dueled with them at a distance of ten yards and directed the fire of the machine gun until enemy resistance was wiped out." On February 5, 1944, he was attacking a Japanese dugout and died from enemy rifle fire. He was on the island of Bigej in the Marshall Islands. He was awarded the Purple Heart in addition to other medals. In February of 2005 the Army named a ship in his honor, Pvt. Clement W. Anderson Catamaran. The ship transports troops around the Pacific.[500]

Arthur Gustafson graduated from Watertown High School in 1931 and the US Naval Academy in Annapolis, Maryland, in 1936. Arthur served on the battleships Idaho and Colorado. He rose through the ranks from midshipman to ensign to lieutenant in 1939. He was on the USS Peary in Port Darwin, Australia, when it was attacked by the Japanese in February of 1942. He stayed with the ship and was one of six crew members who went down with it. He was awarded the Purple Heart. His name is listed on the Tablets of the Missing at Manila American Cemetery in Manila. He was honored in October of 1942 when a Navy destroyer escort, the USS Gustafson, was named after him.[501]

Reinhardt Keppler was from Hosmer. He graduated from high school in 1936 and enlisted in the Navy. He was assigned to the USS San Francisco in 1940. It was on patrol in the Savo Islands, a part of the Solomon Islands and close to Guadalcanal. The battle of Savo Islands took place on November 12, 1942. The ship shook when fifteen large shells tore into it causing a fire. Reinhardt was wounded but continued to fight the fire until it was under control. His bravery saved the lives of some of his fellow crewmen and kept the ship from sinking. Before dawn broke on the 13th, he died from loss of blood. His wife, Elizabeth, accepted the Congressional

Medal of Honor and the Purple Heart for his sacrifice. In 1944 the Navy named a ship after him, the destroyer escort, USS Keppler.[502]

Raymond Kretschmer graduated from Mitchell High School and attended South Dakota State College. He enlisted in the Naval Reserve in 1940 and was called to active duty after Pearl Harbor. Raymond was on duty during the battle of Coral Sea, Midway, and the landings on Guadalcanal. He was stationed on the USS Astoria. The first battle of the Savo Islands commenced on August 8, 1942. Raymond died in action on the 9th. Crew members removed his identification tags so they could be returned to his relatives. He is listed on the Tablets of the Missing at Manila Military Cemetery in Manila. In 1943 Raymond's sister, Betty, was asked to break the traditional bottle of champagne on the bow of the destroyer, USS Kretschmer. Betty joined the WAVES in honor of her brother.[503]

George Philip, Jr. was born in Fort Pierre in 1912. He graduated from high school in Rapid City and the US Naval Academy in 1935. He served on the USS Ellet, USS O'Bannon, and lastly on the USS Twiggs. He rose in rank from lieutenant to lieutenant commander. He commanded the Twiggs. George participated in the battle of the Solomon Islands, the Philippines, Iwo Jima, and Okinawa. On June 16, 1945, the Twiggs was on patrol off the coast of Okinawa when a Japanese kamikaze plane dove into it. George and several crewmen died. George left behind his wife, Margaret, and two children. He was awarded the Presidential Unit Citation, Silver Star, Purple Heart, and several campaign ribbons. There is a memorial marker to George in Black Hills National Cemetery. The USS George Philip was commissioned in 1978. It is a guided missile fast frigate.[504]

Ernest Hilbert was from Quinn in Pennington County. He was the second crewman on a Douglas SBD-3 Dauntless. The morning of June 4, 1942, found Ernest and his pilot, Lieutenant

Weber, fighting for their lives in the Battle of Midway. Ernest's skill at manning the plane's machine guns enabled the pilot to elude attacks from Japanese fighter planes. Hilbert and Weber continued fighting in the afternoon, but both died when the plane was shot down. The Navy awarded Ernest the Distinguished Flying Cross. A new destroyer escort was named the USS Ernest L. Hilbert.[505]

William Wallace Johnson was born in 1904. He was seventeen when he joined the Navy in 1922. After serving four years he was honorably discharged in 1926. Wallace, as he was known, married Marguerite Monroe in 1929. Later he joined the Merchant Marine and was serving on the tanker Australia. His brother-in-law was on the same ship. The ship was close to the coast of North Carolina when it was torpedoed and sank. William was 38. He was honored in 1945 when a Liberty Ship was named after him, the SS Wallace Johnson.[506]

War Bonds Helped to Pay for WW II

War bonds went on sale in December of 1941 and could be purchased in denominations from $25 to $1,000. A variety of methods were used to encourage people to buy bonds. Individuals could sign up for a program at work that allowed their employer to take a certain amount out of each pay- check for a war bond. Several war bond drives were held between November of 1942 and December of 1945. Each one had a sales goal. The drives featured movie stars, popular singers, and war heroes home on leave. Posters were seen everywhere. They all had the same central theme: Buy Bonds. Americans purchased 185.7 billion dollars' worth of bonds.[507]

South Dakota's Poster Boy: U.S. Bond

Urban Selar Bond was from Wentworth. He enlisted in the Army Air Corps and was sent to Randolph Field in Texas for flight training. Somebody from the publicity department noticed his initials. They were almost too good to be true. The government was conducting war bond drives. His youthful looks and initials were a perfect fit for a war bond poster. The poster featured a young pilot in a plane, and the caption read "You buy'em We'll fly'em." His picture also appeared on magazine covers. The gift shop of the USS Lexington, an aircraft carrier harbored in Corpus Christi, Texas, offers memorabilia about the ship and WW II. One item on display was a deck of playing cards featuring this poster.

Urban went on bond drives that crisscrossed the U.S. At a stop in Maine, Jenny McClain introduced herself. In a few weeks they were married. They had been married for thirty years when Jenny died in 1972. Urban completed his flight training and flew planes over North Africa during the invasion of Sicily and in the China-Burma-India campaign.

Urban died at Avera McKennan hospital in Sioux Falls in 2001 at age 82. He was buried at Rose Hill Cemetery in Wentworth.[508]

Native American Code Talkers and the War in the Pacific

In 1942 the war in Europe and the Pacific was not going well for the U.S. and its Allies. Hitler controlled a large portion of Europe, and German submarines had been sinking many supply ships bound for England. The Japanese controlled the major island groups in the Pacific.

American military leaders in the Pacific were faced with another problem. The Japanese were deciphering our military messages. Japanese decoders had gone to school in the United States and knew English. They had also learned our slang terms, Hollywood actors and actresses, base- ball teams and players, and our profanity. They knew where we were going, when, and the number of ships and troops. This information resulted in heavy losses of American lives. Military leaders needed a solution to the problem.

Philip Johnson was a civil engineer living in Los Angeles. He had served in WW I and was too old for WW II but wanted to help the war effort in some way. His parents had been missionaries on the Navajo Indian Reservation. From the age of four he began to learn the Navajo language. As he got older, he became fluent in Navajo and English. As he read about the losses we were suffering, the idea of a secret military code was born. He presented his theory to Lieutenant Colonel James Jones, the Marines' Signal Corps Communications Officer.

Jones was skeptical of the plan saying that no code is completely secure. Philip assured him that a code based on Navajo could not be broken. The Navajo language has words that have as many as four totally different meanings, and the verb forms are complex. Jones agreed to try the plan. After basic training, a few Navajo recruits were ordered to create a new Marine Corps military code. Their first deployment was to Guadalcanal where the code was successful. Because of the success of the code on Guadalcanal, Native Americans from several tribes were recruited to expand the program.[509]

Clarence Wolf Guts was born in 1924 in the Red Leaf Community on the Rosebud Reservation. Growing up, he learned Lakota from his grand- parents. His grandfather gave him some

180 | Charles M. Rogers

prophetic advice, "Study Lakota more in school, you may need it someday." Clarence and his cousin Iver Crow Eagle were juniors at St. Francis School when they left to join the Army in 1942. Clarence was in Ranger Training at Camp Rucker, Alabama, when a captain asked him if he could speak Indian. He said yes. Clarence was instructed to get a haircut, take a shower, and put on his best clothes. The captain and Clarence met with Major General Paul Mueller, Commander of the 81st Infantry Division. Clarence convinced Mueller that he could speak the Lakota language. The captain asked if he knew anybody else who could speak the language. He said his cousin Iver White Bear could.

Roy Bad Hand and Benny White Bear from South Dakota were added to make a group of four. The four were taught how to operate military radios, and they developed a military code based on their language. The procedure for sending and receiving messages went as follows: An officer would give a code talker a message in English; the code talker would translate the message into Lakota code and send it to another code talker who would translate it back into English and give it to another officer. This procedure had to be done under combat conditions.

The Marines were able to move troops and supplies without being detected. The Japanese listened to their transmissions but were never able to decipher them. There was no way of knowing how many lives were saved; it could have been hundreds or thousands. Military leaders did see a drop in casualties once the codes were in place.

General Mueller selected Clarence as his personal code talker and was with him as the 81st Division moved throughout the Pacific. Iver became the code talker for the General's Chief of Staff. Every code talker was protected by two bodyguards. In the movie "Windtalkers" starring Nicolas Cage there was one bodyguard.

The eleven Lakota code talkers listed in the Congressional Record (2002 Code Talkers Recognition Act) are Eddie Eagle Boy, Simon Broke Leg, Iver Crow Eagle, Sr., Edmund St. John, Walter C. John, John Bear King, Phillip "Stoney" LaBlanc, Baptiste Pumpkin Seed, Guy Rondell, Charles White Pipe, and Clarence Wolf Guts. Roy Bad Hand and Benny White Bear are not included on the list.

After the war, code talkers were asked not to talk about what they did, and their written reports were classified. When the military declassified information about code talkers, they were finally honored for their service. Clarence was honored by Senators Tim Johnson and John Thune in a ceremony on Capitol Hill. Clarence passed away in June of 2010 and was buried in Black Hills National Cemetery.[510]

Acts of Bravery

Master Sergeant Clifford C. "Red" Hills was from Sioux Falls. He was stationed on the Solomon Islands in the Pacific. Putting his life at risk, Hills made an attack on a machine gun position and destroyed it. He continued his acts of bravery on Okinawa in the Ryukyu Islands. Admiral Chester Nimitz presented Hills with the Navy Cross.[511]

Rear Admiral Ingolf Kiland was from Sioux Falls. He was commander of the USS Crescent City during the battle of Guadalcanal in 1942. The ship protected American troops and shot down four enemy aircraft. He was awarded the Navy Cross.[512]

Don Talcott was born in Winner on November 6, 1924. He grew up in Witten, South Dakota, and enlisted in the Army in 1943. After basic training he was sent to the Pacific. Don was awarded three Purple Hearts and two Bronze Stars for his bravery in combat. Don and Marty Connot were married on December 27, 1947, in

Winner. He taught and coached in several towns in South Dakota. After a thirty-eight year career, he retired in 1991. Don passed away in 2008 at age 84.[513]

Vitalis "Vic" Cole was born in 1913 in Bon Homme County. Vic graduated from Tyndall High School in 1930. Vic graduated from Southern Normal School with a bachelor's degree and a teaching certificate. Later he graduated from South Dakota State University with a master's degree. Vic and Rachel Barber were married in May of 1941. They had four children.

Vic entered the military and served in China with the "Flying Tigers". He returned to the U.S. and served four years at the Pentagon. His military career included all of WW II, the Korean Conflict, and part of the war in Viet Nam. Vic was in the military over twenty years.

After retiring from the military, he taught in rural and city schools for twenty-one years. He retired from Brookings Middle School in 1978. Vic passed away in 2008 at age 94.[514]

A Long Boat Ride to Safety

Rear Admiral John Morrill was from Miller. His ship, the USS Quail, had to be scuttled during the battle of Corregidor. John and his crew escaped in a thirty-six foot motor launch. They made it to Port Darwin, Australia, a distance of 2,000 miles. John was awarded the Navy Cross.[515]

American POWs

The September 21, 2008, issue of the *Argus Leader* carried the stories of twelve servicemen who were German POWs and returned home.

Lee Bevers was living in Watertown. He was in the Army Air Corps when his plane was shot down, and he became a POW. Lee was a POW from April 13,1944, to May 13,1945. He was held in Germany. Fate is a funny thing: he met the German pilot who had shot them down; they had shot him down. Upon entering the prison camp, he was surprised by two fellow fliers he knew. They had also been shot down in bomber planes. Lee was liberated by the Russians.

Don Brommer was living in Sioux Center, Iowa. He was in the Army when he became a prisoner. Don was a POW from December 17,1944, to April 28,1945. He was held in Germany. Late in the war POWs were being moved in railroad cars. Don remembered being locked in a boxcar four days and four nights with a loaf of black bread and nothing to drink. He was liberated by the 45th Infantry Division.

Lyle Davis was living in Brookings. He was in the Army. Lyle was a POW from December of 1943 to the spring of 1945. He was captured in Italy and then spent time in two German camps. He was liberated by the Russians. They were ordered to start marching in the middle of the night as heavy snow was falling. Civilians were also on the move. There were no young people: it was only old men, old women, and kids. Lyle and other prisoners tried to help them by pushing their carts. He often wondered what happened to them as he never saw them again after that night. They marched in the snow, and their feet were never dry during the day. At night they slept in barns. They took their boots off and stuffed them with straw to try to dry them out. Red Cross packages supplemented their meager rations.

Ron Davis was living in Sioux Falls. He was in the infantry when he became a prisoner. He was a prisoner from September 27,1944, to April 29,1945. With the passage of time he tried not to remember the bad things that happened and dwell on the funny things. The Germans were also holding Russian prisoners. One day they sent dogs into the Russian barracks, and the dogs did not return. One unfortunate incident he remembered related to the Dachau Concentration camp. There was a bombed-out car in the vicinity of their camp at Dachau. There was flour in the car, and prisoners were taking it. Ron took as much as he could. Some other guys got caught and were shot on the spot. He was liberated by the 99th Infantry Division.

Charles Dawes was living in Mitchell. He was in the infantry when he became a prisoner. Charles was captured near Strasburg, Germany. He was a prisoner from November of 1944 to April 29, 1945. The Allies had bombed Munich. Charles and other prisoners used wheel barrows and shovels to clean up debris. They had to work in order to get fed. Red Cross food parcels helped keep them alive. The parcels were also a great morale booster. Charles was liberated by General Patton's forces.

Bernard Hoffman was living in Harrisburg. He was in the Army when he became a prisoner. Bernard was a POW from December 23, 1944, to April 15, 1945. He was held in Germany. Bernard was captured in Belgium. He was assigned to a work detail. His group had to walk 15 kilometers to reach Bad Orb, Germany. During the walk they were not given anything to eat, and they slept in a snowbank. The only food they were given in the camp was potato soup. Bernard lost 80 pounds in 103 days. He was liberated by General Patton's troops.

Harry Kelly was living in Kansas City, Missouri. He was in the Navy. Harry was a POW from 1942 to 1945, a total of three and one-half years. He was held in the South Pacific. Salt was a valuable commodity. Harry was accused of having salt and was put a tin box with one cup of water per day. A Korean friend of his found out where he was and broke him out of the box. Then the Korean beat the guards with bamboo sticks. Harry was liberated by American Soldiers.

Truman Kittleson was living in Sherburn, Minnesota. He was with the 34th Infantry Division when he was captured. Truman was a prisoner from February 17,1943, to May 1945. He was held in Italy and Germany. The Italians took their clothes away, and they had to dig holes to stay warm. Truman came down with influenza in the German camp and was sick for a year. He was liberated when they were forced out of the camp by advancing Russian troops. They had the good fortune of encountering American troops.

Morris Magnuson was living in Sioux Falls. He was serving in the Army Air Corps and became a POW from March 14,1945, to April 29,1945. The prisoners' main topic of discussion was food and the lack of it. They talked about the day when they could have hamburgers and ice cream again. Girls were not a topic of discussion. He was liberated by Patton's Army.

George Sterler was living in Sheldon, Iowa. He was in the Army Air Corps and on his 29th mission when he was shot down. One more mission and he would have been eligible to go home. Eight of his crew members did not survive. George was a POW from May 8,1944, to April 29,1945. He was held in Germany. George was on a train on D-Day. The German guards were afraid that they would be killed. George was liberated by the 14th Armored Division.

Art Van Moorlehem was living in Marshall, Minnesota. He was serving in the infantry prior to becoming a prisoner. Art was a POW from December 19,1944, to April 8,1945. He was held in Germany. Lice was a constant irritation and nearly impossible to get rid of. Art and other POWs survived on soup that was not good. Their poor diet contributed to development of dysentery. Art was in

Camp Bad Orb near Frankfurt, Germany. At one time there were 6,000 in the camp. To make room for the Americans, the Germans had gassed 1,300 Serbs and buried them in a big hole. Art wasn't sure why the Germans treated the Serbs more harshly than they did the Americans. He was liberated by a group from Patton's Army.

Bill Vermillion was living in Beresford. He was serving in the Army Air Corps when he was shot down. Bill was a prisoner from February 4,1944, to April 1,1945. He was held in Germany. During the last three months of his imprisonment he was on the march. The marching would begin in the middle of the night. Most of the time they slept outdoors. The German guards marched them into American troops. They knew their chances of survival were far greater with Americans than with the Russians. Thousands of German POWs did not survive Russian prison camps. Art was liberated by American forces.[516]

A Camp and a Movie

Major General Marvin McNickle was from Doland. He was commander of the 78th Fighting Group. Marvin was shot down in September of 1943. He was a POW in Stalag III and became leader of the group. Marvin succeeded in getting concessions from the Germans for his fellow POWs. Stalag III is remembered as the location of the movie "The Great Escape."

Thomas Oliver

Thomas Oliver and his family moved to Rapid City in 1967. He had taken a teaching position in the Electrical Engineering Department at the South Dakota School of Mines and Technology. Thomas had graduated from the U.S. Military Academy at West Point in 1943. After graduation he entered the Army Air Corps and became the pilot of a B-24 bomber. Thomas passed away in 2019 at age 96.

Thomas wrote an account of his last flight, capture, and road to freedom. His story is reprinted here with the permission of his son Rob Oliver. Rob served as President of Wells Fargo Bank and Augustana University.

Unintended Visit to Yugoslavia
by Thomas K. Oliver

May 6, 1944, was the fateful day. I was a B-24 pilot in the 756th Squadron, 459th Bomb Group, 15th Air Force, Flying out of southern Italy. My crew and I had finished about half of our missions and considered ourselves veterans. That day we were breaking in a new copilot, Camillus Rechtin, taking him on his first mission. Little did he know what was to come.

The remainder of my crew were:
Pilot-Thomas K. Oliver
Navigator-John Thibodeau
Bombardier-Charles Gracz
Engineer-Jodie Oliver
Radio Operator-Donald Sullivan
Ball Turret-Franklin Bartels
Tail Turret-Edgar Smith
Nose Turret-Griffin Goad
Funner-William Keepers

The airplane normally flown by my crew was the Fighting Muscat, so named because the catfish is a survivor. It must have been out of commission that day as we few a borrowed airplane. my wife tells me I should never borrow things.

I had a little superstition going. At the briefing before the mission I always made it a point to enter the estimated time of arrival back at our home base on the briefing sheet or pilot's flimsy and carry the sheet in my pocket on the mission. If for some reason I missed getting the official pilot's flimsy, I wrote the time of arrival on a scrap of paper and carried that. It seemed good to have an estimated time back at home base written down somewhere on my person. As we taxied out of takeoff on May 6 the paper blew out the open cockpit window. I remember the flight engineer saying "We didn't need that, did we?" I bravely said "No" and on we went. It was 96 days before we saw home base again. It was enough to make one wonder.

The mission was to the Campina Marshalling Yards, near the Ploesti oil fields. Our group led the 15th Air Force over the target and caught the full benefit of flak and German fighters before the gunners or the fighter pilots got tired. The fighters came right through their own flak to make a nose attack on us. One FW-190 had our airplane singled out. After he passed just beneath us the gunners on my crew said he went down trailing smoke. We will never know for sure whether we hit him fatally or not.

We will also never know whether the damage to our plane was done by the fighter or by flak. Shortly after "bombs away" number three engine was losing oil pressure. I tried to feather it, without success. A look at the engine showed why. The prop governor had been hit and was hanging by one bolt. The drag and vibration forced us to slow down and lag behind the formation. Two P-38's came and flew alongside us until we were beyond danger from German fighters. I would like to have hugged those pilots, whose names I probably will never know.

The next excitement came when number three engine seized from turning over without any oil. The vibration was horrendous. The right wing shook in a sine wave pattern as though one took one ned of a rope and tied it to a tree, and then gave a good shake to the other end. Finally something snapped. I was later told that the reduction gear must have failed. The propeller now spun freely on just its own bearing and things went more smoothly for a while.

But not for long. Number four engine now began to lose oil pressure. Not wishing to repeat the experience with number three, we got it feathered in a hurry. With two engines dead on the same side we threw out guns, flak suits, etc., anything to reduce weight.

We managed to maintain about 8000 ft. altitude, just enough to clear the Dalmatian Alps near the Adriatic Sea. I was figuring that I might be the first to bring a B-24 back from the Ploesti area with two engines dead on the same side. That should be good for a distinguished flying cross and a little respect back at home base. But all that was not to be.

John Thibodeau, the navigator, was trying to keep us on a course that would not take us over any flak batteries. Just after we crossed the Danube River near Turnul Severin and the Iron Gates we encountered flak at the Yugoslavian town of Bor. It had not been noted on our charts. One blast set the number two engine on fire. The crew said that the bomb bay doors looked like the top of a salt shaker. With only one good engine and no way to put out the fire, the only course of action was to bail out.

I gave the order to bail out on the intercom and hit the bail out bell. Then I took one more look at the burning engine. It did not look any better. I turned and looked back to see how the crew were coming along at bailing out. All were gone except John Thibodeau, who was standing in the bomb bay motioning me to come on. I waved to him to get out. I did not want anyone in my way when I let go of the wheel. He jumped and I jumped.

As I tumbled through the air I remember saying to myself that even if the parachute did not open, I was no worse off than when I was in the plane. It did open. My attention was drawn to a noise like the loudest siren I ever heard. The free propeller was winding up as the plane dove toward the ground. The plane hit ground and there was a huge fireball. Cecile B. DeMille never put on a better show. After the fireball cleared, all I could see was a large black spot.

At first I seemed to be descending very slowly. I feared the Germans would have time to have a patrol waiting for me when I reached the ground. As the ground came closer I realized that it was approaching at an alarming speed. I made a good landing, but did have a sore ship for a week or so.

I almost landed on top of a group of Yugoslavian peasants who were having a picnic lunch. The table was set near a farmhouse. on the table was a sheep's head, eyeballs and all. As the honored, if uninvited, guest I was offered the eyeballs. Somehow I lost my appetite. Then they offered me a glass of wine and it seemed like a marvelous idea.

Probably within ten minutes or less a couple of men approached wearing military caps, with rifles slung over their shoulders, and leading a horse. They mentioned Draza Mihailovic and indicated that I was to mount the horse. It had not taken the guerrilla organization long to find me.

That afternoon we kept moving rather steadily and a few times I heard shots fired over the hill. Once we stopped for a few minutes to talk with a Yugoslavian medical doctor who had been educated in France. I discovered that it is much easier to communicate in French with a Yugoslavian educated in France than with a Frenchman. He was very helpful at putting the words in my mouth. For example he would ask in French "Is it that you are worried about your comrades?" All I had to supply was "Oui". He told me that all were well with one slightly wounded. It was to be two days before I saw the rest of the crew again.

In the evening we stopped at a peasant farmhouse. The lady of the house offered me a cup of hot goat's milk with some kind of scum all over it. I was getting very hungry. So I said to myself "You have to eat to live. Furthermore these people eat it and they survive." It tasted better than it looked.

After supper I was put to bed on a pile of straw. At some time during the wee small hours they woke me up and it was time to move on again. By this time there were about six Chetniks escorting me. We all rode horses with about three of them in front, then me, then three more of them bringing up the rear. We proceeded single file winding through the hills by moonlight. The Chetniks wore Cossack style fur hats and tight jackets. Each had a rifle slung over his shoulder. The only sound was of the horses' harness jingling. I pinched myself and silently asked "What am I doing in the middle of this Grade B, black and white move?"

The next day our pace was more relaxed. We seemed to go from one outdoor cafe to the next, with a round of drinks at each. I was carrying two hunting knives, one on my belt and one strapped to my leg. The Chetniks would ask, via gestures, "Why two knives?" Then one of them supplied the answer. He pointed to one and said "Ah Hitler" with a throat-cutting gesture and an appropriate noise like a death rattle.

Then he pointed to the other and said "Ah Mussolini" with the same gesture and noises. I later used the same line among other groups and it always went over well.

That evening there was a religious ceremony. They took me to what obviously were the graves of two American airmen who had been shot down and killed. A Serbian Orthodox priest conducted the service. A cup of wine was passed around. Each person took a sip and spilled a small amount on the grave.

That night I was put to bed in a house in a little village. In the wee small hours I was roused again. There was alarm that the Germans were coming. "Heidi, heidi" they cited to me, which by that time I had learned meant "Hurry, hurry". In my underwear I was taken out and hidden in the woods until the danger was over. The stark terror conveyed by their voices is something I will never forget.

The next day I was reunited with the rest of my crew. There were in fact parts of three crews, about 24 of us, all billeted in one place, a peasant farmhouse. We had an interpreter, an old man who much earlier in life had spent several years in the United States. He had worked in Wisconsin in the logging business, obviously surrounded with Swedes. It was unusual to find a Yugoslavian who spoke English with a "My name is Yon Yohnson, I come from Visconsin" Swedish accent.

The local Chetnik commander was a man called Kent. He was young, handsome and dynamic, a Chetnik's Chetnik. We were in the region of the Timok corps.

Nothing great occurred for about a month. We were still fairly close to the Danube River, close to the eastern border of Yugoslavia. The local Chetnik commander was hoping to get us evacuated from there and hoping to get some sort of aid or supplies from the allies in return. Finally he was persuaded to send us west to the center of old Serbia, the region where General Mihailovic's headquarters was.

Captain Ivan Milac was assigned the job of leading us over about 150 kilometers to the middle of old Serbia. He was a Chetnik who had been an officer in the Yugoslav Regular Army. He had learned English on his own, largely by listening to radio broadcasts in English. A finer gentleman has never lived.

We were issued rifles to carry on the march west. It began on a section of mountain railroad with evidently was considered safe. We traveled for some distance and then got off just before the train went into a town of some size.

That was the only easy part of the march. The rest is all mixed together in my memory: walking in the sunshine, walking in the rain, sleeping on haystacks, sleeping on hardwood schoolhouse floors. John Thibodeau reminded me of one incident. About lunchtime we came upon a place where there were three city girls. The usual peasant girls in their babushkas were not all that attractive. But these were beautiful and they invited us to lunch and indicated that we could spend the night. It seemed like heaven. As we sat down to lunch the Chetniks indicated that we had to leave immediately, the Germans were coming. That was the last we saw of the three beautiful city girls.

We arrived in the general area of General Mihailovic's headquarters and were divided up into small groups and billeted at various peasant farmhouses. We had lots of time to kill and would whittle out corncob pipes and smoke whatever local blend of tobacco we could lay our hands on. It was explained to us that cigarettes were in short supply because we had bombed the cigarette factory at Nis.

I remember watching a peasant lady baking bread. It was in a little square house made of timbers. The roof sloped up steeply on all four sides with a hole at the top. The floor was of clay and in the center a fire had been burning. Most of the smoke rose and went out the hole at the top of the roof. The lady swept hot coals away from a spot not he hearth. The bread dough, on a plate, was then set on the clay hearth. She then placed a large earthenware bowl upside down over the plate with the bread dough. Finally hot coals were shoveled over the inverted bowl. That way the bread got baked.

In Yugoslavia we saw real genuine gypsies. I never saw anyone who needed a bath more than they. They would come into the village carrying an accordion and a couple of violins. Then that evening the whole village had a party. Food was brought out and everyone had dinner. Then the gypsies played and there was dancing in the public square. Next day the gypsies moved on.

It was an impressive event each time the 15th Air Force flew overhead on the way to targets in the Ploesti area. We would first hear a faint buzzing sound, like bees. The sound would get louder and louder until it became a roar and the sky was filled with airplanes. We knew we could count on another two or three crews to join us on the ground. Once we saw a B-24 overhead flying in large circles. All four engines were running. It kept flying in large circles until it eventually went out of sight. Clearly the plan has been abandoned. I would love to have had a long rope ladder to climb up into that airplane and fly it home.

Meanwhile, no great progress was being made at getting us back to Italy. One reason for this was that the British, who controlled the Mediterranean Theater of operations, had recalled their mission and severed all relationship with Mihailovic. Some of the Yugoslavian officers who spoke English would tell us that they had notified the British, and that was all they could do. We gradually got the idea that we ought somehow to get a message to the 15th Air Force as to how many of us were in Yugoslavia, and that they would be more likely to act than the British in Cairo.

To send a message involved getting General Mihailovic's personal approval. By this time (late July, 1944) there were close to 150 allied airmen in our group including the crew of one British Wellington. So far as I knew, as a first lieutenant I was as high-ranking as any of our group. So I started saying that as the commander of the Americans I wanted to see the commander of the Chetniks, General Mihailovic himself.

Finding the general in a guerrilla outfit is not easy and it is not supposed to be easy. The lieutenant knows where the captain is and no more. The captain knows where the major is, etc. Finally I got to see general Mihailovic himself. We spoke through an interpreter. He assured us that he had notified his government in Cairo, etc., but was very willing to help us to send a message directly to Italy.

Now it turned out that among the downed airmen the idea of sending a message to Italy was very controversial. Some said "Don't send any message. The Germans will intercept it and home in on it and capture us." Those on my side felt that the Germans already must have known that there were allied airmen in the hills. But the Germans were taking a beating on two fronts and did not have their finest troops stationed in Yugoslavia. They probably did not want to pay the price involved in trying to capture us.

My right hand man in the whole process of getting to see General Mihailovic and composing and sending a message was a fighter pilot named Jack Barrett. If we accomplished anything worthwhile he deserves a full measure of credit.

Partially as a concession to the cautious group we decided to formulate a message in American slang which would accomplish our purpose and at the same time be as puzzling as possible to any Germans who might pick it up.

The resulting Message went something like this (explanations are in parentheses): **Mudcat driver to CO APO520** (My airplane was named The Fighting Mudcat. APO520 was the 15th Air Force.)

150 Yanks are in Yugo, some sick. Shoot us workhorses. (The workhorse of the US Air Force was the C-47. We hoped the literal-minded Germans would picture executing old dobbin.)

Our challenge first letter of bombardier's last name, color of Banana Nose's scarf. Your authenticator last letter of chief lug's name, color of fist on wall. (The challenge and authenticator were to be done with signal lights and could be transmitted ground-to-air or air-to-ground so that each party would know they were dealing with the right people. Banana Nose was Sam Benign, a pilot in our squadron who wore a white scarf. The commander of the 459th Bomb Group, Col. Munn, once wrote on the wall of the officers' club at our base "Each lug in the 459th sign here" and the signed "M. M. Munn, Chief Lug". The fist on the was a red fist on the club wall, part of the 15th Air Force emblem.)

Must refer to shark squadron, 459th Bomb Group for decoding. (Our squadron had shark teeth painted on the noses of our B-24s.)

Signed, TKO, Flat Rat 4 in lug order. (My tent mates and I back at our base called our tent "poker flat". When I signed on the wall below Col. Munn's signature, I had signed "T. K. Oliver, Flat Rat 4".)

This message was sent by a Yugoslav radio operator and picked up by a British operator in Italy. Eventually it came to Walt Cannon, who was then the CO of the 756th Squadron. He deciphered it and recognized it as genuine. This led to a reply which we got from the 15th Air Force Hq.

Someone in the escape and evasion office of 15th AF Hq. had a great idea. They asked us to transmit our longitude and latitude, coded by adding the numbers to my radio operator's serial number. This we of course did. The task leads to a digression in my story. I had to get longitude and latitude off some German maps which the Yugoslavians had. The Germans did not use Greenwich as the reference point for longitude. They used Berlin. I had to figure out a conversion. I remember that at West Point I thought the two most useless things I had to learn were: (1) How to ride a horse, and (2) How to use all the ground-troop type contour maps. After all, the only thing I would need would be aeronautical charts. In Yugoslavia, what do you suppose were two of the most valuable things I had learned at West Point?

This leads to my small world story. About the time we were sending longitude and latitude to Italy I ran across my West Point roommate, Leo C. Brooks, in Yugoslavia. He had been shot down flying a B-17.

Using the serial number code, 15th AF sent us a message saying what day and hour an OSS team would be dropped in to join us. It was about midnight and I remember the beautiful silhouette of a C-47 against the sky. The team was led by George Muslim, an American of Serbian parentage who spoke the language well.

He had an assistant who also spoke the language and a radio operator. They were equipped with radio, code books, and everything necessary to arrange the evacuation.

The Chetniks prepared a short sod-covered runway along the top of a hill. I paced it off taking short steps to be as optimistic as possible about its length. I got 600 yards. The Chetniks filled holes with dirt and stones and tamped it all down by hand.

The evacuation started about midnight on August 10, 1944. C-47s landed, one at a time. The firs took off before the second landed. We sent out sick and wounded first. After that whoever had been in Yugoslavia longest had priority. I was scheduled for the third airplane. The first got off nicely. The second went off the end of the strip and disappeared into the valley below. Fortunately it climbed out again. As we got on the airplane most of us threw our shows out as a parting gift to the Yugoslavs who had risked their lives for us. We had to admire those people. They had something hard to explain. For lack of better words I will call it character and integrity.

I was told the evacuation continued into daylight hours the next morning. Some P-51s flew cover in daylight. I know that there were several ME-109s at a field at Kraljevo not far from the evacuation strip. I saw them there at one time. Evidently they wisely chose to stay on the ground.

As it turned out, about 250 of us were evacuated and flown back to Italy. Back at 15th AF Hq. in Bari, Italy, we were deloused and all our remaining clothes were burned. We were issued a set of khakis and given orders to return to the U. S. via the next convoy. So ends our Yugoslavian tale.

One postscript might be added. Our tail gunner, Edgar Smith, hit his head getting out of the airplane. He evidently had sense enough to pull the ripcord, but he remembered nothing until he woke up lying on the ground. He used to complain about a sore neck. We suggested he have another drink of racchia, the potent local plum brandy. After we returned to the U. S. he wrote me that on the occasion of his mustering out physical exam, his neck was X-rayed. He had had a cracked vertebra. I am just as glad that we did not know about it at the time. THE END[517]

German POWs

At the end of WW II there were nearly 400,000 German POWs in the United States. The main base camp for surrounding states was in Algona, Iowa, with branches in Minnesota, North Dakota, South Dakota, and Iowa. The exact number of POWs housed in Sioux Falls is not known. The records at the National Archives show the number was between 174 and 218. They were held at the Sioux Falls Army Air Base from August to November of 1945.[518]

A POW's Personal Story

Erich Glowania had been drafted into the German Army at age 17. He became a prisoner after D-Day. Erich was relieved to be held by the Americans. He no longer faced hunger on a daily basis. The U.S. followed the Geneva Convention relating to prisoners of war. It states that prisoners must be given the same amount and quality of food as civilians in the host country. After landing in New York and being processed, he was put on a train to Algona, Iowa. In Europe Erich had traveled in box cars. He was pleasantly surprised to ride in a Pullman car in his own seat. After being placed in a camp, he worked for farmers de-tasseling corn and harvesting grain and potatoes.[519]

POWs worked at a variety of jobs. Because of the war, farmers were short of help. The War Manpower Commission approved a request from east river farmers to employ POWs during the fall harvest. In 1945 prisoners from the camp at Ortonville, Minnesota, worked for farmers in Grant and Roberts counties in South Dakota. Others worked in meat packing plants and logging operations. They did their own laundry and laundry that was trucked in from camps in Iowa and Minnesota. Between 100 and 125 were sent to Yankton and worked to stabilize the shoreline along the Missouri river. They slept in a hangar at the Chan Gurney Airport and were there from April to July of 1945.[520]

Louis Baete, one of the founders of Baete-Forseth Inc., was working in the sheet metal department at the air base in Sioux Falls. He remembered POWs being in the area where he worked.[521] Harvey Gildemeister was fifteen in 1945. He had a part-time job selling the *Minneapolis Tribune*. A bicycle was his mode of transportation. He remembered seeing POWs mowing grass and cutting weeds around the barracks. They were dressed in denim uniforms with PW on their backs.[522]

In 1951 Dan Peterson was putting up hay on land that was formerly part of the air base in Sioux Falls. Curt Eggers wanted to buy some of the hay. When Curt went to check it out, Dan offered to show him the graves of German POWs. The crosses had German names on them. The graves were along the banks of the Big Sioux River. The graves can no longer be located.[523]

A museum in Algona, Iowa, dedicated to preserving the history of the POW camps opened in 2004. It covers the time period of 1944 to 1946. A model of the camp, POW uniforms, and chairs built by the prisoners are among the artifacts on display.[524]

German POWs in Western South Dakota

POWS were sent from a base camp at Fort Robinson, Nebraska, to a branch camp at the former CCC barracks at Orman Dam. Some worked in the sugar beet fields near Belle Fourche. A few worked on Jack Rathburn's near Nisland. David Rathburn was a boy at the time. He rode in the truck when prisoners were picked up and then returned to their barracks. A group was sent to Sturgis. Their job was to help remodel Fort Meade, a former military post, into a veteran's hospital. Another group went to Newell and Vale where they worked in the sugar beet and potato fields.[525]

In 1943 the prisoners were still confident that Germany would win the war. They refused to believe what the guards were telling them about the war. Their attitudes began to change when POWs arrived who had been captured after D-Day. They told them how the war was going for Germany. By Christmas of 1945 most of the German POWs in South Dakota had returned to their homeland.[526]

South Dakota's Connection to Two Atomic Bombs

Ernest Lawrence of Canton developed the cyclotron or "atom smasher" that led to the development of the atomic bomb. He was awarded the Nobel Prize in 1939 for his work. An element, Lawrencium, was named after him.[527]

Myron Domsitz graduated from Washington High School and Augustana College. He was attending the University of Iowa in a program to earn a doctorate in physics prior to working for the government. Myron was employed by the National Bureau of Standards in the ordinance development division. Myron was part of a group that developed a radio proximity fuse. Once the atomic bomb was dropped from the plane, the fuse picked up radio waves, causing it to detonate and the bomb to explode. The fuse, smaller than a pack of cigarettes, helped us to win the war.[528]

A Civilian POW and the 2nd Atomic Bomb

The depression and drought led Harold Bridgman to a job with the CCC in Pierre. The project was to create a state park on Farm Island. In search of another job Harold and a friend from Witten, Merle Williams, headed west to look for jobs in the orchards of Washington and Oregon. Always looking for a better job and pay, they heard about a construction company in Idaho that was looking for workers. Morrison-Knutson needed workers for a job in the South Pacific. Wake Island was advertised as a tropical paradise. It didn't take long for Harold and Merle to sign up, and on May 23, 1941, they were on their way. Harold's job was operating a dredge in the harbor.

Everything changed on December 7, 1941. Japanese bombers brought death and destruction to the island. The Marines and sailors, along with some civilians, kept the Japanese at bay for two weeks. Their resistance became legendary. A television movie in 2003, "Wake Island Alamo of the Pacific", tells their story.

The Americans surrendered on December 23,1942, and a civilian worker from South Dakota became a POW. In a matter of weeks most of the POWs were sent to a camp in China. Harold was part of a group allowed to stay. They were supposed to teach the Japanese how to operate the heavy equipment. The Americans tried to limit their instruction and sabotage the equipment whenever possible. They had to be careful as the penalty for sabotage was death. Harold and his fellow POWs were forced to watch when a POW was beheaded. The POW had been warned several times not to break into the area where the alcohol was stored but did not the warnings.

Harold was fortunate to be among more than two hundred POWs who were sent to the Japanese island of Kyushu in October of 1942. They were assigned to build a dam. In October of 1943, ninety-eight Americans who had been left behind were executed. On Kyushu, his standard ration per day was a small cup of uncooked rice. From time to time there might be a piece of vegetable or spoiled fish mixed in. Grasshoppers added protein when they could be caught. The poor diet led to death from starvation and beriberi. Gary

Rogde from Philip worked on the dam with Harold. Gary helped bury fifty-eight of their fellow POWs near the dam.

Harold had been moved to a camp a few miles from Nagasaki. He was preparing rice for Japanese officers when he saw a bomb descending, and in a split second there was a flash of light. The concussion knocked him down, and a hot wind took his breath away. It was August 9, 1945, and Nagasaki was destroyed.

Harold returned home and married Margaret Worcester in 1947. He continued to experience tragedy throughout his life. His wife of twenty-two years died of cancer. His son Scott, his daughter-in-law, and two grandchildren died in a car crash near Sioux City, Iowa. His son Barry said that his dad was a hard worker, a good provider, and interested in their school activities. He did not complain about the circumstances of his life. Harold lived the rest of his life near Witten. Harold died of natural causes on August 9, 2007. He had seen the atomic bomb go off sixty-two years earlier.[529]

A South Dakota Casualty on the Last Day of the War

Ronald Williams was born on East 6th St. in Sioux Falls. He graduated from Washington High School in 1939. Ronald and Phyllis McCormick were married in 1943. He worked for the U.S. Postal Service and at the John Morrell plant prior to entering the military. Ronald was trained to be a paratrooper. He was assigned to the 11th Airborne Division. Ronald perished when his plane hit a mountain on Okinawa. The date was August 13, 1945, the last day of the war. He is buried in a military cemetery on the island of Oahu, Hawaii. Ronald was awarded a Purple Heart.[530]

The Fields Family of Egan

Ord and Anna Fields lived in Egan. Three of their sons—Lyle, Lloyd, and Dale—served in WW II. They were all in the military at the same time.

Lyle enlisted in the Army and fought in New Guinea. Lyle, like many veterans, never talked about his experiences.

Lloyd enlisted in the Army. He was with an artillery unit that was part of the 29th Infantry Division. The 29th was known as the "Blue and Gray" Division. Lloyd was with his unit from D-Day through the Battle of the Bulge. One war story that he related to his nephew, Doug Fields, was about fox holes. His artillery unit followed the infantry who had already dug fox holes, so they just used the ones that were there. The fox holes were covered with wood and dirt for protection. The Germans set their artillery shells to explode in the air so that shrapnel would hit the ground and Soldiers if they were not protected. Lloyd stayed in the Army after the war ended. He was assigned to guard German POWs until they were released. Lloyd collected German artifacts that he brought back with him. A German luger and holster were among the items given to the Museum in Flandreau.

Dale graduated from Egan High School in 1944 and enlisted in the Navy. He took his basic training in San Diego. He was assigned to the USS Santee, CVE-29, an aircraft carrier. The ship had been an oil tanker before it was converted to an aircraft carrier. All Dale's service time was on the USS Santee. The ship and its crew were in a war zone for two hundred and seventy-five days. They fought in the Battle of Leyte Gulf, Okinawa, and other major battles in the Pacific.

The USS Santee was the first naval ship to be hit in a Kamikaze attack. It was also torpedoed by the Japanese. Several Sailors and airmen died in the attacks, and many others were injured.

The USS Santee picked up over four hundred survivors of the Bataan Death March. They were being held on the island of Formosa. Every Sailor had to adopt a survivor and help with showering, shaving, and getting the lice off. Dale adopted a Scottish Soldier. He was six feet tall and weighed between one hundred and one hundred—twenty pounds.

When the POWs first came abroad, they were given limited amounts of food. If they were given too much, they might die. This lesson was learned earlier in the war when POWs and survivors from the death camps had been given too much too soon. As their bodies adjusted, the survivors were gradually given more. They were on the ship about two weeks. Their destination was the Philippines. When Dale went ashore, he had not been on land for two hundred and seventy-five days.

All three brothers returned to the United States.[531]

A Japanese Balloon Bomb that Changed the Lives of a Sioux Falls Family Forever

The date was May 5, 1945. Elyse Mitchell and her husband, The Reverend Archie Mitchell, were living in Bly, Oregon. He was the pastor of the Christian Alliance Church. Elyse was from Sioux Falls. They had planned a Sunday picnic to Gearhart Mountain. The area was covered with a pine forest that was owned by the Weyerhaeuser Timber Company.

Elyse was in the fifth month of her pregnancy and had been dealing with morning sickness. Archie wasn't sure she wanted to go on the picnic. She had baked a chocolate cake, and the weather was good on Sunday, so she decided to go. They picked five members of the church youth group — Dick Patzke (14), Joan Patzke (13), Jay Gifford (13), Eddie Engen (13), and Sherman Shoemaker (11)— to go with them. At the camp site Archie saw what he first thought was a pile of snow but upon closer inspection decided it wasn't snow. The kids found the object and were told not to bother it. Nobody knows for sure what caused the bomb to explode, but one of the youths may have kicked it. Elyse and the five kids died from the explosion. They were the only American civilians to die from a Japanese attack in the Continental United States.

Why Did This Happen?

The development of the balloon bomb was a response to Doolittle's surprise attack on Japanese cities.

How Did This Happen?

The balloons were made of silk and paper. They were filled with hydrogen and could float 6,000 miles by using high altitude air currents. The heat of the day caused the hydrogen to expand, and a balloon would rise. As the air cooled at night, the ballast was released, enabling a balloon to stay at an altitude of at least 30,000 feet. When a balloon reached the U.S., the ballast was gone, and a bomb was released. Approximately 1,000 devices reached the U.S. In seventeen states 120 balloon recoveries were made. States along the west coast recorded the most. South Dakota recorded eight.

In 2002, on the 57th anniversary of the explosion, three members of the Baldwin family were together and talked about the aunt they never knew. Siblings Vanessa Boy, Brad Baldwin, and Carl Baldwin were all living in Sioux Falls.

In August of 1950, the Weyerhaeuser Timber Company had a stone monument placed at the site of the explosion.[532]

Letters About the War, Revealed Many Years Later

Gilbert "Gib" Bohlman was raised in Ramona in Lake County, He was drafted in 1944 at the age of 26. He trained at Fort Snelling and Fort Hood in Texas. Gilbert was sent to the Pacific in February of 1945. His wife, Macky, and their three-year-old daughter, Pattie, lived in the Whittier neighborhood on East Fourth St. The streets were gravel then. Pattie remembers that Western Union couriers riding bicycles delivered the news of war casualties. When they heard the sound of a bicycle on gravel, silence descended on the neighborhood.

Gib and Macky knew that his letters would be censored. So before he left, they created a code. The following tells how the code worked: "When he was in Saipan, he wrote, 'It's too bad John fell into the sow's pen.' That was our code. That's how I knew where he was," his wife said. During his time in the service Gilbert wrote 108 letters to Macky. She put the letters away as she thought they were too personal and private to share.

Gib was a typical veteran. After returning home, he got a job. Gib and Macky raised six children. He did not talk about his war experiences for a long time. Gilbert passed away in June of 2001 at age 83.

Sixty years after they were written, Macky brought out the letters and began to share them with their children. Gib had served on Luzon, Mindoro, Mindanao, and Okinawa. The letters revealed what he had gone through. Gib described marching through the mud, drinking water from holes created by artillery shells, and sleeping in tombs on Okinawa that the locals had dug into the sides of hills.

The tombs contained urns with ashes in them. One day he crawled up to the top of a ridge, and when he looked over, he saw a battlefield covered with bodies from a previous battle. Dead Japanese Soldiers had been left on the hillsides. If a Soldier slipped and slid down a hill, his clothes would be covered with maggots when he hit the bottom.

Gib was on Mindoro when he was assigned a gruesome task. He, along with others, had to remove the bodies of Americans from a mass grave. The bodies were to be reburied in the U.S. He thought that most of the men were Navy pilots. It was the worst thing he had to do. The smell lingered with him many years.

Only in the last years of his life did Gib talk to his family about his war experiences. The family was grateful for the letters. They understood why their mother had kept them hidden away. They understood why their father had not wanted to talk about his war experiences.[533]

Medal of Honor Recipients

Woodrow Wilson Keeble was a member of the Sisseton-Wahepton Oyate Tribe and his birthplace was Waubay. Scouts for the Chicago White Sox were trying to recruit him because of his pitching ability when WWII called. He became a member of the North Dakota 164th Infantry Regiment. The unit fought on Guadalcanal and Keeble was awarded both a Purple Heart and a Bronze Star for his actions. Keebler volunteered for duty when war broke out in Korea. When asked why he volunteered, his response was "somebody had to teach these kids how to fight." He was assigned to George Company of the 24th Infantry Division. Heavy fighting took place near the town of Kumsong and Keeble sustained wounds on multiple days in October 1951. The doctors removed over 70 pieces of shrapnel from a concussion grenade. Although his wounds were starting to show signs of infection and a medic advised against him fighting Keeble did not take the advice. He led his men up the mountain and on his own took out three enemy machine gun bunkers. He was recommended for the Medal of Honor twice but the paperwork was lost.

Keeble's men attempted to submit the recommendation a third time but officials informed them that it was too late because the 24th Division had reached its quota for Medal of Honor recipients. Senators from North and South Dakota worked for several years to make sure that Keeble was posthumously awarded the Medal the Honor. In May 2007, legislation was passed granting the Department of Defense authority to consider awarding Keeble the Medal of Honor. A White House ceremony was held on March 3, 2008 with President Bush presenting the Medal to Keeble's stepson Russell Hawkins. Keeble became the first full-blooded Sioux Indian to receive the nation's highest military award.[534]

Arlo Olson was born in Iowa and at the age of ten moved to South Dakota with his parents and sister. He graduated from Toronto High School in 1936 and enrolled at the University of South Dakota where he was a member of the Reserve Officers Training Corps. (ROTC) until he graduated in 1940. The United States was not at war when Olson enlisted in the Army. His ROTC training earned him the rank of Second Lieutenant. His leadership abilities were obvious and he was promoted to First Lieutenant and then Captain. Arlo's military training took him to Louisiana where he met and married Myra Bordeaux of Baton Rouge on Christmas Day of 1942. Their time together was limited to a few months and he never saw his daughter, Myra (Sandra) Lavern Olson who was born in December 1943. Arlo's first combat experience came on October 13, 1943 when he led his company across the Volturno River in Italy. The water was up to his chest and a machine gun was firing directly at him. He made it across and used two hand grenades to silence the machine gun crew. For the next thirteen days Captain Olson and his men attacked the enemy. Captain Olson was wounded on October 27, 1943 but refused medical treatment until the medic had taken care of all the men under his command and he did not survive the trip down the mountain. Captain Olson was buried in Minneapolis, Minnesota and the American Legion Post #81 in Toronto bears his name. A ceremony was held in his honor in Toronto on June 20, 1999.[535]

CHAPTER 6

Major Battles of the War

D-Day and Beyond

The invasion of Europe began on June 6, 1944. The planning had begun in 1943. Thousands of American troops had been stationed in England. They had spent their time training, frequenting British pubs, and waiting, some patiently and some impatiently, for the day to come. When Eisenhower decided it was time to go, over 13,000 troops from the 82nd and 101st Airborne Divisions parachuted into the darkness of June 6th. The 82nd was assigned to block movements of enemy reinforcements. The 101st was assigned to destroy bridges that could be used by the Germans and secure those that could be used by the Allies.[536]

Ralph Aljets farmed with his parents prior to enlisting in the Army in 1942. He was assigned to the 29th Infantry Division and sent overseas. Ralph was in the second wave that went ashore on D-Day. He was wounded and died that day. He is buried at Fort Snelling.[537]

Fred Baker entered the Army in March of 1942. He was serving as an instructor at the base in Nashville, Tennessee. He volunteered for overseas duty and was shipped to England. Fred was a member of the 8th Infantry Regiment, 4th Infantry Division. He was killed in combat in France on July 24, 1944. Fred is buried in Brittany American Cemetery at St. James, France.[538]

Roland Becker was working in Chicago when he met Beulah Harrison from Virginia. They were married in October of 1942. Roland was drafted in February of 1943. After completing basic training, he was sent to England where he trained for D-Day. Roland landed on Omaha Beach on June 7th and was wounded on the 8th. He returned to duty on June 20th. While he was recuperating, nearly 100 percent of his company had been wounded, killed in combat, or taken prisoner. There are about 100 troops in a company. After winning the battle of St.-Lo, Roland's company was sent to Brest, France. The Germans had submarine pens there. His unit was assigned to take the facility. Roland was wounded again and died on September 17, 1944. He left behind his widow, Beulah.[539]

Robert Benson joined the Army in November of 1942. He volunteered for paratrooper duty. After basic training he was sent to North Ireland and then to England. He was a member of the 508th Parachute Infantry Regiment that was part of the 82nd Division. Robert's regiment parachuted over Normandy. He was injured during the invasion and died from his wounds on June 11, 1944. Robert is buried in Normandy American Cemetery.[540]

William Bird Horse enlisted in the Army. He died in action on June 11, 1944, at Sainte-Mère-Église. His remains were returned and buried at the Long Hill Cemetery west of Wakpala.[541]

Woodrow Blase had seven siblings. He farmed with his father before entering military duty in January of 1942. He trained at several locations and went overseas in October of 1943. Woodrow was part of the invasion force on D-Day. He was an ambulance driver in the 23rd Infantry Regiment. His unit was engaging the Germans near Murriagen, Belgium, on February 11, 1945. Because of intense enemy fire Woodrow was ordered to abandon his ambulance. Later he braved continued enemy fire to return to his ambulance and drive it to safety. Woodrow was awarded a citation for his bravery. Five days later Woodrow was wounded and died. He was buried in Belgium. At the request of his family his remains were returned and buried in the United States.[542]

Leon Boes was born on the family farm near Herrick in Gregory County. He had seven siblings. Leon worked on the family farm until he was drafted on December 9, 1941. He reported for duty in February of 1942. Leon met Joyce Zimmer when he was in training. They were married in November of 1942. They had a daughter, Bonnie Lynn. Leon was part of the 8th Infantry Division when he was sent to England. He went ashore on Utah Beach and was wounded on June 6th. He returned to his unit and was fighting at St.-Lo when American bombs were dropped on his unit. Leon died from friendly fire. It was July 24, 1944. His remains were returned on January 13, 1948, and buried in Herrick. His daughter was ten months old when Leon died.[543]

Wayne Collins volunteered for military duty. He trained at several locations and went overseas in December of 1943. His unit went ashore on D-Day. They continued to fight the enemy through France, Belgium, and on into Germany. Wayne was in Germany when he died in combat.[544]

Charles Cooper farmed with his parents until he enlisted in the Army in 1939. He was stationed at Camp Meade in South Dakota. Charles would have been discharged in January of 1942, but Pearl Harbor changed his plans. In 1943 Charles was sent to Texas where he and Margaret Peterson were married. They had a daughter, Sharon. Charles never got to see her. In England Charles became part of the 4th Cavalry Reconnaissance Squadron. He went ashore on Normandy and was killed on the beach. It was June 18,

1944. Charles was returned in June of 1949 and buried in Faulkton.[545]

Glenn Cox reported for duty in December of 1943. He shipped out for England in February of 1944. He was attached to the 119th Infantry Regiment of the 30th Infantry Division. Glenn's division landed on Omaha Beach where they suffered heavy losses. The division moved off the beach head and pushed the Germans deep into France. The official notice from the War Department stated that Glenn had died in combat on March 31, 1945. Glenn is buried at Netherlands American Cemetery, Margraten, Netherlands.[546]

John Curtis Jr. was drafted in 1942. He was sent to Africa, then to Sicily, and on to England. John landed on Normandy on June 6th. He died in combat on June 9th. His remains were returned in 1947 and buried at Fort Snelling. He left behind his widow, Mildred, and a daughter who had been born in May of 1944. John never got to see her.[547]

Albert Estes joined the military and was assigned to the 502nd Parachute Infantry Regiment that was part of the 101st Airborne Division. He died in combat on June 7, 1944. Albert is buried in Normandy American Cemetery.[548]

Julius Davis had ten siblings. He joined the Army in March of 1942 and was sent to England in March of 1944. Julius was assigned to the 358th Infantry Regiment, 90th Infantry Division. A sniper took his life near Sainte-Mère-Église, France, on June 16, 1944. His remains were returned in May of 1948 and buried at Gracehill Cemetery in Tripp. Two of his brothers, Harold and Francis, were also in the 90th Division.[549]

Jake Den Ouden entered the military in July of 1942. He was sent overseas in 1944 as part of the 357th Infantry Regiment, 90th

Infantry Division. Jake died in action on June 12th in Normandy. He is buried in Normandy American Cemetery.[550]

Bennie DeWitt enlisted in the Army in July of 1942. He was sent to Africa where he fought in the Tunisian Campaign and in the invasion of Sicily. His next assignment was to England where he trained for D-Day. He was killed during D-Day.[551]

Glen Dow joined the service in June of 1943 and went overseas in March of 1944. He was a rifleman in the 116th Infantry Regiment that was part of the 29th Infantry Division. He went ashore on Omaha Beach. Glen was moving up the beach when he stepped on a land mine and died before he could be evacuated to a field hospital. Glen is buried in Normandy American Cemetery.[552]

Anton Elvesaeter was born in Trondheim, Norway, in 1906. When he was in his late teens, he came to America and lived with his uncle. Anton changed his name to Tony Sather. After the Germans invaded his homeland, Tony enlisted in the Army and became a naturalized citizen. In England he trained with a hook and ladder unit. The Isle of Marcouf is located close to Utah Beach. Tony, along with other Rangers, was assigned to secure the island so that troop transports could get closer to shore and avoid enemy fire. There were mines on the island. During their cliff approach, a mine exploded, killing Tony. There is a marker for him in Normandy American Cemetery.[553]

John Fjeseth entered military duty in June of 1942. In October of 1942 he was sent overseas as a member of the 175th Infantry Regiment in the 29th Infantry Division. He went ashore on D-Day and was killed on June 12th. John is buried in Insigny, France.[554]

Theodore Hanson graduated from South Dakota State College in 1943. Theodore and Evangeline Prange were married in Brookings in that same year. He was a second lieutenant in the

Infantry and was sent overseas in April of 1944. He died in Normandy on July 15, 1944. Theodore's final resting place is in Parkway Cemetery in Brookings.[555]

Harvey Henle was born in Sioux Falls and graduated from Washington High School in 1936. He joined the military in March of 1942. Harvey was trained as a paratrooper and became part of an Infantry Airborne Division. He died in combat on June 16, 1944. His remains were returned to Sioux Falls and buried in St. Michael's Cemetery. He left behind his widow, Elida.[556]

Joseph Henry Jr. enlisted in the Army in April of 1943. He trained at Fort Benning, Georgia. and was assigned to the 505th Parachute Infantry Regiment, part of the 82nd Division. He went overseas in December of 1943. Joseph was wounded on D-Day and died on June 8th. He is buried in Normandy American Cemetery.[557]

Elder Herman was born in 1919. He had eight brothers and three sisters. Elder joined the military on March 27, 1942. After basic training he was assigned to the 358th Infantry Regiment, 90th Infantry Division. He landed in France on June 10, 1944. A sniper took his life six days later on the 16th. Elder is buried in Normandy American Cemetery.[558]

George Hevlin was from Tuthill in Bennett County. He joined the military in October of 1943. After basic training he was sent to France. He died in combat on June 19, 1944.[559]

Charles Joslin was born in 1923 and enlisted in the Army in 1942. He was sent overseas as part of the 58th Armored Field Artillery Battalion, 8th Armored Division. Charles was serving in France when he was killed in combat on June 6, 1944. He is buried in Normandy American Cemetery.[560]

Edwin Larson was born in 1917. He had nine siblings. Edwin was drafted in 1942. He served at a camp in Texas until his division, the 90th, was called to active duty in March of 1944. Edwin landed on Utah Beach where he was wounded on June 14th and died the next day. His remains were returned and buried in the Vivian cemetery.[561]

William McCormick entered the military in June of 1942. He attended Officers Candidate School and became a second lieutenant. He was promoted to first lieutenant and sent overseas in May of 1944. William was in the 119th Infantry Division. William and three other soldiers were in a jeep that drove over a land mine on the 6th of June. His body was returned and buried in St. Stephen's Catholic Cemetery in Bridgewater. William left behind his widow, Maxine, and his daughter, Mary, who was born after he died.[562]

Walter Moran joined the military after Pearl Harbor. After basic training he was assigned to a tank battalion. His tank unit landed on Normandy on June 9th. Walter's tank was hit by enemy fire, and his body was not found.[563]

Harold Morgen was born in Mellette in Spink County. The year was 1908. He farmed with his brother prior to military duty. He joined the service in 1942 and was sent to France. Harold died in combat on June 14, 1944. He is buried in Calvary Catholic Cemetery near Mellette.[564]

Raymond Oehler graduated from South Dakota State College in 1943. Raymond and Alice Larson were married in 1942. He joined the military in 1943 and enrolled in Officers Candidate School. Upon graduation and becoming a second lieutenant, he volunteered for parachute school. He was sent to England with the 101st Airborne Division. On June 6th the 101st parachuted into France. Raymond landed safely and was in combat near Caretan, France, where he died from a sniper's bullet. His body was returned and buried in Milbank City Cemetery.[565]

Nels Peterson was born in Yale in Beadle County. He joined the Army in 1942 and after basic training was sent to England. Nels was part of an infantry unit that went ashore in France. He was wounded in combat on June 15th and died from his wounds. Nels is buried in Normandy American Cemetery. He left behind his widow, Betty, and son, Jimmy.[566]

Elmer Reitz was from Ralph in Harding County. He enlisted in the Army in May of 1941. After basic training he attended Officers Candidate School in Virginia. He became a second lieutenant and went to Normoyle Ordinance School in Texas. Elmer was promoted to first lieutenant and was sent to England in 1943. Elmer was a member of the 207th Engineer Combat Battalion. Elmer died in combat on June 19, 1944.[567]

Elmer Rusch served in the CCC until he enrolled at South Dakota State College. He was in the ROTC in 1941 and was trained at Fort Leonard Wood. Elmer was sent to England and was assigned to the 101st Airborne Division. He was in a glider plane that crash-landed on D-Day. He died in combat near Sainte-Mère-Église in France. Sainte-Mère-Église was one of the towns in the movie "The Longest Day" based on the book by the same name. He died on June 7th. Elmer left behind his widow, Mary, and two children. Elmer's body was returned and buried in Clark.[568]

Philip Stands entered military duty in 1943. He was assigned to the 502nd Parachute Infantry Regiment of the 101st Airborne Division. Philip was killed on June 6th. His remains were returned and buried at St. Francis Catholic Cemetery.[569]

George Sund was born in Iona in Tripp County. He did farm work in the Hamill area before enlisting in the Army. After basic training he was sent to Germany and assigned to the 358th Infantry Regiment of the 90th Infantry Division. His unit was in combat in Normandy when he died on June 16, 1944. After the war his body was returned and buried in Winner cemetery.[570]

George Voelsch was born in Hartford in 1918. He had five brothers and four sisters. George farmed with his brother Willie before entering the service. He enlisted in the Army in 1943. George was sent to the European Theatre as part of the 29th Infantry Division. George was in France on June 11, 1944, when he and another soldier were sent ahead on scout duty. He was killed by a sniper near St.-Lo, France. He was buried overseas but was returned and buried at Mount Hope Cemetery in Watertown.[571]

The Following Went Ashore at Normandy and Survived

Leslie Boner of Wagner went ashore on Omaha Beach. He and his fellow Soldiers came face to face with pill boxes, encountered land mines, and were exposed to artillery fire. The dead and wounded floated in the water and lay on the beach. Every Soldier was trying to survive, fight the enemy, get ammunition ashore, and get the injured to boats and taken to hospital ships.

Myron Abraham was part of the second assault wave on Omaha Beach. A boat near his took a direct hit, and everybody perished. When he left his boat, the water was up to his neck. Myron manned a machine gun and carried 150 pounds on his back. He left the beach and crawled up a hill. John Jensen of Sioux Falls was on a boat with what was supposed to be amphibious tanks. When the tanks hit the water, they sank. The crews had to swim to shore. John made it to shore, through a mine field, and to safety at the top of a hill.

Nelson Lagendyk of Avon was a glider pilot. His glider held a Jeep, machine guns, ammunition for a 57 MM gun, men from the 82nd Airborne Division, and his co-pilot. The total weight of the cargo was about 8,000 pounds. As they were being towed over the beachhead by a C-47 cargo plane, they could see Allied troops going ashore. His glider was scheduled to land about ten miles behind enemy lines near Sainte-Mère-Église. They hit the ground hard and were greeted by machine gun fire.

Jerald Swartz of Chester served on a merchant ship, M.S. Potter. His ship, along with several others, was sunk to create an artificial harbor. They did stay on board five days and manned antiaircraft guns. When he returned to Omaha Beach in September, no signs of the ships remained. Some of the crew went ashore to play ball, but went sightseeing instead. Two died when they stepped on land mines.

Al Shock of Sioux Falls went ashore on June 6th. The beach was littered with trucks, tanks, and other vehicles that had been destroyed in the initial landing.

George Wallenstein of Sioux Falls landed on Normandy three days after D-Day. His most vivid memory was of bodies and body parts covering the beach.

Oliver Carlson of Beresford was on a Liberty ship when dawn broke on June 6th. His ship was in the middle of the action. Bomber and fighter planes were overhead, some of which were being shot down. Ships were being hit and sinking. Battleships several miles off shore were firing 2,000 pound shells to soften up the enemy for the landing on Utah Beach. He saw dead soldiers in the water and on shore. They were under constant fire by the Germans. Oliver was sent ashore in a truck pulling a 105 Howitzer gun. Their job was to lay down an artillery barrage ahead of the infantry.

C.N. Fath of Elkton was in the second wave to go ashore on Utah Beach. They did not encounter any opposition as the first wave had cleared the way. When they reached the town of Sainte-Mère-Église, it was vacant. There was evidence that the locals had left in the middle of a meal. The hedgerows of rural Normandy were mounds of dirt covered with vegetation that divided farmer's fields.

They provided cover for the Germans and were hard to get around. Tanks were modified and became bulldozers to penetrate the hedgerows. His unit was encircled in the Battle of Bulge. Their second enemy became the cold weather.

Glenn Jespersen of Wagner was part of the second wave to go ashore. He was with an engineer company that built bridges. Glenn served under Generals Bradley, Patton, and McAuliffe.

Orval Sievers of Canton was part of a 90mm gun crew whose job was to destroy enemy tanks. He was below deck on a LST landing craft as it crossed the English Channel. Orval did not see daylight until the doors opened on Omaha Beach. He was greeted by the sight of body parts on the shore. There were many American and German planes dueling for control of the skies.[572]

The Lives of Duane Miller, Howard Wood, Bob Burns, and Ben Rossow Before, During, and After the War

Duane "Stub" Miller was eighteen when he left Canova and entered the military. He was a replacement in a unit that had suffered a lot of casualties on D-Day. As he went ashore on Omaha Beach, he encountered unburied American soldiers who had died on D-Day. Duane was wounded near St.-Lo on July 29, 1944. He was sent to London to recuperate. He had just turned nineteen. Duane returned to his unit and fought across Europe until the war ended. It was 1946 when he returned to South Dakota.

Duane spent his entire life in and around Canova. Duane and Marcella raised nine children. He was instrumental in starting The Canova Gang Amateur Baseball team. Duane was involved in baseball many years and was elected to the South Dakota Baseball Hall of Fame.

Duane, like many veterans, had nightmares for years, and most of his memories about the war were not good. He could still recall the odor of decomposing bodies and the destruction of farms and villages. He was still saddened by the loss of six members of his unit to a sniper in one day, by the sight of an enemy Soldier dying when he was hit-point blank by a shell from a tank. He could not watch the movie "Saving Private Ryan" as it brought back bad memories. One good memory of the war was the generosity of the French people who brought wine to the Soldiers.

For many years he had not given much thought to returning to France. His son Ed convinced Duane after some persuasion to return to Europe. They went with a reunion group from the 29th Division. While Ed was planning the trip, he discovered that Duane's military service met the requirements for the French Legion of Honour. Ed filed the paper work, and Duane became a Knight in the Legion of Honour. The medal arrived in June of 2012.[573]

Howard Wood of Sioux Falls was twenty-two when he went ashore on Omaha Beach on June 6, 1944. He had made it to the hedgerows beyond the beach when shrapnel ripped open his stomach. Howard was seriously wounded when he heard one of his fellow soldiers say, "He's a goner", but as they were leaving, one of his fingers twitched. Howard survived and returned to Sioux Falls. Howard and his wife had four daughters.[574]

Robert "Bob" G. Burns was born in Des Moines, Iowa, on February 8, 1921, and grew up in Sioux City, Iowa. He participated in the Golden Gloves boxing program and became a city champion. At Sioux City Central he played fullback and was honored with a place on the All City Team. Bob enrolled at the University of South Dakota and played football for coach Harry Gamage. During his junior year he led the North Central Conference in scoring. While attending USD he enrolled in the ROTC program. He graduated in 1942 and was commissioned a second lieutenant in the Army.

Bob was sent to Fort Benning, Georgia, for basic training. He volunteered to become a paratrooper, and he was further trained at Fort Bragg, North Carolina. He was assigned to the 502nd Parachute Infantry Regiment, which was part of the 101st Airborne Division. His unit parachuted into Normandy during the night before D-Day. As he was dropping into France, he was wounded. He also parachuted into Holland during Operation Market Garden. The weather prevented his unit from parachuting into the Battle of the Bulge. They had to be trucked in and dropped off the back of the trucks.

Bob was awarded several medals, including a Silver Star, two Bronze Stars, two Purple Hearts for wounds suffered in combat, the Croix de Guerre from Belgium for Bastogne, and the Orange Dutch Lanyard from Holland for Operation Market Garden.

Bob and Alice Drabeck of Winner had met at USD. They were married on December 1, 1945. Bob's first coaching job was at Yankton High School. In two seasons their won-loss record was 16-3-1. Two of those wins came at the expense of Washington High School. Bob was credited with starting the Quarterback Club in Yankton. Bob's next position was head football coach at Washington High in Sioux Falls. At one point the team enjoyed a 37 game winning streak.

Dr. L. M. Stavig, president of Augustana College, had taken note of Bob's coaching success. Augustana's football record for the previous season was 0-10. Bob was hired to turn the program around. In his first year Augustana defeated rivals USD and SDSU. The 1959 season brought the first North Central Conference Championship in the school's history. Bob returned to USD in 1962, but only coached one year as high blood pressure forced him to the sidelines.

Bob worked in private business and did television broadcasting for several years. He kept his hand in coaching with a Sioux Falls junior football league team. Meanwhile, new medications had been developed, and he was able to keep his blood pressure under control. He returned to coaching in 1976 at O'Gorman High School. They had not won a game the previous season. Bob was 53 when he coached the Knights to the first ever South Dakota High School football championship. Bob's legacy at O'Gorman is celebrated every year with the Dakota Bowl. Bob passed away in 2000 at age 79. He is buried at Arlington National Cemetery.[575]

Colonel Ben Rossow was born in Herreid in Campbell County in 1905. He graduated from the University of South Dakota. Ben taught German at Washington High School in Sioux Falls from 1933 to 1941.

Ben went ashore on Utah Beach. He was serving with General Patton's Army when he was wounded by a German hand grenade. A piece of shrapnel struck one of his legs. Ben was promoted to colonel in the field. He was awarded a Purple Heart and Silver Star. Ben's unit was the first to cross the Rhine river into Germany.

Upon returning to Sioux Falls, Ben served as Principal of Hawthorne Elementary during the 1946-1947 school year. Ben returned to Washington High School in the fall of 1947 as Assistant Principal and served in that position until he became Principal in the fall of 1958. He served in that capacity from 1958 to 1971. Ben retired in 1971. Ben was highly respected by the faculty. He passed away in 1980 at age 74.[576]

The following veterans did not want to relive the scenes that had brought them so close to death. Talking about the war might bring up the question of why they lived when the Soldier in front, beside, or behind them died.

Howard Wood had seen the Soldier in front of him die from an explosion.

Ray Brockhoft was in a jeep when enemy fired killed the Soldier next to him.

Oliver Carlson and another Soldier were taking a break. The Soldier next to him took his helmet off and almost instantly a sniper's bullet killed him.

There were not any counseling services available to veterans. They had to deal with their experiences in their own ways. Oliver Carlson of Beresford spent several weeks picking corn by hand by himself. His son Lee said he needed the time alone.

Wartime experiences manifested themselves later in life in different ways.

Ray Brockhoft of Winner was having a flashback late one night, and when his wife startled him, he threw her against the wall. She suffered some broken ribs.

Oris Hove of Beresford was milking a cow. The sound created by a woodpecker on the side of the barn took him back to a battle scene and the sound of machine gun fire. His survival instinct kicked in, and he ended up in the nearest hay stack. The bucket of milk was lost.[577]

A Surprise Attack that Resulted in Massive Casualties

The Battle of the Bulge started on December 16, 1944, and lasted into January of 1945.

In September of 1944 Hitler called a meeting of his generals. He announced there would be a counterattack starting in the Ardennes Forest with the main objective being the capture of Antwerp. The counterattack would divide Allied forces and provide the Germans with a much-needed port.[578] German Field Marshals Gerd von Lundstedt and Walter Model both objected to the plan. They did not agree with the timetable that Hitler had outlined and offered alternatives that were not heard. Model gave the plan a small chance of success.[579]

This location was selected as there were not many American troops defending the area, and it would conceal the buildup of troops, tanks, and artillery pieces.[580] The success of the attack would depend on surprise. Only the very top officials knew about the attack; several orders were given to keep it a secret. Troops could move only at night. There were not to be any fires during the day. Radios were to be silenced. Maps were not to be given out until the last minute. Officers were not to brief their troops until the evening of December 15th.

The surprise was aided by several factors on the Allied side. In November, there were rumors of an attack by forty-six divisions, some divisions being made up of 10,000 troops or more. The Allies did not believe the Germans could amass that many troops. A warning from German POWS went unheeded. The Allies held a common belief that an attack would not come before Christmas. They also thought that not enough fuel and ammunition would keep the Germans from mounting an attack. Air superiority was on the side of the Allies. Because the Americans did not believe an attack was imminent, they did not fly reconnaissance missions over the Ardennes. On December 14th a German-speaking woman reported on troop buildups behind enemy lines. There was no follow up on the report.[581]

The Surprise

When the attack started, there were not enough American forces in place, and they were too scattered out.[582] Poor phone communications between Major General Alan Jones and General Troy Middleton led to the surrender of 6,500 troops under Jones's command. It was one of the largest mass surrenders of U.S. troops in WW II.[583]

The Importance of Bastogne

Bastogne was located at the intersection of several roads. The main road was N15, and the Germans needed control of it and the town on their way to the Meuse River and then Antwerp.[584] By December 21st the Germans had surrounded the town. The 101st Airborne Division was cut off with no way out, and nobody could get in to help them. They were outnumbered and suffered many casualties before General Patton's Third Army broke through German lines on December 26th. The tenacity of the troops in the 101st is legendary.[585] The book *Those Who Hold Bastogne* vividly describes the intense fighting that took place in Bastogne and neighboring towns.

Factors that Led to a German Defeat

The Air Force played a significant role in defeating the Germans. C-47 cargo planes dropped thousands of tons of supplies, ammunition, medical supplies, food, and winter clothing. The P-47 Thunderbolt was a fighter- bomber. P-47 attacks destroyed hundreds of German tanks, anti-tank guns, transport vehicles, artillery pieces, and Soldiers. The Germans were afraid of the P-47 and its destructive power.[586] Most important was that the Germans had underestimated the will power of the American Soldiers in all units to fight on against all odds. Another factor was that the Germans ran out of fuel for their tanks.[587]

On January 16th the bulge was cut. General Patton's Third Army linked up with Lieutenant General Courtney Hodges's First Army at Houffalize, Belgium.

The battle for Bastogne took a heavy toll on both sides as a total of 45,000 troops were lost.

The Mardasson Memorial was dedicated in July of 1950. It is located on a hill northeast of Bastogne. It is a tribute to the American Soldiers who defended the Belgians against the Germans in December of 1944 and January of 1945. The American units that participated in the Battle of the Bulge are listed on supporting columns.[588]

The total casualties in the Battle of the Bulge were about equal. German losses, including those who died, were wounded, and were missing were around 80,000. The American forces suffered 75,482 causalities with 8,407 killed.[589]

South Dakotans Who Perished in the Battle of the Bulge

Arvid Anderson was born in Lilly in Day County. The year was 1918. He had eight brothers and sisters. Arvid enlisted in the Army in 1940. After basic training he was assigned to Troop B of the 4th Cavalry Reconnaissance Squadron. He went overseas in December of 1943. His unit was on a reconnaissance mission when they were attacked by a tank.[590]

On December 24 their vehicle was hit, and as he was pushing it, a mortar shell killed him.

Francis Anderson was born in 1915 in Moody County. He worked on the family farm until he was drafted in 1942. Francis trained in Kansas and Wisconsin. He was in the Second Division of the First Army. He was sleeping in a house near the front lines when it was struck by a bomb. Francis died, along with nine other Soldiers.

It was December 29th. His final resting place is in Nelson Cemetery northeast of Dell Rapids.[591]

Lloyd Belmont was born in 1918. His birthplace was Hill City in Pennington County. After high school graduation he attended auctioneer school and worked with his father's auctioneering business before entering the service. Lloyd and Corliss Jones were married before he was sent overseas. He never got to see his son. Lloyd was in combat in Belgium. Lloyd was a medic and was taking a Soldier to an aid station when he was killed on January 15th. Lloyd is buried in Luxembourg American Cemetery.[592]

Chris Jumping Bull was from Oglala in Shannon County. He was born in 1925 and joined the military in 1944. After basic training he was assigned to the 26th Infantry Division. His unit was fighting in Germany when the Battle of the Bulge erupted. They were sent to Belgium. Chris was killed in combat in Belgium on December 22nd. His remains were returned and buried at St. Peter Episcopal Cemetery.[593]

Robert Carlow was born in Hot Springs in 1921. He enlisted in the Army in 1939. He was part of the 507th Parachute Infantry Regiment. Robert experienced combat in the Aleutians. He was fighting in Germany when he died on January 8th. Robert is buried in Black Hills National Cemetery.[594]

Merlin Christiansen was from Gettysburg and graduated from high school in 1943. He enlisted in the Army the same year. After basic training he was assigned to the 394th Infantry Regiment of the 99th Division. He was in action in Belgium when he was killed on December 18th. Merlin is buried in Fort Snelling National Cemetery.[595]

Arnold Clements was born in Belle Fourche in 1907 and graduated from Deadwood High School in 1925. Arnold and his brother Kenneth owned and operated a Conoco gas station in Deadwood. Arnold was drafted in 1942 and completed basic training at Fort Leavenworth, Kansas. He was sent overseas in May of 1944 as a member of the 144th Infantry. His unit was in combat on December 16th in Luxembourg when he was killed. His body was returned and buried at Mt. Moriah Cemetery in Deadwood.[596]

James Crisp was born in Willow Lake in Clark County. His family moved to Ipswich where he attended high school. He entered the military in 1943. After basic training he was sent overseas in August of 1944. James was part of the 28th Infantry Division. He was killed in combat on December 20th in Germany. James was buried by the Germans.[597]

Quentin Eymer was born in 1922 in the farm home northwest of Reliance. He graduated from Reliance High School. Quentin enlisted in the Army Air Corps in 1942. He trained at Luke Field in Arizona where he earned his wings and became a second lieutenant. He completed combat training in Texas and Louisiana. Overseas, he was based in Nancy, France, with the 512th Fighter Squadron of the 100th Wing. Quentin was the pilot of a P-47 Thunderbolt fighter-bomber during the Battle of the Bulge. Quentin was on a mission over Bastogne when his plane was hit by antiaircraft fire, spun out of control, and crashed. It was December 22nd. His body was returned to the U.S. for burial.[598]

Henry Gleaner, Jr. was born on the family farm in Sully County. The year was 1910. He worked on the family farm from 1928 to 1933. Henry and Doris Dennis were married in February of 1944. Henry enlisted in the Army and became part of a tank unit. He died in combat on December 21st in Luxembourg. He left behind his widow.[599]

Robert Grosz was born in Tolstoy in Potter County. He graduated from high school in 1940. Robert fought in France and

Germany. He was with the 273rd Field Artillery Battalion. His unit was in combat in Luxembourg when he was killed during the Battle of the Bulge. Robert is buried in Luxembourg American Cemetery.[600]

Dominic Gruba was born in Grenville in Day County. He had four sisters and five brothers. Dominic farmed with his father and brothers until he enlisted in June of 1941. He was sent overseas as part of the 87th Calvary Reconnaissance Squadron. His unit was fighting in Belgium when he was wounded on December 23rd. He died from his wounds on January 11, 1945. His body was returned in 1949 and buried at Grenville. Dominic and Clara Sichmeller had been married in March of 1944.[601]

Harold Keller was born in Thomas in Hamlin County. He had seven brothers and sisters. Harold worked on the family farm until he was drafted in 1942. After basic training he was sent to France. He was a member of the 589th Field Artillery Battalion of the 106th Infantry Division. Harold's unit was in combat in Belgium when he died on December 17th. His body was returned in 1949 and buried at Mount Hope Cemetery in Watertown.[602]

Gerald Kerber was born in 1925. He had five sisters and four brothers. The family lived in Hand County. Gerald worked on the family farm until he enlisted in September of 1943. He was in the infantry. His unit was fighting in Belgium when he was killed on January 20, 1945. His body was returned and buried in Howell Cemetery in the Polo area of Hand County.[603]

Inar Lellelid was born in 1925 in Colman. He had three brothers and two sisters. He graduated from high school in 1943 and joined the military the same year. Inar trained in Texas and Kentucky before being sent overseas in October of 1944. He was a member of the 289th Infantry Regiment, 75th Infantry Division. Inar died in combat in Belgium on January 17, 1945.[604]

Francis Metz was born in Miranda in Faulk County. He graduated from Faulkton High School. Francis farmed with his father and brother. He was a rural mail carrier from 1940 to 1944. Francis and Betty Ford were married in 1940 and had a daughter, Virginia. He joined the military in 1944. After basic training he received further training in Maryland before going overseas. He was assigned to the 119th Infantry Regiment. His unit was fighting in Belgium when he was killed on December 21st. His remains were returned in 1947 and buried in Miranda.[605]

Milo Oihus was born in Sherman in Minnehaha County. He graduated from Washington High in Sioux Falls and Augustana College. Milo was a teacher and basketball coach before entering the service. Milo and Doris McKinney were married in 1941 and had a daughter, Marsha. He enlisted in the Army Air Corps in 1943. Milo trained in Kentucky and Texas before he was sent overseas with the 28th Infantry Division. His unit was in action on the border of Luxembourg and Germany when he was killed on December 20th. His body was returned in 1948 and buried in Sioux Falls.[606]

Robert Pennington graduated from Watertown High School in 1938. He became a member of the 134th Infantry Regiment, 35th Infantry Division. The 35th was part of General Patton's Third Army. Robert died in combat on December 29th. He is buried in Luxembourg American Cemetery.[607]

LaVern Redman was born in 1924 in Milbank. He entered the military in February of 1944. After basic training he became a member of the 56th Battalion of the 11th Armored Division. He went overseas in September of 1944. His unit was sent to Belgium in December of 1944. LaVern was killed by a sniper on January 18th. His body was returned and buried in Milbank.[608]

Robert Riddle was born in White Butte in Perkins County. He went to Europe in 1944 and was assigned to the 4th Armored

Division in General Patton's Third Army. He died on January 10th when his unit was defending Bastogne. His body was returned and buried in Fort Snelling National Cemetery.[609]

Matthew Schultz was born in White in Brookings County. He graduated from White High School in 1940. He was trained in Louisiana, Texas, and California. Matthew was in action in Belgium when he was killed on January 1st. His body was returned and buried in Fairview Cemetery in White.[610]

David Simpson was born in Butte County. He was drafted in 1943. After basic training he was sent to North Carolina for paratrooper training. He joined the 17th Airborne Division. His unit was in combat in Belgium. David died when a mortar shell exploded. David was buried in Luxembourg American Cemetery.[611]

Carroll Smith graduated from high school in Rapid City in 1940. He went to the University of Nebraska two years and in 1942 enlisted in the Army. Carroll and Marjorie were married and had a daughter, Carolyn. Carroll trained in Louisiana and California. He was assigned to the 21st Armored Infantry Regiment in the 11th Armored Division. His unit was sent to France in December of 1944. The division was told to move east and help defend Bastogne against the rapidly advancing Germans. Even though the Germans had more tanks, the division stopped their advance. Carroll was helping a fellow soldier who was suffering from frozen feet when a German artillery shell killed both Soldiers. They were close to Bastogne. His body was returned and buried in Rapid City.[612]

Le Roy Stokes was from Codington County. He was a member of the 24th Reconnaissance Squadron. Le Roy died in combat on December 20, 1944, in Belgium. He is buried in Ardennes American Cemetery.[613]

Harvey Strobel was born in Eureka in McPherson County. He joined a family of four sisters and three brothers. Harvey taught school and worked in the implement business before entering the service in 1942. Harvey and Rose Dickhaut were married in May of 1943. He was in the 34th Infantry fighting in Belgium when he was killed in action on January 1, 1945. His body was returned and buried in the Eureka cemetery.[614]

Edmund Timmons was from Ramona in Lake County. Edmund and Dorothy Schwartz were married in 1937. He worked on the Milwaukee Railroad before enlisting in the Army in 1944. Edmund was trained at Fort McClellan in Alabama and in Alaska and was sent to Europe in October of 1944. He died in combat in Belgium on January 18, 1945. Edmund is buried in Henri-Chapelle American Cemetery in Belgium.[615]

Earl Wanke was born in Yankton. He was with the 411th Infantry Regiment, 103rd Division of the 7th Army. General Patch was commander of the 7th Army. Earl died in combat on December 19, 1944. His body was returned to the U.S. for burial.[616]

Bernard Williams graduated from Ipswich High School in 1942. Bernard and Maxine Guthert were married in August of 1942. He trained in California, Mississippi, and South Carolina. Bernard was sent overseas as part of the 312th Engineer Battalion, 87th Infantry Division. He was killed in combat on January 11th near Lebramont, Belgium.[617]

Louis Wise was from Spencer in McCook County. He worked for local farmers before entering the military. Louis was in the 35th Infantry Division. His unit was in combat in Belgium on January 1, 1945, when he was killed. His body was returned and buried in Parker.[618]

Egrid Zacher joined a family of seven brothers and two sisters. He worked on the family farm near Onaka in Faulk County before he was drafted in June of 1944. Egrid was killed in combat on January 7th. His body was returned and buried at St. Mary's Cemetery in Aberdeen.[619]

Survivors of the Battle of the Bulge

Larry Kirk of Sioux Falls served in the Army as a liaison to the 8th Corps. He had a brush with death near Mersh, Luxembourg. Larry and seven other Soldiers had come off patrol duty and were settling into their sleeping bags when a German patrol broke through American lines and started shooting. In the chaos of the shooting, six of his fellow Soldiers died before they could get their bags unzipped. In an interview conducted in December of 1994, Larry stated, "Til this day, I still sleep at night with my hands and feet uncovered by the blankets on my bed."

When the Battle of the Bulge started, Larry was traveling between Liege and Bastogne. The members of his unit scattered, and it was every man for himself. Larry headed for the woods. He traveled only at night and finally got back to his unit in Mersh. Along the way he was more than a little concerned about stepping on a land mine and about mortar shells that were exploding in the area. His rations consisted of two chocolate bars and whatever he found on dead German Soldiers along the way. It took five days to get back to his unit.

Upon returning to his unit Larry was assigned to patrol duty around Bastogne. Larry and four other Soldiers spent five days in foxholes. Their job was to protect the city's perimeter. December of 1944 was the coldest December in seventy-years in Western Europe. When his group of five were pulled off the line, three became double amputees. Two months after the Battle of the Bulge ended, Larry's unit helped to capture the bridge over the Rhine River at Remagen, Germany.

After the war Larry and his brothers operated Kirk's Cafe for many years. On the 50th anniversary of the battle, the Belgium government asked Soldiers to return so that they could thank them for what they had done. Larry declined. He did not want to relive the death and destruction he had experienced.[620]

William Srstka Sr. was born on the family farm near Geddes in Charles Mix County. The year was 1914. The family moved to Jerauld County, and he graduated from Wessington Springs High School in 1933. He attended Northern State College for one year, but the economic conditions of the Depression prevented him from continuing. William went to Notre Dame Academy and earned a teaching certificate. He became a rural school teacher in Jerauld County. William was attending a teachers' convention when he met Elvira Welter, who was also teaching in Jerauld County. They were married in 1941. Teacher pay was still low for country school teachers so they moved to Washington, D. C. in search of better jobs and better pay. Elvira started working in the State Department, and William found a job in the Veterans Administration. Life was good.

Pearl Harbor changed their lives along with thousands of others. William had joined the South Dakota National Guard before the war. He was part of the 147th Field Artillery Regiment. He was called to active duty in late 1942. Before he could report to duty, he had to get his wife and seven-week-old son back to South Dakota. They ran into a snow storm in Maryland, and he had to put them on a train to South Dakota. Elvira and newborn son were going to live with her parents near Woonsocket. William drove the rest of the way by himself.

Upon entering active duty, he became part of the 915 Field Artillery Battalion in the 90th Division. The 90th was part of Patton's Third Army. The unit fought in the Battle of the Bulge. They were in Czechoslovakia when the war ended.

After the war he decided to attend law school at the University of South Dakota. The G.I. Bill enabled him to do that. He graduated from law school in 1949. His first job was with the Charles Hatch Law Firm in Wessington Springs. He was also the States Attorney for Jerauld County. In 1958 he became an assistant U.S. Attorney in Sioux Falls. His next position was Clerk of Courts for the U.S. District Court of South Dakota. He retired in 1980. Elvira passed away in 1990 and William in 2009.[621]

Dr. Robert Giebink could see war clouds on the horizon and enlisted in the Army Reserves. Upon being called to active duty with the U.S. Medical Corps, he trained in Pasadena, California. Robert was sent to Europe in December of 1943. His first assignment was to a U.S. Military hospital in Paris. In the fall of 1944 a battalion surgeon was killed in action. A replacement was needed, and Robert became a part of a medical battalion of the 120th Infantry Regiment, 30th Infantry Division. The 30th was sent to help stop the German advance in the Battle of the Bulge. Robert was instrumental in creating a plan for handling casualties during the initial fighting. This plan helped to save the lives of wounded soldiers. Later he led his medical group across the Rhine River through intense artillery and mortar fire to a town where an aid station was set up. As a result, the wounded were treated as soon as possible. For his actions in battle he was awarded a Bronze Star and oak-leaf cluster. He was wounded in battle and was awarded a Purple Heart.

After the war he returned to medical school and studied the field of orthopedics. In the early 1950's he set up a solo practice in downtown Sioux Falls. In 1962 Dr. Giebink and Dr. Phil Gross joined forces and opened Orthopedic Associates. Dr. Giebink was instrumental in founding the Sioux Vocational School for the Handicapped (now S. D. Achieve) in the late 1950's. He donated land for a permanent building on South Western Avenue. Robert served in the S.D. State Legislature as a representative and a senator.

He introduced bills for three years in a row until a four-year medical was authorized. Robert passed away on January 27, 2008. His wife, Mary, had preceded him in death.[622]

Forrest Lothrop was born on June 16, 1924, in Redfield. He graduated from Redfield High School and in the fall of 1942 enrolled at South Dakota State College. Because he had joined the Enlisted Reserve, he was called to active duty before the end of the school year in 1943. His induction into the Army was held at Ft. Snelling in Minnesota. Camp Clairborne in Louisiana was the location of his basic training.

After basic training he was assigned to the 84th Infantry Division which had been reactivated in October of 1942. The division had participated in WW I. It was known as the "Railsplitter Division." The division was made of three infantry regiments, the 333rd, 334th, and 335th; four field artillery battalions, 325th, 326th, 327th and 909th; one tank battalion, 771st; an engineer combat battalion, 309th; and a medical battalion, 309th.

The 84th Division landed on Omaha Beach in November of 1944. It was commanded by Major General Bolling. Colonel Timothy A. Pedley Jr. took command of the 333rd Infantry Regiment on October 1, 1944. Company A was led by Captain Prophet. The commander of the 4th Platoon was Lt. Ken Ayers.

Forrest shipped out to England on a military vessel. He was assigned to the 1st Battalion and was part of a machine gun and mortar squad. His position was to man a machine gun. The 1st Battalion was part of Company A. Company A was one of the units in the 333rd Infantry Regiment.

The division was involved in several battles in Germany before moving to Belgium on December 18th to help slow down the

German winter offensive known as the Battle of the Bulge. In the area between Verdenne and Bourdon, Belgium, there was a German force of five tanks and two infantry companies, about four hundred soldiers. The 84th Division took the town of Verdenne on Christmas Day, 1944.

Lothrop's squad was engaged in combat when he was wounded on December 26, 1944. A piece of shrapnel hit his left leg below the knee and came out above his knee. Another piece hit his left arm below the elbow and came out above it. A third piece hit his left hand. The wound resulted in the loss of his index finger on his left hand. A medic treated his wounds on the battlefield. He received further treatment at an aid station behind the front lines. Further treatment took place in Marche, France. Forrest was sent to Paris and then to England. He was there from January to March of 1945. Camp Kilmer in New Jersey was his next stop. From there he was sent to Dibble General Hospital in Menlo Park, California. He was discharged from the Army there in October of 1945.

After the war Forrest spent his entire career teaching and coaching. His name is on a plaque at the Pavilion for having taught American History and American Government at Washington High School for over twenty years.[623]

Bernard Olson was born at Nunda in Lake County. The year was 1924. He served in the Army. His unit fought in the Battle of the Bulge. Barnard was wounded in the fighting. Bernard and Deloris Paul were married in 1956. They had a son and two daughters. After the war Bernard worked for the Lake County Highway Department many years. Bernard and Deloris also ran the B&B Cafe ten years. Bernard passed away in September of 2010.[624]

South Dakota/ Iwo Jima/ Famous Photos

The island of Iwo Jima is located about 650 miles south of Tokyo. American military leaders viewed its location as vital to their battle plans. Control of the island would provide a staging area for attacks on the main islands of Japan. Its three airfields would shorten the flight time to Japan.

The battle to take the island started on February 19, 1945. When the Soldiers hit the beaches and began to make their way inland, they met numerous obstacles. The beach itself was black volcanic ash. It is hard to dig a foxhole in a sand pit. Farther inland they encountered eleven miles of underground tunnels, fortified bunkers, and hidden artillery positions. These obstacles resulted in some of the bloodiest fighting in the Pacific.

The battle lasted five weeks until March 26, 1945. By the time it was over, 6,821 American Soldiers had died. Of that total 5,931 were Marines.

Famous Photos

Jack Thurman grew up on a dairy farm not far from Mitchell. He had fourteen siblings. Horses did the farm work until they purchased a tractor in 1939. Jack attended Notre Dame School in Mitchell. After Pearl Harbor he wanted to enlist but was only seventeen, and his father would not sign the permission form. Jack turned eighteen on September 27, 1943, and headed for the recruiter to enlist in the Marine Corps. After basic training he was on a ship in the Pacific. His unit was informed that they were headed for Iwo Jima. Jack was part of the 27th Marine Regiment of the 5th Marine Division. His regiment landed on February 19th. As they moved inland, they faced the reality of war when they had to step over dead Japanese Soldiers.

His unit was supposed to take an airfield while the 28th Regiment was to secure Mt. Suribachi. By the 23rd an American flag was raised on the mountain. The first picture was taken by a Marine photographer. Later in the day another group replaced the smaller flag with a larger one. Joe Rosenthal, an Associated Press photographer, took the second picture of six Marines raising the flag.

The second picture became one of the most famous photos of WW II. The six Marines in that photo are memorialized in the Marine Corps War Memorial in Arlington, Virginia. Later Rosenthal took a picture of Soldiers from the 28th Regiment. Jack was nearby and was invited to be in the picture. He said that he was in the 27th Regiment. A Soldier from the 28th said it did not make any difference. Rosenthal identified all the Soldiers in in the 28th, but not Jack. Jack remained unidentified until 2000.[625] The book *Flags of Our Fathers* was published that year, and the picture of the larger group is in the book. Jack is on the left holding his helmet in the air and listed as unknown. Family members saw the photo and knew it was Jack. In 2006 Clint Eastwood directed a movie based on the book. After the movie came out, Jack got to meet with Lieutenant Keith Wells whose men were putting up the flag in the photo. Lieutenant Wells was glad to meet the Soldier whose name they had not known all those years.[626]

Grady Dyce grew up in Chamberlain. He was identified in the Gung Ho photo by Marilyn Gunnare. Grady was her husband's uncle. It is hard to believe that two South Dakota Soldiers who grew up less than seventy miles from each other could travel seven thousand miles and both be in a WW II photo that is recognized the world over.[627]

Ira Hayes was a Pima Native American from Arizona. Jack Thurman and Ira met when they were training in the Hawaiian Islands. Later they were stationed on Camp Tarawa. Jack asked Ira to teach him how to speak Navajo. The lesson was not successful, but they became friends. Their friendship was based on things they had in common—both grew up on farms, both took pride in being a Marine, and both had a love for their country.

Jack and Ira met again on Iwo Jima. They fought side by side on February 23, 1945, when the Marines were in combat on Mt. Suribachi. Ira is one of the Marines in the Marine Corps War Memorial, Arlington, Virginia. Ira passed away in 1955 and was buried in Arlington National Cemetery. Jack visited Ira's grave in February of 2017.[628]

South Dakotans Who Perished on Iwo Jima.

Eli Haas was born in Canton. His family moved to the Miller area where he graduated from high school in 1935. He moved to Washington and worked on the Grand Coulee Dam project three years. Eli and Mary Grant were married in 1940. He enlisted in the Marines in 1941. Eli was sent to the Pacific and died in combat on March 8th.[629]

Gerald Hill was from Yankton. Gerald and Vione Larson were married in 1938 and had a daughter. He worked for the Rio Grande Railroad prior to enlisting in the Navy. Upon arriving in Omaha for induction, he discovered that he was in the Marines and not in the Navy. He was sent to San Diego to be trained as a Marine. Gerald was assigned to the 3rd Marine Division and sent to Guam and later on to Iwo Jima. He never got to see his second daughter. Gerald wrote his wife a letter dated March 2nd in which he noted that he was going into combat the next day. He was wounded the next day and died from his wounds. He was buried on Iwo Jima. In 1948 his remains were returned and buried in the Yankton cemetery.[630]

Ernest Hladik was from Tabor in Bon Homme County. He was employed as a junior statistician in the Labor Department in Washington, D.C. Ernest and Mary Ann Zitka were married in December of 1937. They had three children. He enlisted in the Marines. Ernest completed his training at Camp Pendleton and was sent to Iwo Jima in 1944. He died there on March 10, 1945. His body was returned and buried in the Catholic cemetery in Tabor.[631]

Donald House was born in Sioux Falls and graduated from Cathedral High School. He worked at a Sunshine Food Store from 4:00 to 6:00 pm. After supper he worked at the USO Club until midnight. Then it was time to do his homework. After his graduation he took two days off and then enlisted in the Marine Corps. Donald completed his basic training and was sent to Iwo Jima. Donald was killed by a Japanese sniper on March 23rd. His body was returned and buried in St. Michael's Cemetery in Sioux Falls.[632]

Leonard Kloiber was from Parkston where he attended school. He worked at aircraft plants in Omaha, Nebraska, and Warren, Wyoming. Leonard enlisted in the Army Air Corps in 1943. After completing his training, he received his wings and became a second lieutenant in the Army Air Corps. Leonard went overseas in February of 1945. He was a pilot in the 457th Fighter Squadron. Leonard was reported as missing in action on June 1st. He was in the vicinity of Iwo Jima, but his plane was not found. Leonard is listed on the Tablets of the Missing at Honolulu Memorial.[633]

Howard Kopke was born in his grandfather's log home near Pukwana in Brule County. In 1937 the family moved to a farm in Jerauld County. Howard graduated from Wessington Springs High School in 1941. He worked at a CCC camp in the Black Hills. Howard enlisted in the Marines in 1943. He was assigned to the 5th Division and fought on several Pacific Islands. He was wounded on Iwo Jima and sent to a military hospital in Pearl Harbor where he died on February 23rd. Howard was buried on Iwo Jima, but his remains were returned and buried in the Catholic cemetery in Kimball.[634]

Donald Long was born in Bison in Perkins County. He graduated from high school in 1943. Prior to entering the military, he worked for his father in the Long Trucking Service. Donald enlisted in the Marines in June of 1944. He was assigned to the 4th Marine Division and sent overseas in November of 1945 and died five days later. His remains were returned and buried at Fort Snelling National Cemetery in Minneapolis. His brother Clifton served in the South Pacific.[635]

Merle Lorenzen was born in Bath in Brown County. He was employed by the Milwaukee Railroad before entering the service at Fort Snelling. Merle was a Marine. He was sent overseas in June of 1944. He died in combat on June 17, 1945. His remains were returned and buried in Black Hills National Cemetery.[636]

Max Malloy was born in McCook County. The family moved to Sioux Falls, and Max went to Washington High School. He enlisted in the Marines in March of 1944. Max trained in San Diego and Camp Pendleton in California. He was sent overseas as a private in the 5th Marine Division. Max was part of the first invasion wave on February 19th. He died in combat on the 20th. His brothers Gene and Virgil were also in the military.[637]

Francis Mitchell was born in Gann Valley in Buffalo County. The year was 1918. Prior to entering the military, Francis and Mary Durr were married and had a son. Francis enlisted in the Marine Corps in March of 1942. He served in the Asiatic-Pacific Theatre from March of 1943 to February of 1944. Francis fought in several major campaigns in the Pacific. He died in combat on March 15th. His remains were returned and buried in Black Hills National Cemetery.[638]

Wayne Mortensen was born in Sioux Falls and attended Washington High School. He was a fireman at the Sioux Falls Army Air Field. Wayne and his wife had two sons. He enlisted in the Marine Corps in March of 1944. Wayne was trained and sent overseas that same year. He was wounded on February 26th when a mortar shell exploded near him. Wayne was taken to a hospital ship for treatment but died on the ship.[639]

Kenneth Olson, his wife, and two children lived in Sioux Falls. He managed the Granada Theater. Kenneth enlisted in the Marines in December of 1943. He trained at Camp Pendleton in California and was sent overseas. Kenneth died in combat and is listed on the Tablets of the Missing at Honolulu Memorial.[640]

Glen Smith was born in 1919 and was from Eagle Butte in Dewey County. He joined the Marines in September of 1941. He was assigned to the 4th Marine Division and sent to Iwo Jima. Glen had been promoted to staff sergeant. Glen died in combat on February 23, 1945.[641]

Leonard Stricker was born on a farm southwest of Iroquois in Beadle County. He worked on the family farm but because of the Depression moved to Minneapolis in search of work. Leonard joined the Marines and was sent to the South Pacific. His next assignment was to Iwo Jima. Leonard was killed by a Japanese sniper on March 2nd. His body was returned and buried in the De Smet cemetery.[642]

Leonard Trudo was born in Elk Point. He joined the Marines in 1943 when he was sixteen. Leonard needed parental consent. He trained at Camp Pendelton in California. He was sent overseas as part of the 3rd Battalion of the 4th Marine Division. Leonard participated in five island invasions. Leonard died during the invasion of Iwo Jima on February 24, 1945. His eighteenth birthday would have been on March 13th.[643]

Luster Walker was born in Oelrichs in Fall River County. He worked at the 7-11 Ranch in Hot Springs prior to entering the military in March of 1945. After basic training he was sent to Alaska and served with the 81st Army Air Service. His next assignment was to Iwo Jima. Luster was killed when an artillery shell exploded above him. His remains were returned and buried at Fort McPherson National Cemetery in Maxwell, Nebraska.[644]

Delmar Westerman graduated from Chancellor High School in 1942. He farmed with his father until he enlisted in the Marine Corps in December of 1943. After boot training in San Diego, he was assigned to the 5th Marine Division. His unit trained on the ship en route to the Pacific. Delmar's unit was fighting the Japanese for control of Mount Suribachi when he was wounded. He was taken to a hospital ship for treatment but died on the ship on February 22nd. Delmar was buried at sea. Delmar is listed on the Tablets of the Missing at Punch Bowl Crater in Honolulu.[645]

South Dakotans Who Fought and Died on the Islands of Leyte, Luzon, Saipan, Tarawa, and Okinawa.

Leyte

American forces invaded the island of Leyte in the Philippines in October of 1944. The fighting continued until July of 1945 when American forces gained control of the island.

Several South Dakotans lost their lives on the island.

John Meyer was born in Armour in Charles Mix County. He joined seven brothers and one sister. John worked on the family farm until he entered the military in September of 1942. He was sent to the Pacific in February of 1942. He died in combat on October 26th. His body was returned and buried in Armour Cemetery.[646]

James Petrik was born in Geddes in Charles Mix County. He had six brothers and five sisters. James worked on the family farm prior to entering the military. He was sent overseas in May of 1943. James was killed trying to get off the beach on Leyte.[647]

Elmer Reyelts was born near Wilmot in Roberts County. He had ten brothers and three sisters. Elmer enlisted and after basic training was sent to the Pacific. He died in combat.[648]

Wilbert Rhodes was born in Rapid City. He worked in Rapid City before entering the service. Wilbert was trained at the Great Lakes Naval Training Center. He was trained at several other locations before being sent to the Pacific. Wilbert died in action on November 18, 1944. He is listed on the Tablets of the Missing at Manila American Cemetery.[649]

Lloyd Rundell was born on a farm near Hurley in Turner County. He graduated from Hurley High School in 1934. Lloyd enlisted in the Army in 1942 and went overseas in 1943. He was stationed in Australia and New Guinea before being sent to Leyte. Lloyd was in combat when a mortar shell exploded killing him. He was buried in an American cemetery on Leyte.[650]

Edward Ruzicka was born near Winner and attended school there. He was a truck driver prior to entering the service in 1943. After basic training in Corvallis, Oregon, he served in the U.S. until March of 1944. Edward was in the infantry and sent to the Pacific in 1944. A Japanese sniper took his life on October 23rd. His remains were returned and buried in the family plot at ZCBJ Cemetery south of Winner.[651]

George Sorbel graduated from Wilmot High School in 1943. He entered the military in September of 1943. After basic training he was enrolled in officer's training school. George and his classmates did not get to finish the course as they were sent to train for an amphibious landing. He was assigned to the 382nd Infantry

Regiment of the 96th Infantry Division and sent to Leyte. He died in combat. George's remains were returned in 1948 and buried in the Wilmot cemetery.[652]

Rolland Steele was from Lake Norden. He was a second lieutenant in the Army. Rolland fought in the Marshall Islands and then was sent to Leyte. He died in combat on December 6, 1944.[653]

Robert Stowe was born in Jefferson in Union County. He joined eleven brothers and sisters. Robert enlisted in the Army in December of 1942. He trained at Fort Riley in Kansas and was sent to Leyte. Robert died in combat on December 29, 1944. His body was returned and buried at St. Peter's Cemetery in Jefferson.[654]

Earl J. Two Bulls was born in Shannon County. His first job was helping his father care for cattle and horses. His next employment was at the Black Hills Ordinance Depot in Igloo. Earl worked there until he entered the service in March of 1943. After basic training he was sent to Ft. Bragg, North Carolina, and trained to fly a glider plane. Earl and Tillie Moeller were married and had a son in September of 1943. Earl was sent to Leyte in September of 1944. He was assigned to the 465th Field Artillery Battalion. His unit was in combat when a Japanese plane attacked their position killing Earl on November 30, 1944. His remains were returned and buried at Christ Church at Red Shirt Table.[655]

Marvin Tystad was born in Sisseton. He worked for a local farmer and farmed on his own before entering the military. Marvin enlisted in the Army and after basic training was assigned to the 382nd Infantry Regiment of the 96th Infantry Division. On Leyte he was part of a machine gun squad. He died in combat on November 4th. Marvin was buried in Manila American Cemetery.[656]

Barton Walter was born in Clark County. He had six sisters and two brothers. His family moved to Lemmon where he graduated from high school in 1940. Barton enlisted in November of 1942.

After basic training in Louisiana and California, he was sent to college in Illinois and Michigan. He graduated in 1944. Barton was sent to Leyte. He was helping a wounded Soldier when he was killed by a sniper's bullet. His body was returned in 1945 and buried in the Lemmon cemetery.[657]

Luzon

The fighting on Luzon lasted from January 9, 1945, until August 15, 1945. The cost in American lives was 10,640 dead and 36,550 wounded. The estimate of civilian deaths was 120,000 to 140,000. South Dakotans who lost their lives are listed below. Their biographies can be found in *Fallen Sons and Daughters of South Dakota in WW II*, volumes one through six, at a public library.

Edwin Meyer, LaVerne Napier, Lloyd Nedved, William Neilan, Wilfred Neuroth, Douglas Olinger, Clarence Olson, George O'Neal Jr., Gayhard Reede, Orville Rogers, Stanley Rogers, Emmens Sand, George Schwartz, Clarence Seefeldt, Clarence Siebrecht, Arthur Sump, Charles Swimmer, Elton Thompson, Stewart Turnwall, Albert Van Overschelde, Frank Wahl, and Thomas Waters.[658]

Saipan

Lyman Schmidt was a graduate of Aberdeen Central High School. He joined the Army in 1943 and was trained at Camp Walter. He was assigned to the 27th Infantry Division which was sent to the Pacific. The Battle of Saipan lasted from June 15th to July 9th of 1944. The invasion force consisted of the 2nd and 4th Divisions of the Marines and the 27th Division of the Army. Lyman died in combat on June 26th. Nobody in Lyman's platoon survived the battle. His remains were returned in 1948 and buried in Sacred

Heart Cemetery in Aberdeen. His brother Stan was in the Army Air Corps.[659]

Emil Vasknetz was born in Alpena and graduated from Wolsey High School. He joined the Marines in October of 1943. His training took place at Camp Elliot in San Diego. Emil was assigned to the 4th Marine Division and sent to the Pacific in March of 1944. Emil died in combat in July of 1944. His body was returned and buried in St. John's Lutheran Cemetery near Wolsey.[660]

Crichton Walker was born in Pierre. At age eighteen he enlisted in the Marines. After basic training he was sent to the Pacific. Crichton died in combat in June of 1944. He had attained the rank of lieutenant.[661]

Saipan was one of the bloodiest battles of the Pacific. More than 2,900 Soldiers died, and over 10,000 were wounded.

Tarawa

Vincent Traversie was born at White Horse in Dewey County. He graduated from Wakpala High School in 1942 and joined the Marines later that year. His basic training was held in San Diego. Vincent was assigned to the 2nd Marine Division and sent to the Pacific Theater. He died in combat on November 20, 1943.[662]

Fay Moore was from Pine Ridge. He enlisted in the Marines. After basic training he was assigned to the 2nd Marine Division and sent to the Pacific. He died in action on November 20, 1943. Fay was buried in the military cemetery in Honolulu.[663]

The 2nd Marine Division was awarded the Presidential Unit Citation for its sacrifices on the battlefield. Over 1,000 Marines died on Tarawa, and more than 2,000 were wounded.

Okinawa

The battle of Okinawa lasted from April 1 to June 22, 1945. It was the biggest amphibious assault in the Pacific Theater. One hundred eighty thousand troops were committed to the battle. When it was over, more than 12,500 Americans had died, 36,000 had been wounded, 36 ships had been lost along with 800 planes. The total of civilian lives lost was 149,193.[664]

South Dakotans who lost their lives are listed below. Their biographies can be found in *Fallen Sons and Daughters of South Dakota in WW II,* volumes one through six, at a public library.

Melvin Allen, Robert Allen, Nels Bach, Havard Baker, Daniel Baughman, Lewis Behrend, George Carr, James Cobb, Ralph DeBauche, Alvin Ellingson, Richard Fielder, Bernard Foote, Keith Frank, August Frankenstein, Jacob Gayken, Norbert Geaghan, Marvin Gunderson, Rosswell Halse, Gordon Hanes, Eli Hargens, Raymond Harrington, Melvin Hunker, William Jaspers, Cullen Johnson, Harvey Luke, William Mance, Cyril Manthey, Arthur Nelson, Clayton Nessan, Glenn Olson, Selmer Pederson, Joseph Poss, Kenneth Rearick, Ervin Rieck, Quinten Robel, Marion Rounds Jr., Eldon Siefken, John Sinning, Lyle Skillingstad, Kendall Smith, Gerald Tellinghuisen, Donald Wallace, Ewald Widmann, Lyle Windherst, Leonard Wolff, and Harry Ziegler.[665]

The Cost of Invading Japan and the Decision to Drop the Atomic Bomb

The Joint Chiefs of Staff estimated 149,000 casualties including 28,981 dead and missing. As American troops moved closer to Japan, the number of civilian deaths increased. One estimate of Japanese civilian deaths was 250,000. Based on the estimates, Truman decided to approve dropping the atomic bomb.

Memorial to Those Who Died on Okinawa

The memorial was dedicated in 1995. Listed on the memorial are all the known names of those who died in battle; civilian, military, Japanese and foreign. As of June 2008, there were 240,734 names on the memorial.[666]

CHAPTER 7

Ship Disasters and Kamikaze Attacks

The USS Houston

Edward O'Leary was from Roscoe. He was stationed on the USS Houston. Edward died because of enemy action on February 4, 1942. His brother Richard was in the Marines.

The USS Houston engaged the Japanese Navy late at night on the 28th of February. The battle continued through March 1st. The battle took place in Sunda Strait southwest of the island of Borneo. The Houston was out- numbered and at the very end was surrounded by ships of various sizes. She was hit at close range by several five-inch shells and torpedoes.

There were 1,168 crew members on board. Seven hundred died in the battle. One hundred and fifty went into the water but did not survive.[667] The Commander, Albert Rooks, died when he was struck by shrapnel[668], and the South Dakotans who died were John Bell from Watertown in Codington County, Sylvester Shemanski from Grenville in Day County, Meredith Hall from Artesian in Sanborn County, and Elra Barringer from Alpena in Jerauld County. They are listed on the Tablets of the Missing at Manila American Cemetery.

The survivors who made it to shore became POWs. The prison camps were numbered according to their distance from

Japanese headquarters in Burma.[669] Many were forced to work on the Burma-Thailand Death Railway. The railway was the focus of the film "Bridge on the River Kwai." Prisoners died from dysentery, tropical ulcers, malaria, beriberi, infections, and malnutrition. Conditions were the worst from 80 Kilo Camp to the Burma-Thailand border. One hundred thirty-one Americans perished in the camps. Most of the deaths occurred in Kilo Camps 80,100, and 105.[670] A few managed to survive until 1944 only to die on a Japanese Hell Ship. Of the 1,168 on board two hundred ninety-one returned to the U.S.[671] The crew members who died in battle, those who died in prison camps, and those who died on Hell Ships are listed in the book *Ship of Ghosts (490- 512)*.

The USS Houston Monument was dedicated in 1998. It is located in Sam Houston Park in Houston, Texas. The ship's brass bell was recovered and is part of the monument. The names of the crew members are listed on the granite pedestal.[672]

The USS Liscome Bay was an aircraft carrier and carried a crew of 916. The ship had been sent to the Gilbert Islands and was part of the invasion force assigned to take the islands from the Japanese. The ship was on its first battle mission when it was torpedoed by a Japanese submarine and sank in minutes on November 24, 1943. There were only 267 survivors.[673] South Dakotans who died that day were Lawrence Adkins of Alexandria, Thomas Bradbury of Howard, Harry Christopherson of Viborg, Edward Schomer of Faith in Meade County, Thomas Shryock of Deadwood, Harry Weiss of Akaska in Walworth County, Lyle Wood of Pukwana in Brule County. Thomas Bradbury, Edward Schomer, Thomas Shryock, Harry Weiss, and Lyle Wood are listed on the Tablets of the Missing at Honolulu Memorial.

Typhoon in the Pacific

William F. "Bull" Halsey was an admiral in the U.S. Navy. He commanded the Third Fleet stationed in the Pacific. The fleet's assignment was to support General MacArthur's invasion of the island of Mindoro and then Luzon. While preparing to support MacArthur, the fleet ran into a typhoon on December 17th of 1944. It lasted into the 18th. The high winds made it impossible for the destroyers to refuel, making it more difficult for them to ride out the storm.[674]

The USS Hull sank on the 18th. There were only 62 survivors out of a crew of 250. Three South Dakotans were lost on the Hull—Wallace Karnopp, Charles McGill, and Alphonsus Weibel.[675]

Thirteen wives of Hull Sailors were pregnant when the ship sunk.[676]

The USS Monaghan also sank on the 18th. There were thirteen survivors while 256 crewmen were lost.[677] Three South Dakotans were lost on the Monaghan—Forest Jones, Simon Larson, and Melroy Morrison.

A third destroyer, the USS Spence, was also lost the same day. There were 24 survivors from a crew of 339. There were not any South Dakotans on the Spence.[678] Over 700 were missing or presumed dead from the three destroyers. There were 90 survivors.[679]

The book *Down to the Sea* by Bruce Henderson has an Appendix: Crew Muster Rolls for Lost Destroyers. The Appendix starts with the Hull (547). The names of those lost on the three destroyers are listed on the Tablets of the Missing at Manila American Cemetery.

The USS Indianapolis departed from San Francisco and delivered the component parts of the A-bomb to the island of Titian in the Pacific. It had left the island of Guam and was on its way to the Philippines when it was struck by torpedoes from a Japanese submarine. It sank in minutes. The date was July 30, 1945. The ship carried a crew of 1,196. Three hundred died from the blast. The rest went into the water.

Ed Brown of Sioux Falls had attended Cathedral High School. He played on the football team coached by Nusier Salem. After his last basketball game on January 17, 1944, he boarded a train and left for naval training in Idaho.

When Brown and others first hit the water, they were swimming in a large slick of oil. The oil may have saved them as it coated their skin and protected them from the powerful rays of the sun. After a day and a half the sharks showed up. They took the dead and wounded first. The air was filled with the screams of the wounded as they were being attacked. Once a sailor was pulled beneath the surface only his life jacket resurfaced. It is estimated that at least 200 died from shark attacks. Ed did not see any shark attacks, but he did have one shark swim between his legs.

Ed was in a group of 366 who hooked their life jackets together to improve their chances of survival. Only 66 of the group survived.

The sailors suffered from weather extremes, hot in the day and cold at night. Dehydration was a problem, and they were told not to drink sea water. Some did, and they died within hours. Hypothermia and lack of food led to death.

Brown and fellow crew members had survived in the water four and a half days when they were spotted by Lieutenant Chuck Gwinn. He was on a mission to spot Japanese submarines. Chuck saw the oil slick and men in the water. He sent out a call, and Lieutenant Adrain Marks responded and rescued Brown and 55 others. Three hundred twenty-one were rescued but four did not live a week. Because of numerous miscommunications the Navy didn't realize the ship was missing.[680]

South Dakotans who perished on the Indianapolis were the following:

1. Wayne Bridge from Wagner
2. Russell Bruce from Redfield is listed on the Tablets of the Missing at Manila American Cemetery.
3. David Driscoll from Lead is listed on the Tablets of the Missing at Manila American Cemetery.
4. Vincent Fast Horse was from Denby in Shannon County. He was survived by his wife, Edith, and three children.
5. Marlo Godfrey from Watertown is listed on the Tablets of the Missing at Manila American Cemetery.
6. Floyd Groce from Ramona in Lake County is listed on the Tablets of the Missing at Manila American Cemetery.
7. Raymond Knudtson from Howard is listed on the Tablets of the Missing at Manila American Cemetery. He was the only son of Julius and Anna.
8. Howard Marttila was from Lake Norden. He was part of the Marine contingent that was on board.
9. Telford Morgan was from Warner in Brown County. There is a marker for him in Black Hills National Cemetery.
10. Darrel Peterson from Waubay in Day County is listed on the Tablets of the Missing at Manila American Cemetery. He was the only son of Marion and Katharine.[681]

The crew members and the Marine contingent are listed on the inside of the front cover and the inside of the back cover in the book, *In Harm's Way*.

An A&E Home Video entitled "Sea Tales: Missing! the Indianapolis" tells the story of what happened.

A memorial to the USS Indianapolis had been a dream of survivors for fifty years. The National Memorial to the ship and crew was dedicated on August 2, 1995, in Indianapolis, Indiana. It is located at the north end of Canal Walk. Names of the crew members are engraved on the south face of the monument. There are small crosses by the names of those who perished. The wreckage of the Indianapolis was located on August 19, 2017, at a depth of 18,000 feet.[682]

The HMT Rhona

Ormand Mattox from Pringle in Custer County and Raymond Soppe from Jordan in Tripp County were on board the HMT Rhona. There were 1,981 Soldiers on the ship. They were on their way to serve in the African Theatre. In late November of 1943 the ship was off the coast of North Africa when it was struck by German shells. Ormand and Raymond were among the 1,015 who lost their lives. The loss of life resulted because not enough lifeboats and rafts were on board, and rescue efforts were hampered by darkness. Ormand is listed on the Tablets of the Missing at North African American Cemetery, Carthage, Tunisia. There is a marker to Raymond in the Winner cemetery.[683]

The USS Leopoldville

The USS Leopoldville was crossing the English Channel on December 24, 1944. On board were 2,235 Soldiers of the 66th Infantry Division. Their destination was Cherbourg, France. They were being sent as reinforcements in the Battle of the Bulge. The ship was struck by a torpedo and sank. They were five miles from

Cherbourg. Five hundred-fifteen Soldiers went down with the ship. Another 248 died from injuries, drowning, or hypothermia.

The loss of life happened because there were not enough life jackets on the ship, lifeboats were not well-supervised, and not many soldiers had participated in the training. After the ship sank, rescue attempts were not well-organized.[684] Three South Dakotans lost their lives in the disaster—Garland Husby from Yankton, Elwood Pauls from Bryant in Hamlin County, and Donald Smith from Aberdeen. The history of the ship and loss of life has been recorded in book and film. Clive Cussler's book *"Cyclops"* was published in 1986. A documentary film "Cover Up: The sinking of the USS Leopoldville" was aired on the History Channel in 1998. The National Geographic Channel aired a special in 2009. A monument to the 66th Infantry Division was dedicated in Fort Benning, Georgia in 1997. In 2005 a memorial was erected in Veterans Park in Titusville, Florida.[685]

The USS Juneau

The USS Juneau has a place in history because five Sullivan brothers were on board when it sank. It was engaged in the battle of Guadalcanal when it sank after being hit by a torpedo. It was November 14, 1942. Three South Dakotans were on board—Robert Mosher from Madison, Theodore Pierce from Heppner in Fall River County, and Julius Zener from Leola in McPherson County.[686] The ship carried over seven hundred crew members. Ten survived. Robert, Theodore, and Julius are all listed on the Tablets of the Missing at Manila American Cemetery.

An Explosion that Registered 3.4 on the Richter Scale

The S.S. E. A. Bryan and the S.S. Quinault Victory were cargo ships. They were docked at the Port Chicago Naval Magazine in Port Chicago, California. Munitions from plants throughout the U. S. were shipped to the magazine on railroad cars. The munitions were moved by hand, cranes, and winches onto the E. A. Bryan. They were destined for the Pacific Theatre. The munitions included 1,000 lb. bombs, 40 mm antiaircraft shells, fragmentation bombs, airborne anti-submarine depth charges, and incendiary bombs set to go off.

The Bryan carried 5,292 barrels of heavy fuel oil for its trip across the Pacific and was loaded with nearly 4,600 tons of explosives. There were sixteen rail cars on the pier waiting to be unloaded. They contained several tons of explosives.

The Quinault Victory was being prepared to take on munitions, but it had taken on some fuel oil that released flammable fumes that may have contributed to the disaster. Witnesses heard a noise at 10:18 p.m. on July 17, 1944. It was followed by an explosion and a fire. In seconds the munitions of the Bryan exploded. Pieces of the Bryan were blown 12,000 feet in the air. The Quinault was blown apart, and sections of it landed 500 feet from the blast site. A large crater was created in the river. Only fifty-one could be identified. A specific cause of the explosion was not determined. Possible causes included defects in the munitions, an extremely sensitive element in the ordinance, or problems with the steam winches. [687]

Woodrow Riff was born in 1913 in Platte. He earned a teaching degree at Southern State Teachers College in Springfield. Woodrow and Mary Westendorf were married in 1939. They had a daughter, Donna Jean. Woodrow taught and coached prior to joining the Navy in 1944. He was assigned to the S.S. Quinault Victory. Woodrow perished in the explosion. [688]

The Port Chicago Naval Magazine National Memorial was dedicated in 1994.

The USS Franklin

The USS Franklin was an aircraft carrier. It was on patrol about fifty miles from the Japanese mainland. On March 1, 1945, a Japanese kamikaze plane dropped two 550 lb. bombs on the ship. When the bombs exploded, they caused planes loaded with fuel to explode. Rockets that were stored below deck also exploded. Over eight hundred Sailors and Airmen died in the explosions and fires. One South Dakotan died, Erle Gillenberg from Wolsey.[689]

South Dakotans and Kamikaze Attacks

In October of 1944 the Japanese unleashed a new military strategy, the kamikaze. The peak period of attacks was from April to June of 1945 during the battle of Okinawa. The attacks inflicted 7,000 casualties on the Americans, Australians, and British, with most of those being Americans. The last attack was on August 15, 1945, after the war had ended.

South Dakotans who died during a kamikaze attack:

1. Charles Barnard/ USS Morrison/ May 5, 1945
2. Paul Bauer/ USS Carrier Curtis/ June 21, 1945
3. Darol Brown/ USS Lindsey/ April 12, 1945
4. Walter Davis/ USS Lindsey/ April 12, 1945
5. John Garhart/ USS Indianapolis/ March 31, 1945
6. Erle Gillenberg/ USS Franklin/ March 1, 1945
7. Donald Glanzer/ USS Callaghan/ July 28, 1945
8. Jack Helbing/ USS Pinkey/ April 28, 1945

9. Arthur Hepper/ USS Suwanee/ October 26, 1944

10. James La Pointe/ USS Laffey/ April 6, 1945

11. Eugene Leonhardt/ USS St. Lo/ October 25, 1944.

12. Curtiss Peterson/ USS Twiggs/ June 16, 1945

13. George Philip Jr./ USS Twiggs/ June 16, 1945

14. Alan Plasma/ USS New Mexico/ May 12, 1945

15. Fred Rauscher/ USS Belleau Wood/ November, 1944

16. Darwin Schmidt/ USS Bismarck Sea/ February 21, 1945

17. Jack Schoener/ Merchant ship: Mary A. Livermore/ May 29, 1945

18. Joe Stangle/ USS Drexler/ May, 28, 1945

19. Louis Strong/ USS Caldwell/ December 12, 1944

20. Norman Thormodsgard/ USS Colorado/ November 27, 1944

21. Vernon Torbet/ USS Mullany/ April 6, 1945

22. Paul Wolf/ USS Zellars/ April 14, 1945[690]

Sylvan Vigness from Egan survived a kamikaze attack. His story is related in another chapter.

CHAPTER 8

After the War: Soldiers Found, Medals Awarded, and Military Cemeteries

Harry Bessler enlisted in the Army and was trained in the Air Corps. He was sent to Italy. Harry was piloting a B-24 Liberator bomber on a mission over Rome when the plane was damaged and crashed. He was declared missing in action in February of 1944. Harry was declared officially dead in May of 1945. Several years later his plane was found. Harry was still at the controls.[691]

Frank Higgins joined the military in 1943 and was trained at Lincoln Air Base. He was the top turret gunner on an A-20 Havoc attack bomber. His plane was on a mission over New Guinea when it was shot down in 1944. The plane was found in 1950. Frank's remains and those of two other crew members were returned and buried at Fort Snelling.[692]

Harris Johnson graduated from Yankton College and was teaching in Winner when he enlisted in the Marines. He died in combat on Makin Island in the Pacific. Harris and eighteen other Marines were buried by locals. A road construction crew discovered their remains in 1999. DNA was used to identify each soldier. Harris's remains were returned to his home town, Little Rock, Iowa, for burial.[693]

Archie Newell of Aberdeen was in a Marine Corps tank battalion when he was killed during the first day of the battle on Tarawa, November 20, 1943. Tarawa is located in the Gilbert Islands. The battle of Tarawa lasted three days and was one of the bloodiest battles in the Pacific. Approximately 1,000 Marines and Sailors were killed and more than 2,000 were wounded. Newell had not been identified when he was buried in National Memorial Cemetery in Honolulu. The Defense POW/ MIA Accounting Agency disinterred the remains and used dental, anthropological, and chest radiograph analysis to match his remains with military records. Newell was buried in Arlington National Cemetery on December 8, 2017. His name is recorded on the Tablets of the Missing at the NMCP, an American Battle Monuments Commission Cemetery, along with others killed or lost in WW II. A rosette will be placed next to his name to indicate that he has been accounted for.[694]

William Punnell graduated from Flandreau High School and studied engineering at South Dakota State College of Agriculture and Mechanical Arts and Purdue University. William joined the Navy in 1940. He trained at Wold-Chamberlain Field, Minneapolis, Pensacola, Florida, and Corpus Christi, Texas. William was sent overseas in March of 1944 and stationed on the aircraft carrier Wasp. His squadron was on a mission over the Palau Islands when the tail of his F6 Hellcat was shot off by antiaircraft fire. He crashed in the ocean, and nobody sighted a parachute. He is listed on the Tablets of the Missing at Manila American Cemetery.

William's Hellcat and his remains were found in 2014. The search had begun in 2004 by the BentProp Project. The group had historical documents and eyewitness accounts of the crash. The actual location of the plane was close to the place they thought it would be. His remains were turned over to the U.S. Government

Defense MIA/POW Accounting Agency for identification. The agency used DNA from a relative to identify William. His remains were laid to rest at Arlington National Cemetery in May of 2018.[695]

Isley Warvick graduated from Britton High School in 1939. He enlisted in the Army Air Corps and was trained as a gunner on a B-24 bomber. In 1943 his plane was shot down over Austria. Eight years later the plane and remains of the seven on board were found. The remains could not be identified individually but were returned, and the seven were buried as a group in Fort Scott, Kansas.[696]

George Winters joined the Army Air Corps in 1942. He was trained to be a gunner in a bomber unit. George was stationed in the Pacific. His plane went down over Borneo. It was eleven years later when his plane was found. His dog tags were returned to his parents.[697]

Paul Wittenberger graduated from Wessington High School in 1936. He enlisted in the Army Air Corps in 1943. Paul earned his commission as a second lieutenant and his wings at Ft. Sumpter, New Mexico. He became the pilot of a B-24 bomber. His plane and crew were sent to the Pacific in 1944. In March of 1945, Paul's squadron, the 403rd, was moving operations to Clark Field on Luzon. Paul flew a mission to Luzon. On the return trip flying conditions had deteriorated, and the plane was not heard from again. The War Department notified the family that the remains might not be recovered. His parents had a headstone placed for him in their family plot in Wessington Cemetery. In 1952 the plane was discovered on a mountain top on Leyte Island. Paul and his four crew members are buried communally at Jefferson Barracks National Cemetery in St. Louis, Missouri.[698]

Veterans Whose Medals were Awarded After the War

Louis G. LaPlant grew up on the Rosebud Sioux Reservation. He enlisted in the Army in March of 1941. Louis was in the 10th Armored Infantry Division that was part of General Patton's 3rd Army. He was at Bastogne during the Battle of the Bulge. He was a truck driver and served as a medic when needed. In one battle he treated and helped to evacuate over 400 wounded soldiers. He was recognized for his bravery as a medic, and his name was turned in for an award. Louis was captured by the Germans and became a POW. He was liberated by American troops.

Sergeant Bill Childs was Louis's platoon leader. He praised Louis for his abilities as a Soldier and felt safe with him when they were on patrol. He recorded the medals Louis was entitled to. When Louis was discharged in 1945, he did not receive any medals. Not receiving medals was often the case.

After fifty-five years Louis received his medals. The ceremony was held in Pierre on the shore of Capitol Lake in late 2000. Louis was 80 when he received his Purple Heart and several other medals.[699]

Delmar Strunk was born and raised near Irene. He was 20 when he en- listed in the Army in 1942. Delmar was stationed at Fort Carson, Colorado, when he learned that President Roosevelt was asking for 3,000 men to go on a perilous mission. Delmar signed up; in February of 1944 he was marching into Burma. Delmar was officially part of the 1st Battalion of the 5307th Composite Unit. His commander was General Frank Merrill and the unit became known as "Merrill's Marauders." They fought behind enemy lines. Their main objective was to attack supply and communications lines. Because of the terrain and nature of their mission, they carried what they could on their backs. Mules and horses also carried supplies.

Supplies were air dropped in, but because of the terrain the air drops were not very successful.

The unit engaged the Japanese in five major battles and several smaller skirmishes. They suffered heavy casualties because of the fighting and a variety of tropical diseases. Delmar fought in three of the five major battles before he was hospitalized a second time with malaria and scrub typhus. At the end of their tour of duty, only two in the 5307th Composite Unit had not been shot or afflicted with a disease. In August of 1944, the 5307th was dissolved. Only 200 of the original 3,000 were still fit for combat. The survivors became part of the 475th Infantry Regiment.

Two factors prevented Delmar from receiving his medals when they were due. The first was that the company's records could not be recovered after they went over a cliff with the mule carrying them. The second was that after the war ended, millions of veterans returned, and it was difficult to keep everything straight. Delmar's medals, like those of many others, did not follow him.

The American Legion started the process to make sure that Delmar was finally awarded his medals. His wife, Velma, encouraged him to get involved. In May of 2014 Delmar, age 92, stood on the stage of the Scotland Auditorium and received his Bronze Star along with several other medals. The book *Jungle Stories: The Life of Delmar Strunk* tells the story of his life before, during, and after the war.[700]

Eugene Martinson was born in 1915 in Moody County. He was farming prior to entering the service in January of 1942. His training took place in Texas and Wisconsin. He was trained to make maps, how to scout, gather information, and then form battle plans. Eugene was sent overseas in October of 1943. He completed a course in radio messages. He was stationed in England and Ireland where he was with the 9th Infantry Regiment, 2nd Infantry Division.

Eugene went ashore in France the day after D-Day. The official notice stated that he died in Belgium on December 19, 1944, and was buried in Belgium. No other details were given.

The search for Eugene's records began when Rene Wade, his niece, was listening to a local radio show host who was interviewing a WW II historian. She went to his website and asked for help in locating her uncle's records. He sent her information on the battles her uncle was in as the army moved through Europe and a list of the medals he had not received. The information indicated that on the day the Battle of the Bulge started Eugene was in a hospital tent close to the front lines. He had been hospitalized because of exposure and exhaustion. Eugene died three days later. Eugene's remains were returned to the U.S. in 1947 and buried at Fort Snelling National Cemetery.

With help from Senator John Thune's office, the medals were delivered. Eugene's sister, Marilyn Graber, and his brother, Valire, accepted his medals in August of 2007, sixty-three years after his death. The ceremony was held in Senator John Thune's Sioux Falls office.[701]

Sylvan Vigness: US Navy

Sylvan was born in 1924 in Woonsocket, S.D. He graduated from Egan High School. Sylvan enlisted in the Navy because he did not want to be in the Army and carry a backpack. The Navy sent him to Farragut, Idaho, for basic training. Advanced training took place in San Diego where he trained to be a signalman. He learned how to communicate with ships by using a series of flags and a system similar to a telegraph. The U.S.S. Hinsdale (APA-120) was his first station. It was an attack transport with a crew of over 500. It could hold over 1,600 Soldiers and their equipment along with 20 landing craft. The landing craft carried the soldiers to the beachhead.

The Hinsdale and her crew participated in the attack on Iwo Jima. The Marines went ashore on February 19, 1945, and she stayed in the area over a week. During that time the ship carried out a variety of duties. She served as a hospital when those with serious wounds were brought aboard. Crewmen were kept busy unloading troops and cargo. Sylvan went ashore on Iwo Jima. His job was to communicate with ships close to the beachhead and tell them what was needed by the troops on shore.

Sylvan saw history in the making when he observed the raising of the U.S. flag on Mt. Suribachi. He and some other sailors had been in a foxhole in between their signaling duties. A few minutes after leaving the foxhole it took a direct hit from a Japanese bomb. Sometimes fate is a strange thing. The Japanese continued to attack the ship with artillery fire as they un- loaded men and material. On February 25 a shell hit close enough to kill a Marine captain and wound several others. The Hinsdale left the area on February 27.

After leaving Iwo Jima, the ship stopped at Guam and then at Saipan. At Saipan 1,500 Marines and Sailors were taken aboard for the invasion of Okinawa. The date for the invasion was Sunday, April 1. At 6:00 a.m. a kamikaze plane hit the Hinsdale and ripped into the engine room. The bombs exploded, destroying the engine room. Flying debris from the explosions struck Sylvan in the left eye. He was treated for his wound on a hospital ship and then sent to Brooklyn Naval Hospital in New York for further treatment. Several others were injured, and those who died were buried at sea. The Marines did make it ashore. The ship was repaired and returned to service. One of its final duties was to go to Japan and return Soldiers to the U.S.

Sylvan was discharged in May of 1946. His rank was signalman 2nd class. He received the following medals for his service: a WW II Victory Medal, an American Campaign Medal, an Asiatic Pacific Campaign Medal with two Bronze Stars, and a Naval Occupation Service Medal with a clasp. Because of his wound Sylvan should have been awarded his Purple Heart before he was discharged. His shipmates vouched for him which should have been enough to grant him the award.

For many years Sylvan's son Daniel campaigned to get Sylvan his Purple Heart. Unfortunately, Daniel passed away in 2013 from cancer. Several people took up the cause to get the Purple Heart for Sylvan. There was some confusion about the ship's location when the wound occurred. This confusion added to the delay in awarding the medal. The confusion was finally cleared up, and on January 18, 2018, Sylvan received official notice that he would be awarded the Purple Heart. The award ceremony was held on January 27, 2018, at the Bill Janklow Community Center in Flandreau. Many friends and family members attended.[702]

Military Cemeteries

The American Battle Monuments Commission was established by Congress on March 4, 1923. It is responsible for constructing, operating, and maintaining permanent American cemeteries and monuments in foreign countries. *The Commemorative Sites Booklet* published by the Commission lists the sites. The information for each site includes the location, a description of the grounds, the number buried there, and the Tablets of the Missing. The Ardennes American Cemetery in Neupre, Belgium, is the final resting place of 5,321 Americans; sixty-five percent served in the Army Air Corps. Several South Dakotans are buried there.

The Cambridge American Cemetery near Cambridge, England, is the final resting place of 3,812 Americans. The names of 5,127 are listed on the Tablets of the Missing. Several South Dakotans are buried there.

The Henri-Chapelle American Cemetery is near the village of Henri-Chapelle, Belgium. There are 7,992 Americans in this cemetery. More than thirty-six South Dakotans are buried there. The Belgian people are grateful to the Americans for liberating them from Nazi control. Locals have adopted American graves and take flowers on the Soldier's birthday. The story of the liberation and the gratitude of the Belgians is still taught in their schools. The Military Channel has aired a program about the cemetery. Scenes of the cemetery are on YouTube.

The Honolulu Memorial is located within the National Memorial Cemetery of the Pacific. There are 18,095 names on Eight Courts of the Missing. More than thirty-one South Dakotans are buried there and more than forty-seven are listed on the Tablets of the Missing.

The Luxembourg American Cemetery is located in Hamm, three miles east of downtown Luxembourg. More than twenty South Dakotans are buried there, and some are listed on the Tablets of the Missing.

The Manila American Cemetery contains the remains of 17,191 war dead. There are 36,286 names on the Tablets of the Missing. Fifty or more South Dakotans are buried there, and eighty-seven or more are listed on the Tablets of the Missing.

The Netherlands American Cemetery is in the village of Margarten. The cemetery contains 8,301 Americans. There are forty or more South Dakotans buried there. Over the years locals have adopted graves, and on a Soldier's birthday they take flowers to commemorate his service. *The Margarten Boys* tells the stories of families who have commemorated Soldiers for several generations.

The Normandy American Cemetery overlooks Omaha Beach. There are 9,387 Americans buried there with 1,557 listed on the Tablets of the Missing. Several South Dakotans are buried there. The Sicily-Rome American Cemetery is near Nettuno, Italy, and three miles from Anzio. There are 7,861 soldiers buried there with 3,095 listed on the Tablets of the Missing. The soldiers died in the fighting at Sicily, Salerno, Anzio, and on the Allied movement north toward Rome.

My wife and I, along with our daughter, son-in-law, and granddaughter, visited the cemetery in April of 2018. The beauty of the entire cemetery is breathtaking. As we walked in the cemetery, the serenity was overpowering. The grounds were immaculate. Of the thirty-two or more South Dakotans buried there, we located twelve of the graves.

South Dakotans were laid to rest in the following cemeteries:

1. Brittany American Cemetery near St. James, France
2. Epinal American Cemetery close to Epinal, France
3. Florence American Cemetery, a few miles from Florence, Italy
4. Lorraine American Cemetery, close to St. Avold, France
5. North Africa American Cemetery in Carthage, ten miles from Tunis.
6. Rhone American Cemetery in Draguignan, France, close to Cannes and the Italian border

If requested by a family member, a relative was returned and buried in their home town cemetery, while others were laid to rest in Black Hills National Cemetery near Sturgis, Fort Snelling in Minnesota, and Arlington National Cemetery.

Markers, Memorials, and Monuments to Those who Gave their Lives in Battle

1. Cabanatuan Memorial in the city of Cabanatuan on Luzon. The prison camp held approximately 20,000 prisoners. On January 30, 1945, U.S. Army Rangers, Alamo Scouts, and Filipino guerrillas carried out a night-time surprise attack. Over 500 Allied prisoners were rescued. A movie about the rescue, "Great Raid", came out in 2005. The book *Ghost Soldiers* tells the story of the rescue.

2. Guadalcanal American Memorial on Guadalcanal in Solomon Islands

3. Midway Memorial Marker, The Battle of Midway

4. Papua Marker, Papua, New Guinea, located within the U. S. Embassy in Port Moresby

5. Pointe Du Hoc Ranger Monument located on a cliff eight miles west of Normandy American Cemetery

6. Saipan Monument on Saipan in the Marianas Islands honors the 24,000 American Marines and Soldiers who died recapturing the volcanic islands of Saipan, Tinian, and Guam from June 15, 1944, to August 11, 1944.[703]

Acknowledgments

I would like to thank the following for their contributions to this project. This book was written with the assistance of colleagues, friends and specifically I want to acknowledge and thank Sandra C. Looney, professor emeritus, who has served as a significant editor for this book. Sandra Looney is a 1962 alumni of Augustana University (BA) and earned a Ph.A. in English at the University of Arkansas in 1974. Sandra taught English at Augustana for 54 years. Sandra provided expert guidance on copy edits, content delivery, and overall formatting for this work. She has spent hours offering her expertise throughout this process.

The veterans who shared their stories with me. It was my privilege to listen as they recalled their military experiences.

The individuals who provided me with information about their fathers and grandfathers military service.

The individuals who granted me permission to use photos of their relatives.

Bernie Runoff, publisher of the South Dakota Magazine, for allowing me to use photos from the magazine.
The South Dakota Hall of Fame for the use of photos.

Keely Rees, Ph.D. and Tonja Waring for editing and organizing the bibliography, endnotes, indexing, and publishing.

Alicia Fonder and Bree McCarthy for contributing their word processing and photography skills.

My wife, Paula, for her patience and support throughout the project.

Bibliography

Personal interviews of WW II veterans conducted by Charles M. Rogers

1. Don Crawford: July 2019
2. Sidney Epstein: March 2007
3. Baltus Fritzemeier: July 2018
4. Robert Goodhope: March 2020
5. Wendell Hanson: February 2020
6. Forrest Lothrop: March 2018
7. Sylvan Vigness: January 2018

Obituaries

Clausen, Delmar, Miller Funeral Home, Sioux Falls, 5-20-20

Cole, Hilary, Rapid City Journal, 3-17-19

Cole, Vitalis, Argus Leader, 1-12-08

Conner, Charles, Argus Leader, 3-20-14

Epstein, Sidney, Argus Leader, 11-7-09

Leubecher, Rex, Argus Leader, 3-19-13

Magnuson, Morris, Argus Leader, 3-28-10

Melius, Marvin, Argus Leader, 3-30-08

Mogck, Clarence, Argus Leader, 8-31-10

Muchow, Howard, Argus Leader, 5-6-03

Olson Bernard, Argus Leader, 9-21-10

Ostrander, Ivan, Argus Leader, 11-19-09

Peacock, James, Argus Leader, 4-2-08

Putzke, Kathryn, Argus Leader, 3-15-09

Srstha, William Sr, Argus Leader, 3-2-09

Talcott, Don, Argus Leader, 11-11-09

Wingler, Harold, Argus Leader, 7-23-02

Books

Alexander, Irvin, *Surviving Bataan and Beyond*, Mechanicsburg, Pa.,Stockpile Books, 1999.

Alexander, Joseph, *Utmost Savagery*, Annapolis, Md., Naval Institute Press, 1995.

Ambrose, Hugh, *The Pacific*, N.Y., NAL Caliber, 2010.

Ambrose, Stephen, *D-Day* June 6, 1944, N.Y., Simon & Schuster, 1994.

Ambrose, Stephen, *The Wild Blue*, N.Y., Simon & Schuster, 2001.

Beevor, Anthony, *D-Day*, N.Y., Penguin Books, 2009.

Beevor, Anthony, Ardennes 1944, N.Y., Penguin Books, 2015.

Beevor, Antony, The Battle of Arnhem, N.Y., Viking, 2018.

Blake, Bruce, Twelve Thousand Years of Human History, Sioux Falls, S.D., Ex Machina Publishing Company, 2014.

Borneman, Walter, *The Admirals*, N.Y., Little, Brown & Company, 2012.

Bostick, Douglas, *USS Yorktown* (cv-10) Charleston, Charleston Postcard Company, 2010.

Bradley, James & Ron Powers, *Flags of Our Fathers*, N.Y., 2000.

Brinkley, Douglas, *The Boys of Pointe Du Hoc*, N.Y., Harper Collins, 2006.

Bruchac, Joseph, *Code Talker*, N.Y., Penguin Group, 2005.

Clark, Lloyd, *Anzio*, N.Y., Atlantic Monthly Press, 2006.

D'Este, *Decision in Normandy*, Old Saybrook, Ct., Konecky & Konecky, 1994.

Dewitt, Randall, *Jungle Stories*, Xlibris, 2015.

Fallen sons and daughters of South Dakota in World War II (Pierre, S.D., South Dakota World War II Memorial, 2000) Web.

Retrieved from the Library of Congress, <iccn.loc.gov/2006575207>.

Ford, Daniel, *Flying Tigers*, Smithsonian Books, 1991.

Foss, Joe, *A Proud American*, N.Y., Pocket Books, a division of Simon & Schuster, 1992.

Gee, James & Rosalie H. Smith, *Prisoner of the Samuri*, Philadelphia, Casemate, 2018.

Groom, Winston, *1942*, N.Y., Atlantic Monthly Press, 2005.

Henderson, Bruce, *Down to the Sea*, N.Y., Harper Collins, 2007.

Henderson, Bruce, *Rescue at Los Banos*, N.Y., Harper Collins, 2015.

Holland, James, *Big Week*, N.Y., Atlantic Monthly Press, 2018.

Hornfischer, James, *Ship of Ghosts*, N.Y., Bantam Dell, 2006.

Hornfischer, James, *Neptune's Inferno*, N.Y., Bantam Books, 2011.

Kagan, Neil & Stephen Hyslop, *Eyewitness to WW II*, Washington, D.C. National Geographic, 2018.

Kennedy, *Maxwell, Danger's Hour*, N.Y., Simon & Schuster, 2008.

Kleebe, Woodrow W, in Rogers, Charles, *South Dakota's Challenges Since 1960*, Garrettson,\SD: Sanders Printing Co, 2011, pg 373-374.

Latza, Greg, *Blue Stars*, Sioux Falls, S.D., People Scapes Publishing, 2004.

Larson, George, *South Dakota War Stories*, Bennington, Vt., Merriam Press, 2015.

Lefebvre, Laurent, *They were on Utah Beach*, France, Imprimerie, 2005.

Lefebvre, Laurent, *They Were on Omaha Beach*, americandday.org, 2007.

Lord, Walter, *Day of Infamy*, N.Y. Henry Holt & Company, 1957.

Lucchesi, Emilie, *This is Really War*, Chicago, Chicago Review Press, 2019.

MacArthur, Brian, *Surviving the Sword*, N.Y., Random House, 2005.

Marshall, S,L.A., *Night Drop*, Boston, Bantam Book, 1962.

McClain, Sally, *Navajo Weapon*, Tucson, Rio Nuevo Publishers, 2002.

Miller, Donald, *Masters of the Air*, N.Y., Simon & Schuster, 2006.

Mortimer, Gavin, *Merrill's Marauders*, Minneapolis, Zenith Press, 2013.

Mrazek, Robert, *A Dawn Like Thunder*, N.Y., Little Brown & Company, 2008.

Mundy, Liza, *Code Girls*, N.Y., Machete Books, 2017.

Nez, Chester, *Code Talker*, N.Y., Penguin Group, 2011.

Norman, Michael & Elizabeth Norman, *Tears in the Darkness*, N.Y., Straus & Giroux, 2009.

Olsen, Arlo, In Rogers, Charles, *South Dakota's Challenges Since 1960*, Garrettson, SD: Sanders Printing Co, 2011, pg. 372-373.

Omanson, Oliver, *Prisoner of War Number 21860*, Self-published, 2009.

Oyos, Lynwood, *Reveille for Sioux Falls*, Sioux Falls, The Center for Western Studies, 2014.

Prados, John, *Islands of Destiny*, N.Y., The Penguin Group, 2012.

Ruggero, Ed, *The First Men In*, N.Y., Harper Collins, 2006.

Ryan, Cornelius, *The Longest Day*, N.Y., Simon & Schuster, 1959.

Salazar, Noelle, *The Flight Girls*, Printed in U.S.A., Mira, 2019.

Sanders, Peggy, *The Civilian Conservation Corps: In & Around the Black Hills*, Charleston, Arcadia Publishing, 2004.

Schock, Al, *Brothers in War*, Hills, Minnesota, Crescent Publishing, Inc., 1988.

Schrijvers, Peter, *The Margraten Boys*, N.Y., Palgrave Macmillan, 2012.

Schrijvers, Peter, *Those Who Hold Bastogne*, New Haven, Yale University Press, 2014.

Simmons, L. Bill, *Goddess of War*, Self-Published, 1990. pg. 167-193.

Sledge, E. B., *With the Old Breed*, N. Y., Presidio Press, 2010.

Sloan, Bill, *Brotherhood of Heroes*, N. Y., Simon & Schuster, 2005.

Sloan, Bill, *The Ultimate Battle*, N. Y., Simon & Schuster, 2007.

Smith, Larry, *Iwo Jima*, N. Y., Norton & Company, 2008.

Spaulding, Ted, *Itchy Feet*, Self-published.

Stafford, David, *Ten Days to D-Day*, N. Y., Little Brown & Company, 2003.

Stanton, Doug, *In Harm's Way*, N. Y., Henry Holt & Company, 2001.

Tillman, Barrett, *Forgotten Fifteenth*, Washington, D.C., Regnery History, 2014.

Twomey, Steve, *Countdown to Pearl Harbor*, N. Y., Simon & Schuster, 2016.

Ward, Geoffrey, *The War*, N. Y., Alfred A. Knopf, 2007.

Weintraub, Stanley, *11 Days in December*. N. Y., New American Library, 2006.

Wheeler, Richard, *Iwo*, Annapolis, Maryland, Naval Institute Press, 1980.

Whitlock, Flint, Desperate Valour, N. Y., Machete Book, 2018.

Wilson, Stephen*, Answering the Call*, Bennington, Vt., Merriam Press, 2007.

Yahara, Hiromichi, *The Battle for Okinawa*, N. Y., John Wiley & Sons, 1995.

Associated Press, *Another unexploded bomb found at Igloo dump site*, 1996.

Associated Press, *Live bomb found at Edgemont,* 1996.

Bauske, Gloria, *Span renamed to honor WW II hero*, Argus Leader, December 29, 2002.

Callison, Jill, *A glimpse into their experiences: Twelve former POWS*, September 21, 2008.

Callison, Jill, *B-29 crash near Philip recalled*, Argus Leader, April 19, 2012.

Callison, Jill, *Horror struck far from war for Sioux Falls airman in 1944*, Argus Leader, April 13, 2011.

Callison, Jill, *South Dakota's belle of the battle*, Argus Leader, July 7, 2010.

Callison, Jill, *1940's poster boy, U.S. Bond dies*, Argus Leader, July 7, 2001.

Cunningham, Lloyd, *One of the last Lakota code talkers honored in D.C.*, Argus Leader, July 13, 2006.

Ellis, Jonathan, *A final resting place*, Argus Leader, May 27, 2018.

Ellis, Jonathan, *Harold Thune, fighter pilot, father of US Senator dies at 100*, August 15, 2020.

Ellis, Jonathan, *Hometown hero*, Argus Leader, August 10, 2013.

Ellis, Jonathan, *S.D. duo aided Doolittle Raid*, Argus Leader, April 18, 2012.

Ellis, Jonathan, *WW II ace honored with statue*, USA Today, 2014.

Harriman, Peter, *70 years later, the medals came*, Argus Leader, May 29, 2014.

Harriman, Peter, *USS SD, battleship's propeller home*, Argus Leader, December 7, 2000.

Harriman, Peter, *WW II vet returning to France*, Argus Leader, July 14, 2012.

Harriman, Peter & David Kranz, *S.D. loses legend, American hero, Joe Foss, 1915-2003*, Argus Leader. January 2, 2003.

Hascall, Randy, *Two of Canton's famous native sons will be honored in new museum*, Argus Leader, November 4, 2002.

Nord, James, *Fence of Black Hills depot worries some locals*, Argus Leader, June 26, 2016.

Oechslin, Russ, *Museum to showcase POW camp*, Argus Leader, July 4, 2004.

O'Sullivan, Joe, *S.D. code talkers to receive medals*, Argus Leader, November 8, 2013.

Ramos, Nestor, *Flier finally at rest*, Argus Leader, May 26, 2007.

Randle, Payton, *WW II school leaves legacy*, Argus Leader, July 5, 2012.

Renshaw, Eric, *Dating show can trace roots to our WW II training base*, Argus Leader, June 26, 2016.

Renshaw, Eric, *Looking back: El Matador founder brought authentic Mexican food to Sioux Falls*, October 5, 2017.

Renshaw, Eric, *Women's Army Corp officer found slain near 12th, Grange in 1943*, Argus Leader, November 19, 2017.

Rezac, Jennifer, *Battleship memorial takes its place in history*, Argus Leader, July 7, 2001.

Sanderson, Jennifer, *Radio link to freedom*, Argus Leader, March 14, 2000.

Smorada, James, *Marker to recall fatal WW II crash in city*, Argus Leader, March 29, 2001.

Walker, Carson, *Cleanup planned for Igloo depot*, Argus Leader, November 8, 2013.

Walker, Carson, *Residents fear explosion at Igloo*, Argus Leader, October 13, 1996.

Walker, Carson, *Workers dig up rocket at old Army depot*, Argus Leader, August 28, 2003.

Walker, John, D-Day at Normandy, Argus Leader, June 5, 1994.

Weinstein, Dorene, For Currers, battered Bible more than artifact, Argus Leader, September 3, 2010.

Woster, Terry, *SD veteran accepts WW II medals as symbol of liberty*, Argus Leader, December 7, 2000.

Woster, Terry, *War framed future for South Dakota*, Argus Leader, September 9, 2001.

Young, Steve, *Army honors slain soldier sixty-one late*, Argus Leader, April 7, 2005.

_____, *D-Day: Fine line between life, death*, Argus Leader, June 6, 2014.

_____, *Fallen WW II soldier finally gets medals*, Argus Leader, August 24, 2007.

_____, *France to honor former war nurse of Eagle Butte*, May 16, 2004.

_____, *Goodwill carries gun barrel to SD*, Argus Leader, June 30, 1994.

_____, *History of Navajo Codetalkers*, Historynet.com, Accessed April 4, 2014.

_____, *11 days bobbing in the Pacific, Ocean*, May 26, 2008.

_____, *Letters hid veteran's untold story*, Argus Leader, May 27, 2007.

_____, *Lessons from war served Tyndall native well*, Argus Leader, May 26, 2008.

_____, *Man recalls seven graves of German POWS along Big Sioux*, 1997.

_____, *Nazi POWS did time in Sioux Falls after WW II*, Argus Leader.

_____, *Reviving memories of forgotten crash*, Argus Leader, December 23, 2007.

_____, Sioux Falls scientist among experts behind 2nd secret weapon, Argus Leader, No Date.

_____, *Shattered picnic still sends echoes*, Argus Leader, May 2, 2002.

_____, *SD native finally gets his due*, Argus Leader, March 21, 2008.

_____, Soldiers who went ashore on Normandy and survived, Argues Leader, June 5, 1994.

_____, *South Dakota's 'lost' hero of WW II gets fresh lift*, Argus Leader, May 9, 2010.

_____, *South Dakotan dies sixty-two years after seeing the bomb drop*, Argus Leader, September 1, 2007.

_____, *South Dakotans on the USS Indianapolis: forgotten at sea*, Argus Leader, August 7, 2007.

_____, *South Dakotans left Pearl Harbor days before the bombing*, Argus Leader, December 7, 1998.

_____, *Vet recalls Battle of the Bulge horrors*, Argus Leader, December 15, 1994.

Bahr, Jeff, *Pearl Harbor remembered*, Aberdeen American News, December 7, 2009.

Jerke, Tyler, *A salute to SD's last code talker*, Rapid City Journal, June 24, 2010.

Penzenstadler, Nick, *Veterans to commemorate site of 1944 plane crash*, Rapid City Journal, September 22, 2010.

Aberdeen AM News: Aberdeen Man takes part in sea rescue, July 3, 1945.

KEVN TV: Rapid City, *Sailor killed at Pearl Harbor attack finally identified*, September 25, 2017.

Andrews, John, *Unknown no more: Jack Thurman takes his place in Iwo Jima history*, South Dakota Magazine, March/April 2008.

Antonen, Kathy & Elizabeth Williams, *The Wolsey farm that was public enemy No. 1*, South Dakota Magazine, Jan/Feb 2005.

Higbee, Paul, *Letters home*, South Dakota Magazine, May/June 2002.

_____, Rekindling a memory, South Dakota Magazine, Nov/Dec. 2012.

Holtzmann Roger, *The real hero*, South Dakota Magazine, May/June, 2019.

Hunhoff, Bernie, *The last Lakota code talker*, South Dakota Magazine, May/June 2007.

Jensen, Dave, *Crash of the Flying Sioux*, South Dakota Magazine, July/August 2007.

Nickisch, Curt, *Prisoners of war*, South Dakota Magazine, Jan/Feb. 2001.

Periodicals

Gross, Garrett, Jack Thurman, The Farming Families of Minnehaha County, May 2018.

Mehrer, Katherine, Dakota Images; Helen Anderson Severson, Pierre, South Dakota History, Vol. 33, No. 3, Fall 2003.

Booklet

Radiomen: *The story of the Sioux Falls Army Air Force Technical Training Command Radio Training School*, Old Courthouse Museum, Sioux Falls, South Dakota.

Pamphlet

Home of the WW II Pheasant Canteen, Aberdeen, South Dakota.

Flyer

USS South Dakota: USS SD Foundation.

AV Sources

DVD/ *Pacific*/ Tom Hanks and Steven Spielberg collaborated on the project.

DVD/ *The War*/ A Ken Burns film on the war in Europe and the Pacific.

Video/ Sea Tails: Missing the USS Indianapolis/ A&E Home Video.

Hero Cards

Zerr, Mick and Junior and Senior high school students from Washington High School Research & Archival Records and Interviews, 2000-2001.

Internet

Cohen, Zachary, *U.S. launches most advanced Stealth sub amid undersea rivalry*, U.S. Military, CNN. October 26, 2017, accessed November 15, 2018.

Sherman, Stephen, LT. *Cecil E. Harris*, Acepilots.com, June 1999 updated July 2, 2011, accessed August 4, 2018.

Bataan project.com/Spaulding html accessed December 31, 2017.

Defense POW/MIA Accounting Agency accessed December 1, 2017.

Northern State University/ *Cecil Harris* accessed August 14, 2018

http://clifhullinger.blogspot.com/ accessed June 1, 2018.

Wittenberger, Paul, https://www.chamberlainmccolleys.com/ accessed April, 12, 2018.

http://www.Sarah Sundin.com/ *WW II war bonds*, accessed July 20, 2018.

http://wwwhistory.com/8-things-you-may-not-know-about-the-Battle-of-the Bulge, Evan Andrews, accessed April 14, 2019.

http://en.Wikipedia.org/wiki:/*Battle-of-the-Bulge* accessed April 14, 2019.

http://en.Wikipedia.org/wiki:/Okinawa accessed June 10, 2018.

https://en.Wikipedia.org/wiki/*Ola-Mildred-Rexroat* Accessed September 19, 2018.

https://en.Wikipedia.org/wikii/*Women-Airforce-Service-Pilots* accessed September 19, 2018.

https://en.Wikipedia.org/wiki/*Cecil-E. Harris* accessed August 14, 2018.

https://en.Wikipedia.*GermanSubmarineU-505* Accessed December 28, 2017.

Index

Bataan Death March, 24, 26, 27, 29, 33, 34, 35, 37, 38, 39, 40, 41, 42, 205

Battery B, 4

Battle of Monte Cassino, 171

Battle of the Bulge, 12, 32, 81, 86, 110, 112, 113, 120, 140, 164, 204, 223, 225, 228, 229, 230, 231, 235, 236, 237, 239, 258, 266, 268

Bauer, 23

Bauer, William, 55

Beadle county, 6

Bear Butte Cemetery, 174

Bear King, 181

Beardemphl, Cecil, 106

Beck, Harley, 122

Beck, Howard, 81

Becker, 212

Belgium, 56, 57, 69, 81, 85, 86, 97, 100, 105, 106, 110, 111, 112, 120, 121, 140, 141, 142, 164, 184, 212, 213, 223, 228, 229, 231, 232, 233, 234, 236, 238, 268, 270, 271

Bell, 140

Belmont, Lloyd, 229

Bennett, John, 27

Benson, 94, 212

Beresford, 186, 220, 225

Berg, 94

Bergen, 23

Beri-beri, 25

Bertram, Richard, 138

Bessler, 263

Bevers, Lee, 183

Bianchi, Willibald C., 39

Biberdorf, 23

Biberdorf, Gerhard, 129

Bingham Jr., John C., 37

Bird Horse, 212

Bjertness, 140

Black Hills, 6, 7, 18, 22, 35, 36, 47, 56, 57, 61, 75, 82, 110, 118, 121, 122, 129, 130, 134, 139, 142, 143, 161, 174, 176, 181, 229, 243, 244, 248, 257, 272

Blacksmith, Leonard, 81

Blase, 212

Blind Date, 15, 16

Block, Ernest, 56

Blount, Charles, 123

Boes, Leon, 213

Bohlman, 207

Bonacker,Earl, 1

Bond, Uran Selar, 178

Bondurant, Norman, 82

Boner, Leslie, 219

Bowar, Edmund, 106

Bowling, Maxwell, 106

Bradbury, Thomas, 130

Brammer, Alfred, 56

Brandt, Herbert, 137

Bridgman, Harold, 201

Britton Cemetery, 116

Brockhoft, Ray, 225

Broke Leg, 181

Brommer, Don, 183

Bronze Stars, 89, 163, 181, 223, 270

Brooks, Bruce, 56

Brown, Ed, 256

Bryant, Otis C., 37

Buffalo County, 7

Burdock, Eugene, 130

Burke, Donald, 57

Burke, John, 123

Burns, Robert, 222

Bush, President, 209

Y

Z

Endnotes

[1] (Argus Leader, South Dakotans on USS Holbrook left before attack)

[2] (Gese, Aberdeen American News)

[3] (Sameas) 1

[4] (Marvin Sletten, letter from daughter)

[5] (Hoon, Fallen Sons and Daughters)

[6] (Pingel, Argus Leader South Dakotans on USS Holbrook)

[7] (Porter, G, Fallen Sons and Daughters)

[8] (Smith, M, Fallen Sons and Daughters)

[9] (Thompson, C Fallen Sons and Daughters)

[10] (Peacock, J, Argus Leader)

[11] (Melius, Argus Leader)

[12] (Wikipedia German Sub 505)

[13] (Rogers,W, Rapid City, KEVN TV)

[14] (Dill, Fallen Sons and Daughters)

[15] (Grand PRE, Fallen Sons and Daughters)

[16] (Rich, P, Fallen Sons and Daughters)

[17] (Rich, P, Associated Press March 23, 2018)

[18] (Lehman, M, Fallen Sons and Daughters)

[19] (Nigg, L, Fallen Sons and Daughters)

[20] (Nigg, E, Fallen Sons and Daughters)

[21] (Jarding, G, Fallen Sons and Daughters)

[22] (Henrichsen, J, Fallen Sons and Daughters)

[23] (Houde, E, Fallen Sons and Daughters)

[24] (Anderson, A, Fallen Sons and Daughters)

[25] (Goetsch, H, Fallen Sons and Daughters)

[26] (Roesch, H, Fallen Sons and Daughters)

[27] (B. General Laverne Saunders in SD Hall of Fame)

[28] (Booklet Radiomen) 1-2

[29] (Argus Leader, March 14, 2000)

[30] (Argus Leader, July 5, 2012)

[31] (Reville, book) 130

[32] (Ostrander, I, Argus Leader)

[33] (Wingler, H, Argus Leader)

[34] (Conner, Argus Leader)

[35] (Epstein, S, personal interview)

[36] (Epstein, S, Argus Leader Obituary)

[37] (Hale, Separation Document From Army of US)

[38] (Putzke, Argus Leader, March 15, 2009).

[39] (Reville, book) 127-128.

[40] (Keiser, I, Fallen Sons and Daughters)

[41] (Ronk Jr., J, Fallen Sons and Daughters)

[42] (Mogck, C, Argus Leader)

[43] (Dating Game, Argus Leader, June 26, 2016)

[44] (Women's Army Aircorp Officer, Argus Leader, November, 19, 2019)

[45] (Reville, book) 192

[46] (Reville, Book) 191

[47] (Airbase, Booklet) 15

[48] (Argus Leader, September 9, 2001)

[49] (Argus Leader, October 13, 1996)

[50] (Argus Leader, November 8, 2013)

[51] (Argus Leader, April 13, 2011)

[52] (Argus Leader, December 23, 2007)

[53] (Argus Leader, September 22, 2010)

[54] (Argus Leader, April 19, 2012)

[55] (South Dakota Magazine, 2012) 80-83

[56] (Etc For Her, July 2008) 74

[57] (Argus Leader, May 26, 2008)

[58] (Civilian Conservation Corp, book) 7

[59] (South Dakota History Winter 2005) p.7

[60] (1942, book) 177-183

[61] (Surviving the Sword, book) 87

[62] (Itchyfeet, book) 147

[63] (Surviving the Sword, book) 114

[64] (Surviving the Sword, book) 118-119

[65] (1942, book) 408

[66] (Fallen Sons and Daughters)
[67] (Fallen Sons and Daughters)
[68] (Fallen Sons and Daughters)
[69] (Fallen Sons and Daughters)
[70] (Fallen Sons and Daughters)
[71] (Fallen Sons and Daughters)
[72] (Fallen Sons and Daughters)
[73] (Fallen Sons and Daughters)
[74] (Fallen Sons and Daughters)
[75] (Fallen Sons and Daughters)
[76] (Fallen Sons and Daughters)
[77] (Fallen Sons and Daughters)
[78] (Fallen Sons and Daughters)
[79] (Fallen Sons and Daughters)
[80] (Fallen Sons and Daughters)
[81] (Fallen Sons and Daughters)
[82] (Fallen Sons and Daughters)
[83] (Fallen Sons and Daughters)
[84] (Fallen Sons and Daughters)
[85] (Fallen Sons and Daughters)
[86] (Fallen Sons and Daughters)
[87] (Fallen Sons and Daughters)
[88] (Fallen Sons and Daughters)
[89] (Fallen Sons and Daughters)
[90] (Fallen Sons and Daughters)
[91] (Fallen Sons and Daughters)
[92] (Evans, E., Surviving the Sword) 383-384
[93] (Padilla, J, Argus Leader, October 5, 2017)
[94] (Book of Tears) 305-307
[95] (Book of Tears) 308-316
[96] (Fallen Sons and Daughters)
[97] (Fallen Sons and Daughters)
[98] (Fallen Sons and Daughters)
[99] (Fallen Sons and Daughters)
[100] (Fallen Sons and Daughters)
[101] (Fallen Sons and Daughters)
[102] (Fallen Sons and Daughters)

[103] (Fallen Sons and Daughters)
[104] (Fallen Sons and Daughters)
[105] (Fallen Sons and Daughters)
[106] (Fallen Sons and Daughters)
[107] (Fallen Sons and Daughters)
[108] (Fallen Sons and Daughters)
[109] (Fallen Sons and Daughters)
[110] (Fallen Sons and Daughters)
[111] (Fallen Sons and Daughters)
[112] (Fallen Sons and Daughters)
[113] (Fallen Sons and Daughters)
[114] (Fallen Sons and Daughters)
[115] (Fallen Sons and Daughters)
[116] (Fallen Sons and Daughters)
[117] (Fallen Sons and Daughters)
[118] (Fallen Sons and Daughters)
[119] (Spaulding: Bataan Project Int) 1-6
[120] (1942, book) 170-172, 188, 190
[121] (South Dakota Magazine, May/April 2002) 22, 26, 28
[122] (Argus Leader, April 18, 2012)
[123] (1942, book) 192-193
[124] (Code Girls, book) 144
[125] (Waldron, Fallen Sons and Daughters)
[126] (USS Yorktown, booklet)
[127] (Waldron, Argus Leader 12-29-02)
[128] (Perry, L., Fallen Sons and Daughters)
[129] (Selle, H., Fallen Sons and Daughters)
[130] (Foss, book) 32-34
[131] (Foss, book) 41-42
[132] (Foss, book) 76
[133] (Foss, book) 77
[134] (Foss, book) 79
[135] (Anderson, A, Fallen Sons and Daughters)
[136] (1942, book) 339
[137] (USS SD, pamphlet/flyer)
[138] (Argus Leader, 7-7-01)
[139] (Currier, Argus Leader, 9-30-10)

[140] (USS Military, USS South Dakota)

[141] (Harris, C, Wikipedia) 1

[142] (Argus Leader, 8-10-13)

[143] (Argus Leader, 5-9-10)

[144] (Argus Leader, 8-10-13)

[145] (Argus Leader, 5-9-10)

[146] (Northern State University)

[147] (Argus Leader, 8-10-13)

[148] (Northern State University)

[149] (Argus Leader, 5-9-10)

[150] (Argus Leader, 5-9-10)

[151] (Hedman, Hero Card)

[152] (Masters of the Air) 7

[153] (Masters of the Air) 8

[154] (Forgotten 15th) IX

[155] (Forgotten 15th) X

[156] (Forgotten 15th) 8

[157] (Forgotten 15th) 133

[158] (Forgotten 15th) 250

[159] (Masters of the Air) 316-317

[160] (Bauer, W, Fallen Sons and Daughters)

[161] (Block, E, Fallen Sons and Daughters)

[162] (Brammer Jr, A, Fallen Sons and Daughters)

[163] (Brooks, B, Fallen Sons and Daughters)

[164] (Fallen Sons and Daughters)

[165] (Fallen Sons and Daughters)

[166] (Fallen Sons and Daughters)

[167] (Fallen Sons and Daughters)

[168] (Fallen Sons and Daughters)

[169] (Fallen Sons and Daughters)

[170] (Fallen Sons and Daughters)

[171] (Fallen Sons and Daughters)

[172] (Fallen Sons and Daughters)

[173] (Fallen Sons and Daughters)

[174] (Fallen Sons and Daughters)

[175] (Fallen Sons and Daughters)

[176] (Fallen Sons and Daughters)

[177] (Fallen Sons and Daughters)
[178] (Fallen Sons and Daughters)
[179] (Fallen Sons and Daughters)
[180] (Fallen Sons and Daughters)
[181] (Fallen Sons and Daughters)
[182] (Fallen Sons and Daughters)
[183] (Fallen Sons and Daughters)
[184] (Fallen Sons and Daughters)
[185] (Fallen Sons and Daughters)
[186] (Fallen Sons and Daughters)
[187] (Fallen Sons and Daughters)
[188] (Fallen Sons and Daughters)
[189] (Fallen Sons and Daughters)
[190] (Westby, M, Fallen Sons and Daughters)
[191] (Westphal, E. Fallen Sons and Daughters)
[192] (Williams, H, Fallen Sons and Daughters)
[193] (Wilson, L, Fallen Sons and Daughters)
[194] (Karstens, F, Fallen Sons and Daughters)
[195] (Skoba, J, Fallen Sons and Daughters)
[196] (Conner, C, Hero Card)
[197] (Hanson, W, Hero Card)
[198] (Magnuson, M, Argus Leader, Obituary)
[199] (Muchow, H, Argus Leader, Obituary)
[200] (Wild Blue, book) 29
[201] (Wild Blue, book) 30
[202] (Wild Blue, book) 31-33
[203] (Wild Blue, book) 43
[204] (Wild Blue, book) 45
[205] (Wild Blue, book) 45-51
[206] (Wild Blue, book) 56-57
[207] (Wild Blue, book) 68-70
[208] (Wild Blue, book) 104
[209] (Wild Blue, book) 153-160
[210] (Wild Blue, book) 173
[211] (Wild Blue, book) 175-178
[212] (Wild Blue, book) 179-180
[213] (Wild Blue, book) 187-189

214 (Wild Blue, book) 200-201
215 (Wild Blue, book) 231
216 (Wild Blue, book) 263
217 (Rogers, P, Interview)
218 (Cole, H, Rapid City Journal 3-17-19)
219 (Claussen, D, Miller Funeral Home 5-2-20)
220 (Ellis, J, Harold Thune, Fighter Pilot, Argus Leader 8-15-20)
221 (Jackman,L, Fallen Sons and Daughters)
222 (Women's Air Force Service, Wikipedia) 1
223 (Rexroat, OM, Wikipedia) 1
224 (Anderson, HJ, Fallen Sons and Daughters)
225 (Severson, R, Argus Leader 5-26-07)
226 (Finally at Rest, Argus Leader 5-26-07)
227 (Fallen Sons and Daughters)
228 (Fallen Sons and Daughters)
229 (Fallen Sons and Daughters)
230 (Fallen Sons and Daughters)
231 (Fallen Sons and Daughters)
232 (Fallen Sons and Daughters)
233 (Fallen Sons and Daughters)
234 (Fallen Sons and Daughters)
235 (Fallen Sons and Daughters)
236 (Fallen Sons and Daughters)
237 (Fallen Sons and Daughters)
238 (Fallen Sons and Daughters)
239 (Fallen Sons and Daughters)
240 (Fallen Sons and Daughters)
241 (Clear Lake Courier)
242 (Argus Leader, 5-16-04)
243 (Fallen Sons and Daughters)
244 (Fallen Sons and Daughters)
245 (Fallen Sons and Daughters)
246 (Fallen Sons and Daughters)
247 (This is Really War) XI-XII
248 (This is Really War) XIV
249 (This is Really War) 23-24
250 (This is Really War) 44

251 (This is Really War) 53-55
252 (This is Really War) 77-87
253 (This is Really War) 85-86
254 (This is Really War) 117
255 (This is Really War) 173
256 (This is Really War) 187-189
257 (Rescue at Los Banos, book, Appendix)
258 (This is Really War) 255-257
259 (This is Really War) 260-261
260 (Fallen Sons and Daughters)
261 (Fallen Sons and Daughters)
262 (Fallen Sons and Daughters)
263 (Fallen Sons and Daughters)
264 (Fallen Sons and Daughters)
265 (Fallen Sons and Daughters)
266 (Fallen Sons and Daughters)
267 (Fallen Sons and Daughters)
268 (Fallen Sons and Daughters)
269 (Fallen Sons and Daughters)
270 (Fallen Sons and Daughters)
271 (Fallen Sons and Daughters)
272 (Fallen Sons and Daughters)
273 (Fallen Sons and Daughters)
274 (Fallen Sons and Daughters)
275 (Fallen Sons and Daughters)
276 (Fallen Sons and Daughters)
277 (Fallen Sons and Daughters)
278 (Fallen Sons and Daughters)
279 (Fallen Sons and Daughters)
280 (Fallen Sons and Daughters)
281 (Fallen Sons and Daughters)
282 (Fallen Sons and Daughters)
283 (Fallen Sons and Daughters)
284 (Fallen Sons and Daughters)
285 (Fallen Sons and Daughters)
286 (Fallen Sons and Daughters)
287 (Fallen Sons and Daughters)

[288] (Fallen Sons and Daughters)
[289] (Fallen Sons and Daughters)
[290] (Fallen Sons and Daughters)
[291] (Fallen Sons and Daughters)
[292] (Fallen Sons and Daughters)
[293] (Fallen Sons and Daughters)
[294] (Fallen Sons and Daughters)
[295] (Fallen Sons and Daughters)
[296] (Fallen Sons and Daughters)
[297] (Fallen Sons and Daughters)
[298] (Fallen Sons and Daughters)
[299] (Fallen Sons and Daughters)
[300] (Fallen Sons and Daughters)
[301] (Fallen Sons and Daughters)
[302] (Fallen Sons and Daughters)
[303] (Fallen Sons and Daughters)
[304] (Fallen Sons and Daughters)
[305] (Fallen Sons and Daughters)
[306] (Fallen Sons and Daughters)
[307] (Fallen Sons and Daughters)
[308] (Fallen Sons and Daughters)
[309] (Fallen Sons and Daughters)
[310] (Fallen Sons and Daughters)
[311] (Fallen Sons and Daughters)
[312] (Fallen Sons and Daughters)
[313] (Fallen Sons and Daughters)
[314] (Fallen Sons and Daughters)
[315] (Fallen Sons and Daughters)
[316] (Fallen Sons and Daughters)
[317] (Fallen Sons and Daughters)
[318] (Fallen Sons and Daughters)
[319] (Fallen Sons and Daughters)
[320] (Fallen Sons and Daughters)
[321] (Fallen Sons and Daughters)
[322] (Fallen Sons and Daughters)
[323] (Fallen Sons and Daughters)
[324] (Fallen Sons and Daughters)

[325] (Fallen Sons and Daughters)
[326] (Fallen Sons and Daughters)
[327] (Fallen Sons and Daughters)
[328] (Fallen Sons and Daughters)
[329] (Fallen Sons and Daughters)
[330] (Fallen Sons and Daughters)
[331] (Fallen Sons and Daughters)
[332] (Fallen Sons and Daughters)
[333] (Fallen Sons and Daughters)
[334] (Fallen Sons and Daughters)
[335] (Fallen Sons and Daughters)
[336] (Fallen Sons and Daughters)
[337] (Fallen Sons and Daughters)
[338] (Fallen Sons and Daughters)
[339] (Fallen Sons and Daughters)
[340] (Fallen Sons and Daughters)
[341] (Fallen Sons and Daughters)
[342] (Fallen Sons and Daughters)
[343] (Fallen Sons and Daughters)
[344] (Fallen Sons and Daughters)
[345] (Fallen Sons and Daughters)
[346] (Fallen Sons and Daughters)
[347] (Fallen Sons and Daughters)
[348] (Fallen Sons and Daughters)
[349] (Fallen Sons and Daughters)
[350] (Fallen Sons and Daughters)
[351] (Fallen Sons and Daughters)
[352] (Fallen Sons and Daughters)
[353] (Fallen Sons and Daughters)
[354] (Fallen Sons and Daughters)
[355] (Fallen Sons and Daughters)
[356] (Fallen Sons and Daughters)
[357] (Fallen Sons and Daughters)
[358] (Fallen Sons and Daughters)
[359] (Fallen Sons and Daughters)
[360] (Fallen Sons and Daughters)
[361] (Fallen Sons and Daughters)

362 (Fallen Sons and Daughters)
363 (Fallen Sons and Daughters)
364 (Fallen Sons and Daughters)
365 (Fallen Sons and Daughters)
366 (Fallen Sons and Daughters)
367 (Fallen Sons and Daughters)
368 (Fallen Sons and Daughters)
369 (Fallen Sons and Daughters)
370 (Fallen Sons and Daughters)
371 (Fallen Sons and Daughters)
372 (Fallen Sons and Daughters)
373 (Fallen Sons and Daughters)
374 (Fallen Sons and Daughters)
375 (Fallen Sons and Daughters)
376 (Fallen Sons and Daughters)
377 (Fallen Sons and Daughters)
378 (Fallen Sons and Daughters)
379 (Fallen Sons and Daughters)
380 (Fallen Sons and Daughters)
381 (Fallen Sons and Daughters)
382 (Fallen Sons and Daughters)
383 (Fallen Sons and Daughters)
384 (Fallen Sons and Daughters)
385 (Fallen Sons and Daughters)
386 (Fallen Sons and Daughters)
387 (Fallen Sons and Daughters)
388 (Fallen Sons and Daughters)
389 (Fallen Sons and Daughters)
390 (Fallen Sons and Daughters)
391 (Fallen Sons and Daughters)
392 (Fallen Sons and Daughters)
393 (Fallen Sons and Daughters)
394 (Fallen Sons and Daughters)
395 (Fallen Sons and Daughters)
396 (Fallen Sons and Daughters)
397 (Fallen Sons and Daughters)
398 (Fallen Sons and Daughters)

[399] (Fallen Sons and Daughters)
[400] (Fallen Sons and Daughters)
[401] (Fallen Sons and Daughters)
[402] (Fallen Sons and Daughters)
[403] (Fallen Sons and Daughters)
[404] (Fallen Sons and Daughters)
[405] (Fallen Sons and Daughters)
[406] (Fallen Sons and Daughters)
[407] (Fallen Sons and Daughters)
[408] (Fallen Sons and Daughters)
[409] (Fallen Sons and Daughters)
[410] (Fallen Sons and Daughters)
[411] (Fallen Sons and Daughters)
[412] (Fallen Sons and Daughters)
[413] (Fallen Sons and Daughters)
[414] (Fallen Sons and Daughters)
[415] (Fallen Sons and Daughters)
[416] (Fallen Sons and Daughters)
[417] (Fallen Sons and Daughters)
[418] (Fallen Sons and Daughters)
[419] (Fallen Sons and Daughters)
[420] (Fallen Sons and Daughters)
[421] (Fallen Sons and Daughters)
[422] (Fallen Sons and Daughters)
[423] (Fallen Sons and Daughters)
[424] (Fallen Sons and Daughters)
[425] (Fallen Sons and Daughters)
[426] (Fallen Sons and Daughters)
[427] (Fallen Sons and Daughters)
[428] (Fallen Sons and Daughters)
[429] (Fallen Sons and Daughters)
[430] (Fallen Sons and Daughters)
[431] (Fallen Sons and Daughters)
[432] (Fallen Sons and Daughters)
[433] (Fallen Sons and Daughters)
[434] (Fallen Sons and Daughters)
[435] (Fallen Sons and Daughters)

[436] (Fallen Sons and Daughters)
[437] (Fallen Sons and Daughters)
[438] (Fallen Sons and Daughters)
[439] (Fallen Sons and Daughters)
[440] (Fallen Sons and Daughters)
[441] (Fallen Sons and Daughters)
[442] (Fallen Sons and Daughters)
[443] (Fallen Sons and Daughters)
[444] (Fallen Sons and Daughters)
[445] (Fallen Sons and Daughters)
[446] (Fallen Sons and Daughters)
[447] (Fallen Sons and Daughters)
[448] (Fallen Sons and Daughters)
[449] (Fallen Sons and Daughters)
[450] (Fallen Sons and Daughters)
[451] (Fallen Sons and Daughters)
[452] (Fallen Sons and Daughters)
[453] (Fallen Sons and Daughters)
[454] (Fallen Sons and Daughters)
[455] (Fallen Sons and Daughters)
[456] (Fallen Sons and Daughters)
[457] (Fallen Sons and Daughters)
[458] (Fallen Sons and Daughters)
[459] (Fallen Sons and Daughters)
[460] (Fallen Sons and Daughters)
[461] (Fallen Sons and Daughters)
[462] (Fallen Sons and Daughters)
[463] (Fallen Sons and Daughters)
[464] (Fallen Sons and Daughters)
[465] (Fallen Sons and Daughters)
[466] (Fallen Sons and Daughters)
[467] (Fallen Sons and Daughters)
[468] (Fallen Sons and Daughters)
[469] (Fallen Sons and Daughters)
[470] (Fallen Sons and Daughters)
[471] (Fallen Sons and Daughters)
[472] (Fallen Sons and Daughters)

473 (Fallen Sons and Daughters)
474 (Fallen Sons and Daughters)
475 (Fallen Sons and Daughters)
476 (Fallen Sons and Daughters)
477 (Fallen Sons and Daughters)
478 (Fallen Sons and Daughters)
479 (Fallen Sons and Daughters)
480 (Fallen Sons and Daughters)
481 (Farming Families of Minnehaha County) 22-23
482 (South Dakota Magazine, May/June 2019) 552-557
483 (personal interview)
484 (personal interview)
485 (personal interview)
486 (Roth, information shared from his daughter)
487 (Hullinger, L)
488 (Fallen Sons and Daughters)
489 (Fallen Sons and Daughters)
490 (Fallen Sons and Daughters)
491 (Fallen Sons and Daughters)
492 (Fallen Sons and Daughters)
493 (Fallen Sons and Daughters)
494 (Fallen Sons and Daughters)
495 (Fallen Sons and Daughters)
496 (Fallen Sons and Daughters)
497 (Fallen Sons and Daughters)
498 (Fallen Sons and Daughters)
499 (Fallen Sons and Daughters)
500 (Argus Leader, 4-7-05)
501 (Fallen Sons and Daughters)
502 (Fallen Sons and Daughters)
503 (Fallen Sons and Daughters)
504 (Fallen Sons and Daughters))
505 (Hero Card)
506 (Fallen Sons and Daughters)
507 (Sundin, S,)
508 (Argus Leader, 7-7-01)
509 (Historynet.com) 51-52

[510] (South Dakota Magazine, May/Jun 2007) 583-587

[511] (Hero Card)

[512] (Hero Card)

[513] (Argus Leader, Obituary 12-11-09)

[514] (Argus Leader, Obituary 1-112-08)

[515] (Hero Card)

[516] (A glimpse into their Experiences, Argus Leader, 9-21-2008)

[517] (Oliver, T, personal story) 155-156

[518] (Nazi POWs did Time in Sioux Falls after WWII Argus Leader, 1997)

[519] (South Dakota Magazine, Jan/Feb 2001) 49

[520] (South Dakota Magazine, Jan/Feb 2001) 48-49

[521] (Argus Leader, 1991)

[522] (Man Recalls Seven Graves…, Argus Leader)

[523] (Man Recalls Seven Graves…, Argus Leader)

[524] (Argus Leader, 7-7-04)

[525] (South Dakota Magazine, Jan/Feb 2001) 46-50

[526] (South Dakota Magazine, Jan/Feb 2001) 46-50

[527] (Two of Canton's Native Sons, Argus Leader, 11-4-02)

[528] (Sioux Falls Scientist, Argus Leader)

[529] (Argus Leader, 9-1-07)

[530] (Fallen Sons and Daughters)

[531] (Fields, D)

[532] (Japanese Balloon Bomb, Argus Leader 5-2-02)

[533] (Letters hid vet's untold story, Argus Leader, 5-28-07)

[534] (South Dakota Challenges, Keeble) 372-373

[535] (South Dakota Challenges, Olson) 373-374

[536] (Ambrose D-D) 119

[537] (Fallen Sons and Daughters)

[538] (Fallen Sons and Daughters)

[539] (Fallen Sons and Daughters)

[540] (Fallen Sons and Daughters)

[541] (Fallen Sons and Daughters)

[542] (Fallen Sons and Daughters)

[543] (Fallen Sons and Daughters)

[544] (Fallen Sons and Daughters)

[545] (Fallen Sons and Daughters)

[546] (Fallen Sons and Daughters)

[547] (Fallen Sons and Daughters)

[548] (Fallen Sons and Daughters)

[549] (Fallen Sons and Daughters)

[550] (Fallen Sons and Daughters)

[551] (Fallen Sons and Daughters)

[552] (Fallen Sons and Daughters)

[553] (Fallen Sons and Daughters)

[554] (Fallen Sons and Daughters)

[555] (Fallen Sons and Daughters)

[556] (Fallen Sons and Daughters)

[557] (Fallen Sons and Daughters)

[558] (Fallen Sons and Daughters)

[559] (Fallen Sons and Daughters)

[560] (Fallen Sons and Daughters)

[561] (Fallen Sons and Daughters)

[562] (Fallen Sons and Daughters)

[563] (Fallen Sons and Daughters)

[564] (Fallen Sons and Daughters)

[565] (Fallen Sons and Daughters)

[566] (Fallen Sons and Daughters)

[567] (Fallen Sons and Daughters)

[568] (Fallen Sons and Daughters)

[569] (Fallen Sons and Daughters)

[570] (Fallen Sons and Daughters)

[571] (Fallen Sons and Daughters)

[572] (South Dakotans on Omaha Who Survived, Argus Leader, 6-5-94)

[573] (WWII Vet Returning to France, Argus Leader, 7-14-12)

[574] (Fine line between life and death, Argus Leader 6-6-14)

[575] (Burns, B, information from his son)

[576] (Rossow, B, Hero Card)

[577] (Fine Line, Argus Leader 6-6-14)

[578] (Ardennes, book) 25

[579] (Battle of Bulge, History)

[580] (Ardennes, book) 81

[581] (Ardennes, book) 102-104

[582] (Ardennes, book)120

[583] (Battle of Bulge, History)

[584] (Ardennes, book) 140

[585] (Battle of Bulge, History)

[586] (Those Who Hold B, book) 116-137

[587] (Ardennes, book) 369

[588] (Those Who Hold B, book) 6

[589] (Ardennes, book) 36

[590] (Fallen Sons and Daughters)

[591] (Fallen Sons and Daughters)

[592] (Fallen Sons and Daughters)

[593] (Fallen Sons and Daughters)

[594] (Fallen Sons and Daughters)

[595] (Fallen Sons and Daughters)

[596] (Fallen Sons and Daughters)

[597] (Fallen Sons and Daughters)

[598] (Fallen Sons and Daughters)

[599] (Fallen Sons and Daughters)

[600] (Fallen Sons and Daughters)

[601] (Fallen Sons and Daughters)

[602] (Fallen Sons and Daughters)

[603] (Fallen Sons and Daughters)

[604] (Fallen Sons and Daughters)

[605] (Fallen Sons and Daughters)

[606] (Fallen Sons and Daughters)

[607] (Fallen Sons and Daughters)

[608] (Fallen Sons and Daughters)

[609] (Fallen Sons and Daughters)

[610] (Fallen Sons and Daughters)

[611] (Fallen Sons and Daughters)

[612] (Fallen Sons and Daughters)

[613] (Fallen Sons and Daughters)

[614] (Fallen Sons and Daughters)

[615] (Fallen Sons and Daughters)

[616] (Fallen Sons and Daughters)

[617] (Fallen Sons and Daughters)

[618] (Fallen Sons and Daughters)

[619] (Fallen Sons and Daughters)

[620] (Argus Leader, 12-15-94)

[621] (Argus Leader, Obituary, 3-2-09)

[622] (Information from Robert's granddaughter)

[623] (personal interview)

[624] (Argus Leader, Obituary, 9-21-00)

[625] (SD Native finally gets his due, Argus Leader, 3-21-08)

[626] (Unknown No More, South Dakota Magazine, May/April 2008) 81-83

[627] (The Iconic Gung Ho Photo, Farming Families, May 2018) 30-32

[628] (Ira Hayes and his connection to Mitchell's Jack Thurman, Farming Families, May 2018) 26-27

[629] (Fallen Sons and Daughters)

[630] (Fallen Sons and Daughters)

[631] (Fallen Sons and Daughters)

[632] (Fallen Sons and Daughters)

[633] (Fallen Sons and Daughters)

[634] (Fallen Sons and Daughters)

[635] (Fallen Sons and Daughters)

[636] (Fallen Sons and Daughters)

[637] (Fallen Sons and Daughters)

[638] (Fallen Sons and Daughters)

[639] (Fallen Sons and Daughters)

[640] (Fallen Sons and Daughters)

[641] (Fallen Sons and Daughters)

[642] (Fallen Sons and Daughters)

[643] (Fallen Sons and Daughters)

[644] (Fallen Sons and Daughters)

[645] (Fallen Sons and Daughters)

[646] (Lyte, Fallen Sons and Daughters)

[647] (Lyte, Fallen Sons and Daughters)

[648] (Lyte, Fallen Sons and Daughters)

[649] (Lyte, Fallen Sons and Daughters)

[650] (Lyte, Fallen Sons and Daughters)

[651] (Lyte, Fallen Sons and Daughters)

[652] (Lyte, Fallen Sons and Daughters)

[653] (Lyte, Fallen Sons and Daughters)

[654] (Lyte, Fallen Sons and Daughters)

[655] (Lyte, Fallen Sons and Daughters)

[656] (Lyte, Fallen Sons and Daughters)

[657] (Lyte, Fallen Sons and Daughters)

[658] (Luzon, Fallen Sons and Daughters)

[659] (Saipan, Fallen Sons and Daughters)

[660] (Saipan, Fallen Sons and Daughters)

[661] (Saipan, Fallen Sons and Daughters)

[662] (Tarawa, Fallen Sons and Daughters)

[663] (Tarawa, Fallen Sons and Daughters)

[664] (Okinawa, Wikipedia)

[665] (Fallen Sons and Daughters)

[666] (Okinawa, Wikipedia)

[667] (Ship of Ghosts, book) 149

[668] (Ship of Ghosts, book) 138

[669] (Ship of Ghosts, book) 254

[670] (Ship of Ghosts, book) 289

[671] (Ship of Ghosts, book) 2

[672] (USS Houston Monument, Wikipedia)

[673] (USS Liscome Bay, Wikipedia)

[674] (Down to the Sea, book) XIII

[675] (Fallen Sons and Daughters)

[676] (Down to the Sea, book) 222

[677] (Down to the Sea, book) 290

[678] (Down to the Sea, book) 292

[679] (Down to the Sea, book) 260

[680] (Argus Leader, 9-19-07)

[681] (Fallen Sons and Daughters)

[682] (USS Indianapolis Memorial, Wikipedia)

[683] (Fallen Sons and Daughters)

[684] (USS Leopoldville, Wikipedia)

[685] (USS Leopoldville, Wikipedia

[686] (Fallen Sons and Daughters)

[687] (Port Chicago Disaster, Wikipedia)

[688] (Fallen Sons and Daughters)

[689] (Fallen Sons and Daughters)

[690] (Fallen Sons and Daughters)

[691] (Fallen Sons and Daughters)

[692] (Fallen Sons and Daughters)

693 (Fallen Sons and Daughters)
694 (The Defense PWO/MIA Accounting Agency, 12-1-17)
695 (A Final Resting Place, Argus Leader, 5-27-18)
696 (Fallen Sons and Daughters)
697 (Fallen Sons and Daughters)
698 (Wittenberger, P, internet)
699 (SD Veteran Accepts WWII Medals..., Argus Leader, 12-7-00)
700 (10 Years Later the Medals Come..., Argus Leader, 9-29-10)
701 (Fallen WWII Solider Finally Gets..., Argus Leader, 9-24-07)
702 (Vigness, S, personal interview)
703 (American Battle Monuments Commission/Commemorative Sites, booklet) 18-33

Made in the USA
Coppell, TX
27 February 2021